Television Across Europe

Edited by

Jan Wieten,

Graham Murdock

and Peter Dahlgren

.GE Publications
ıdon • Thousand Oaks • New Delhi

First published 2000

SAGE Publications Ltd
6 Bonhill Street
London EC2A 4PU

SAGE Publications Inc
2455 Teller Road
Thousand Oaks, California 91320

SAGE Publications India Pvt Ltd
32, M-Block Market
Greater Kailash – I
New Delhi 110 048

British Library Cataloguing in Publication data

A catalogue record for this book is available from the British Library

ISBN 0-7619-6884-9
ISBN 0-7619-6885-7 (pbk)

Library of Congress catalog record available

Typeset by Mayhew Typesetting, Rhayader, Powys
Printed in Great Britain by The Cromwell Press Ltd, Trowbridge, Wiltshire

CONTENTS

List of Contributors vii

Preface *Jan Wieten, Graham Murdock and Peter Dahlgren* ix

Part I Television Environments: Traditions and Transitions 1

Introduction *Peter Dahlgren* 3

1 **The Status of TV Broadcasting in Europe** *Kees Brants and Els De Bens* 7

2 **Key Trends in European Television** *Peter Dahlgren* 23

3 **Digital Futures: European Television in the Age of Convergence** *Graham Murdock* 35

Part II Television Trends: Organization and Representation 59

Introduction *Graham Murdock* 61

4 **Programming and Channel Competition in European Television** *Taisto Hujanen* 65

5 **Popular Drama: Travelling Templates and National Fictions** *Albert Moran* 84

6 **Programme Making Across Borders: the *Eurosud* news magazine** *Aurélie Laborde and Michel Perrot* 94

7 **Television Audiences** *Winfried Schulz* 113

Part III Television Genres: Borders and Flows 135

Introduction *Jan Wieten* 137

8 **Music Television: MTV-Europe** *Keith Roe and Gust De Meyer* 141

9 **Arts Television: Questions of Culture** *Marit Bakke* 158

10 **Breakfast Television: Infotainers at Daybreak** *Jan Wieten* 175

11 **Talk Shows: Democratic Debates and Tabloid Tales** *Graham Murdock* 198

12 **Television Current Affairs: The Case of Northern Ireland** *Greg McLaughlin* 221

13 **Television News: The Case of the French Road Blockades** *Sari Näsi* 236

References 253

Index 269

LIST OF CONTRIBUTORS

Marit Bakke is professor at the Department of Media Studies, Universitetet i Bergen (University of Bergen), Norway, and a member of the Euro-Media Research Group.

Kees Brants holds positions at the Department of Communication, Universiteit van Amsterdam (University of Amsterdam) and the Universiteit Leiden (Leyden University) where he is professor of political communication. He is a member of the Amsterdam School of Communications Research (ASCoR) and the Euro-Media Research Group.

Peter Dahlgren is professor of Media and Communication Studies at Lunds Universitet (Lund University), Sweden.

Els De Bens is Professor of Communication Science and Dean of the Faculty of Political and Social Sciences at the Universiteit Gent (University of Ghent), Belgium, and is a member of the Euro-Media Research Group.

Gust De Meyer is senior associate professor at the Department of Communication, Katholieke Universiteit Leuven (The Catholic University Leuven), Flanders, Belgium.

Taisto Hujanen is professor of Electronic Media at the Department of Journalism and Mass Communication, Tampereen Yliopisto (University of Tampere), Finland.

Aurélie Laborde is researcher in information and communication at Université Michel de Montaigne – Bordeaux 3 (Michel de Montaigne University Bordeaux), France.

Greg McLaughlin lectures in Media Studies at the University of Ulster's Coleraine campus.

Albert Moran is senior fellow at the School of Film, Media and Cultural Studies at Griffith University, Brisbane, Australia.

Graham Murdock is reader in the Sociology of Culture at the Department of Social Sciences, Loughborough University, United Kingdom.

Sari Näsi has been research assistant at the Department of Communication, Universiteit van Amsterdam (University of Amsterdam), The Netherlands, and general assistant to the European Module project. She now works for 'Observer Finland' in Helsinki.

Michel Perrot is professor of Media Sociology and Intercultural Communication at the Université de Michel de Montaigne, Bordeaux 3 (Michel de Montaigne University Bordeaux), France.

Keith Roe is professor at the Department of Communication, Katholieke Universiteit Leuven (The Catholic University Leuven), Flanders, Belgium.

Winfried Schulz holds the Chair in Mass Communication and Political Science at the Friedrich-Alexander Universität Erlangen-Nürnberg (University of Erlangen-Nuremberg), Germany.

Jan Wieten is senior associate professor at the Department of Communication, Universiteit van Amsterdam (University of Amsterdam), The Netherlands, and member of the Amsterdam School of Communications Research (ASCoR).

PREFACE

As teachers and researchers of the media at European universities, the editors and authors of this coursebook have over the years felt a growing need for a textbook that would address contemporary developments in television from a European perspective. So much of the available current literature on broadcasting takes as its point of departure the existing system in the United States. While this is immensely important and relevant not least in a global context, we have long felt the lack of a text that is grounded in the particular histories and circumstances of television in Western Europe. Further, we have also come to see the importance of a comparative approach: there is much that unites the character and evolution of television in Western Europe, yet television within each country has its own particular features. Many of these features are significant, yet may be so self-evident they can readily be missed. Cultivating a comparative view helps make visible that which is easily taken for granted.

THE GOALS OF THE BOOK

For practical reasons we restrict ourselves in this book to the Europe that is associated with the original system of public service broadcasting and now with hybrid (mixed) broadcasting systems. There is of course much that can be said about television in the post-communist societies of East and Central Europe – not to mention other parts of the world – but in this book our focus is on the television of the countries and region to which we ourselves belong. This focus also means that we are looking specifically at television, and will not say too much about radio, although many of the general observations we make about 'broadcasting' will often be of relevance for radio as well. It is a coursebook for undergraduate university students in media and communication studies, and related fields, which should also be of interest to students in European Studies and similar areas. Our basic intent here is to enhance the student's *knowledge and understanding* of television. We do this by presenting materials that will provide an *introductory orientation* to television in Western Europe generally, with specific details from several countries.

Further, it is our aim that students will be able to use the book to *conceptually clarify* the factors that have been shaping television's development, and also to help them to *analyse the issues* that are at stake in its future. Finally, we hope the book will serve as a resource for *probing further* particular topics of individual or group interest. We can add that it is our assumption – and it has been our experience – that deepened insight into the television medium will not undermine one's enjoyment of it, but rather enhance it. In this book we do not seek to duplicate the publications of various research efforts to chart these developments – most notably the work of the Euro-Media Research Group[1] – though we certainly make use of such material, as well as our own work and that of other researchers.

The societies and cultures of Western Europe have been undergoing changes in the post-war period, and television has been both a reflection and a catalyst of those changes. Western Europe is thus our historical *setting*, the context for our examination of television. Television is a *medium*, a technology of communication, but it is also an *institution*, an organized societal construction, that is subject to formal and informal controls and influences. Television remains the dominant medium of modern society, continuing to expand in the abundance of its output. As an institution it has both *symbolic* and *material* aspects. The symbolic aspect of television has to do with its output, its representations, including fiction, non-fiction, entertainment, sports, and so forth. It stands at the centre of both popular culture and of the coverage of current affairs. One can say that television is the single most important institution shaping the symbolic environment in which we live (and think and dream). The nature of its output is thus of great social and cultural significance. At the same time, television is a major economic undertaking, a material enterprise of considerable cost; that also has enormous economic consequences for society, not least via its advertising. It should be no surprise that there are various social and economic actors who have vested interests in television.

TELEVISION – AND SOCIETY – IN TRANSITION

Until the 1980s the distinguishing feature of broadcasting in most of Western Europe (as compared to the US) was that it was highly regulated in the form of public broadcasting monopolies. At the beginning of the 21st century the organization of broadcasting in Europe is still easily distinguished from the predominantly commercial system in the United States. Public service broadcasting has not been replaced by commercial broadcasting in the major upheaval since the 1980s, but public and commercial broadcasting have come to exist side by side, in a new equilibrium. Dual broadcasting systems are now the most common organizational form in Europe and competition, not between commercial networks only as in the US, but between public and commercial television is one of the main factors shaping broadcasting in Europe.

It is not only the dialectical relationship between public and commercial arrangements that one is confronted with when studying changing television in a changing Europe. Europe itself is full of contradictions. European unity exists in the form of the European Union (EU) yet the region is still characterized by a multiplicity of nation states. There is one large, EU market, but an immense cultural heterogeneity. We find considerable linguistic diversity and at the same time a dominance of the lingua franca of our days, English. Europe, like the rest of the world today, manifests in compelling ways both global and local trends. Looking at the media, one could further argue that we witness today a relatively uniform European or Anglo-American mass media culture, while we increasingly find multicultural nation states. Our identities as citizens are becoming more problematic, not least in relationship to our identities as consumers. Mass consumption prevails, yet marketing and advertising aims at ever smaller target groups. We have access to more and more television channels, yet the diversity of the programming seemingly does not increase.

Talking about Europe, especially in the field of media, means talking about the ambiguous relationship between Europe and America, about Americanization. Over two decades ago, Caroline Heller, in *Broadcasting and Accountability*, wrote: 'Throughout the history of radio and television [in Britain] the American example has provided an immensely influential devil's advocacy of alternatives: hellfire accounts of chaos and tastelessness, stirring images of freedom, enterprise and imagination' (London: British Film Institute, 1978: 12). This observation is no less true today: television in Europe is still trying to come to terms with American television.

USING THIS COURSEBOOK

Writing a coursebook for European use is a complicated affair. There are huge differences in the curricula and in the organization and forms of media studies courses in European universities. On top of that, ways of teaching are (still) different too. We have adapted the book to the semester- or trimester-long types of courses that are most common, but we have taken care to keep the book's pedagogic approach flexible. This with an eye to enable it to fit into a more compact course or a more extended one.

The book could stand on its own in a short course or it could provide the basic structure for a programme in which each part of it could be extended to encompass related interests. The lists of recommended reading that accompany each chapter offer ways to broaden the programme, to impose different emphases in the course or to vary (raise) the level of difficulty. Another rather obvious way of extending the use of the book would be to narrow down the European, comparative and cross-boundary perspective that we have adopted, and instead take a more nationally focused approach by adding locally oriented studies to the course.

Given that the text is designed as a coursebook, our discussion of television across Europe moves from more general and theoretical to more specific and empirical. The chapters in the first part about 'Television Environments' discuss the profound transition that television has gone through in the last decades. It has moved from an era of public service domination to a multichannel environment commanded by commercial providers and is now on its way to a still uncertain digital future. 'Television Trends', the second part of the book, debates the consequences of these developments for the relationship between television and its audience. Audiences are more and more addressed as consumers instead of as citizens. The operating philosophy of broadcasting has shifted from programmes to programming, i.e. from a concern with the quality of each unit of the output to a strategic concern with capturing and holding audiences. In the case studies that form the third part of the book, 'Television Genres', the developments, problems and issues raised in the first two parts are addressed both explicitly and implicitly. This helps to illustrate and understand the more abstract discussions in the previous chapters. We would expect the different parts of the coursebook to be read sequentially, but the chapters in the last part especially allow for selective use and different sequences.

The book is not just a book for reading (or to suggest further reading), and not even a book for discussing and reading. It is more inquisitive than positive. It is meant to stimulate thinking but also 'doing'. For it is our conviction that the best way to help students get a deeper insight and critical understanding of the fundamental changes that television in Europe is going through, is by activating them to ask questions and find out for themselves. There are numerous relatively simple means by which this can be achieved. This is the purpose of the sets of 'activities' that we have added to several chapters. They are not just points to discuss, but exercises to enable the reader to engage actively in finding answers to questions and to get the taste of media research.

We trust that the exercises (perhaps with minor adjustments) can be done in most places where the coursebook will be used. But it is up to the users in the first place to decide to what extent the proposed activities will be incorporated in the course. This may also be adapted to local circumstances and adds to the overall flexibility of the programme.

THE EUROPEAN MODULE

It is more than a coincidence that most of the people behind the plan to create this media studies coursebook with a European perspective have been engaged in the development and organization of student and staff exchanges between universities in Europe. It is partly from this experience that the idea of a programme that could be used, with local variations, in different European countries originated.

In the opinion of the editors and authors, existing programmes on broadcasting and broadcasting developments share 'an emphasis on national systems and developments. This may lead to a certain one-sidedness in the treatment of complex media questions, but could also be made productive in developing a comparative course in which national orientations are brought into relation with each other and to which a supranational European perspective is added. Apart from this, the international nature of developments in the fields of media and communication has made an emphasis on strictly national situations obsolete' (application European Module 'Comparative analysis of broadcasting in Europe', Amsterdam, summer 1996).

The plan was realized thanks to the financial support of the European Union for so-called European modules as well as the enthusiasm of the authors and the facilities and additional funding provided by their departments and universities.

At the start ten universities participated: Universiteit van Amsterdam (Kees Brants and Jan Wieten), Universiteit Gent (Els De Bens), Universitetet i Bergen (Marit Bakke), Katholieke Universiteit Leuven (Keith Roe and Gust De Meyer), Universitat Autònoma de Barcelona (Rosario de Mateo), Loughborough University (Michael Pickering and later Graham Murdock), University of Ulster – Coleraine (Des Cranston and later Greg McLaughlin), Friedrich-Alexander Universität Erlangen-Nürnberg (Winfried Schulz), Lunds Universitet (Peter Dahlgren), and Université Michel de Montaigne, Bordeaux 3 (Michel Perrot). Tampereen Yliopisto (Taisto Hujanen) and Helsingin Yliopisto (Terhi Rantanen, later Ritva Levo-Henriksson) later joined the group. The Universiteit van Amsterdam acted as coordinating university. As author and co-author of chapters in this book Sari Näsi (Universiteit van Amsterdam) and Aurélie Laborde (Université Michel de Montaigne, Bordeaux 3) should also be mentioned. A most welcome contribution from outside our group came from Albert Moran of Griffith University, Brisbane, whose study of European adaptations of the Australian soap *The Restless Years* is reprinted here in a revised form with permission of the University of Luton Press.

Our special thanks go to Chantal van Mourik, Sari Näsi and Franca Jonquière for their invaluable assistance at various stages of the project.

NOTE

1 E.g. Euromedia Research Group (ed. Bernt Stubbe Østergaard) (1997) *The Media in Western Europe: The Euromedia Handbook*, 2nd edition, London: Sage; Denis McQuail & Karen Siune (eds) (1998) *Media Policy. Convergence, Concentration & Commerce*. London: Sage.

TELEVISION ENVIRONMENTS: TRADITIONS AND TRANSITIONS

INTRODUCTION

Peter Dahlgren

When we switch on our television sets, we gain access to a number of different channels and the programming that they provide. In our everyday lives this is of course self-evident and seemingly unproblematic. Yet, behind our experience of watching television there are many factors at work that shape the number and kinds of channels that are available to us and the types of programmes they offer. Moreover, these factors have in recent years been increasingly altering the character of television environments in most European countries. Television in Europe today is very different from what it was in the early 1980s, and – perhaps of even greater relevance – we can anticipate that in a few years it will be quite dissimilar from what it is today. Obviously today's television carries forward many recognizable programming and scheduling traditions from earlier decades, but television, as a medium and as a complex institution, is in profound transition. The chapters in this section address these developments, specifying the various forces at work.

In approaching television as an institution, it is of central importance to grasp the basic logic of the two fundamental systems for organizing and financing television: the public service model and the commercial model.

In Chapter 1, Kees Brants and Els De Bens provide an introduction to television in Europe and sketch the basic differences between these systems. In almost all Western European countries, the principles of public service shaped the emergence of television in the post-war years (even in the few cases where there were channels with commercial financing). Indeed, European television was typified by public service monopolies until relatively recently. The aims of public service broadcasting are more complex than those of its commercial counterpart, and it has a more complicated system of accountability. Since public service television is in part structured by the specific political culture of any given country, it has varied somewhat within Europe.

The public service channels are still with us, but they lost their monopoly position in most countries during the 1980s and today television in

Western Europe is characterized by mixed systems. Not surprisingly, the emergence of commercial competitors has had an impact on the programming of public service broadcasters. As Brants and De Bens indicate, the response has varied somewhat between countries, but it is fair to say that in most cases there still remains a significant difference in the programming profiles between commercial and public service television.

Why did television in Western Europe evolve the way it did? What are the factors behind the emergence of commercial broadcasting? And what are the major trends in the new television landscape? These are the questions that Peter Dahlgren takes up in Chapter 2. He suggests that the changes in television have been brought about by the interplay of several factors. At the most immediate level, what is called deregulation opened the doors for commercial broadcasting, terminated public service monopolies, and removed or weakened many rules and regulations for television. In Dahlgren's presentation, deregulation is understood as part of a larger ideological shift away from the traditional model of the welfare state and toward an emphasis on market forces as the key mechanism for societal development. Given that public service broadcasters were all facing fiscal crises and many of these institutions were seen as stagnant and paternalistic, the time was ripe for introducing market mechanisms in television.

This shift toward market forces can in turn be related to widespread changes in society. For example, increasing cultural diversification, especially in regard to lifestyles and consumption, had helped promote a desire for greater choice among television viewers. This growing diversity made it more difficult for public service television, with its limited number of channels, to fulfil its mission. Further, public service was very clearly a product of nation states, and many argued that the world – not least markets and television itself – was becoming increasingly transnational.

In the new media landscape that took shape in the 1980s, cable networks and satellite transmissions became key features, though there is still great variation between different countries as to the degree of penetration of cable and satellite. Public service has generally responded vigorously to these changes. Yet there are lingering questions concerning its role in a situation where all growth within television will be in the commercial sector, and where public service will comprise a shrinking portion of the overall television environment. For the future, it is likely that entertainment programming will continue to increase and that audiences – and the shared public culture – will become more fragmented. Dahlgren ends his chapter with reflections on the implications of these developments for democracy.

The future of television is digital. In Chapter 3, Graham Murdock discusses the emerging digital technology. Digital television is on the immediate horizon, but already we are seeing strong connections being made between the technologies of television, telecommunication and computers. According to Murdock, there is an optimistic rhetoric about the digital development that promises several things. Audio and visual signals will be made clearer. We will have yet more channels via the digital technology. We will see the convergence of a variety of services, such as television programming, telephony, shopping, banking, etc., via a new 'universal box' that will replace today's television receivers. Finally, viewers will have more control over what they see and when they see it, given the increased interactivity made possible by the digital systems.

At the same time, Murdock warns that there are some very problematic aspects about the emerging digital systems. Already we see a clear pattern of a few major firms dominating the communication industries. The linking of television and computer technologies will accelerate this tendency, resulting in fewer choices for the consumer and a massive concentration of power. Further, given the commercial character of these enterprises, they will proceed on the logic of market niches, not social community. Diversity for minorities and for specialized tastes cannot be expected. Indeed, Murdock sees the main drive-shaft of these developments to be the realm of electronic commerce, to encourage people to make economic transactions. Digital television will be addressing the population as consumers, not citizens.

Finally, digital television will be an expensive proposition; many people will not be able to afford it. But since these people are weak consumers, digital television will have little interest in them. The virtue of universality – accessibility for all citizens – that was one of the hallmarks of public service, will have no place here. Murdock foresees that for the sake of democracy, public service television will have to become active in the digital domain. He suggests that in the new digital age public service television should join forces with other public institutions, such as schools, libraries and museums, to develop a 'digital commons' that would provide universal access. This is one possible future scenario; we can speculate about others. In the meantime, our television environments are undergoing rapid change, even if the future, for the time being, is still open.

CHAPTER 1

THE STATUS OF TV BROADCASTING IN EUROPE

Kees Brants and Els De Bens

In an average West European household television viewing is an intense and varied affair. In the sitting room members of the family will be watching a game show, a documentary or a soap. With the remote control in hand, every now and then one of them zaps along the channel supply to see whether a sports programme or the national news has already started. In another room one of the children will be watching a music channel with the latest video clips or decides on a video or film, on offer via the pay TV channel. This picture may differ across households and across countries – often depending on the availability of cable or a satellite dish which allows for a multiplicity of channels – but the choice and the variety of watching opportunities is enormous, and still extending.

At the same time, while members of one family may have different viewing experiences, there is also a cross-national familiarity and sometimes even similarity in what is on offer. TV news will have a national emphasis or angle, but going abroad and watching TV from a hotel room, one can see a familiar programme dubbed in another language, or a format like *Wheel of Fortune* adopted to the national taste with a different presenter and a slightly different style. And everywhere American sitcoms and films fill the small screen. Looking at a listings magazine and comparing the different channels, one is astounded to see how often one and the same film, talk show, serial is shown on different channels in different countries in the same week.

This complex and constantly changing picture of European broadcasting is relatively recent. In fact, it is a picture of the last ten, twenty years. In this chapter we present an overview of the history, system and changes of television in Europe, comparing the different countries' and different systems' media economics, organizational structure, goals and programming.

A PUBLIC BEGINNING

With the notable exception of Luxembourg, where a commercial system has always been in place, the history of broadcasting in Europe is rooted in an idea of public service. There is, however, not one theory or generally accepted notion of what public service broadcasting (PSB) stands for, and the variations in form according to national priorities and traditions are manifold. But even though there might be a different organizational structure and typical national programmes, that patchwork quilt we call the West European broadcasting system was, roughly until the 1980s, based on a belief that the programmes produced one way or the other had to be in the public interest. It usually meant that there was an explicit reference or implicit assumption of diversity and quality, catering for all while not forgetting minorities. It is only recently, with the system more or less in crisis, that decision makers are consciously referring to and nostalgically embracing what are seen as the functions of public broadcasting. For decennia the system had been self evident, unchallenged and heralded as a dam against what were considered to be the evils of commercial television: the mediocre and the popular, of which US television was the prime example.

In that history of public broadcasting in Europe it is not always clear what is fact and what is fiction, because the spectacles of hindsight are sometimes coloured by wishful thinking now that the creation seems to be overrun by avalanches of commercialization. In the 'good old days', first radio and later television was considered to provide 'public goods' which should be available to all, wherever they lived, for the same price. Most of us are familiar with water, electricity and the telephone as goods falling under this principle of universal service. But contrary to the USA, where broadcasting started as a commercial venture left to the freedom of the market, in most European countries the supply of radio (from the 1920s) and TV (roughly from the 1950s) was considered to be in the public interest. As such, the public goods of radio and TV had to be produced and distributed by institutions and by mechanisms guaranteed by the state and other than that of a market economy.

Why this deviation from a 'normal' pattern of capitalist production in which the ultimate aim is the maximization of profit and which dominates for instance that other mass medium, the press? There is a mixture of reasons. First of all, the sky had its limits. There were more demands for terrestrial space than there were frequencies at the time. So someone had to decide who could go on air and who not. To have a fair system of frequency allocation in a situation of scarcity, the state should be intimately involved, as it is both the representative and the guarantor of the general interest. Secondly, public broadcasting is a pragmatic compromise, comparable to and in line with the treatment of the welfare state. It has been 'firmly rooted, as a belief system and a set of institutional practices, in the optimistic, humanistic Enlightenment idea that the world can be made a humane place for all, and that the collective (the nation, the region) is important in order to allow the individual to flourish. Public good and public service converged in broadcasting' (Corcoran, 1996: 10). Shocked by the experiences of the Second World War, where the German Nazis under propaganda minister Goebels used radio to indoctrinate the people, the post-war development of broadcasting involved both protection from and intervention by the state.

Finally, partly due to this state intervention but also because governments saw the benefits as well as the dangers of this powerful new medium, public service broadcasting corporations were highly politicized organizations. There would usually be an uneasy balance between, on the one hand the ideal of editorial independence, which went with the Enlightenment ideal of the public sphere, and on the other hand the political reality of (sometimes direct) powers over finance and appointments, and a claim for easy access to the TV channels by representatives of what Golding (1994) has already described as the 'public relations state'.

The link between politics and broadcasting was not the same everywhere in Europe. Countries like Britain, Ireland and Sweden had more formally autonomous systems, in which mechanisms for distancing political organs from broadcaster decision-taking had been adopted. Germany, Denmark, Belgium and the Netherlands could be described as politics-in-broadcasting systems, in which the governing bodies of the broadcasting organizations included representatives of the country's main political parties as well as of social groups loosely affiliated with them. And in countries like Greece, Spain, Italy and France, state organs were in the past authorized to intervene in broadcaster decisions (Kelly, 1983: 73).

In spite of these political differences, we have seen a striking resemblance in European television of specially mandated, non-commercially driven organizations, publicly owned and funded, and publicly accountable. In 1994 the Council of Europe, in light of the threat to public broadcasting, summarized the cultural and social goals which justify such strict structures:

- a common reference point for all members of the public;
- a forum for broad public discussion;
- impartial news coverage;
- pluralistic, innovative and varied programming;
- programming which is both of wide public interest and attentive to the needs of minorities;
- reflection of the different ideas and beliefs in multi-ethnic and multicultural societies;
- a diversity of national and European cultural heritage;
- original production by independent producers; and
- extended viewer and listener choice of programmes not provided by the commercial sector (Council of Europe, 1994).

Quite a mouthful. And it will not always be easy to recognize one's own national public broadcasting system in it. It should be read, paradoxically, both as an idealization of 'days gone by' and as an ideal worth striving for. As such, it could be read as a statement, a definition contrasting what Europe is supposed to stand for culturally with the economic primacy of commercialization, epitomized by the private model of (US) broadcasting. But what does the situation in Europe look like, now that we have entered the 21st century and public TV stations are just one from among many?

THE LANDSCAPE

Indeed, the picture has changed dramatically in the last decennia of the previous century. The technological developments of cable and satellite and a changing political climate have opened up opportunities for television to flourish as a commodity-selling industry. Gradually commercial channels – which can be local, national or international, general or special interest, a copy of the familiar or a completely new experience – are beginning to dominate the television landscape. Up to the early 1980s the public broadcasting system dominated in the 17 countries of Western Europe. Against some 40 public channels in 1980 there were only four commercial channels, in only three countries (Luxembourg, Finland and the UK). At the end of the 20th century the balance has shifted. In spite of the fact that there are still no private companies in the national terrestrial television stations in Austria, Denmark, Ireland, the Netherlands and Switzerland, cable, satellite and a wind of liberalization have opened up markets for private companies in most West European countries and created a different broadcasting system (see Table 1.1).

Looking at national channels, both terrestrial and cable or satellite, we see in the 17 countries almost 60 public and over 70 private channels intended for a national audience and reaching more than 50 per cent of households. Moreover, there are now hundreds of mostly private cable and satellite channels that reach a smaller size audience per country, with a special interest character (music, sports, all news) or aiming at local or regional audiences. Only Austria, Ireland and Switzerland seem to hold on to a 'pure' public system, but in reality the last two already have a number of smaller private channels and Austria has some 19 local private TV stations. It is only a matter of time until Europe has no country without national private television.

The level of cable penetration and satellite dish sales still gives a rather scattered picture, which also explains the level of 'advance' in the different countries. Although potentially there are hundreds of satellite channels available (via Astra, Eutelsat, Hispasat and Intelsat, to name the most important ones), the penetration of dishes exceeds 20 per cent only in Austria and Germany. In cable infrastructure Belgium, Switzerland and the Netherlands stand out, while in large countries like Italy, Spain, Greece, the UK and France it is virtually absent. In Spain and the UK infrastructural

TABLE 1.1 Television in Western Europe

	Number of national terrestrial, cable & satellite channels (>50% reach) (1999)		Market share national channels in % (1998)		Cable penetration in % (1998)	Satellite dishes penetration in % (1997)
	Public	Private	Public	Private		
Austria	2	–	50	–	37	40
Belgium	5	5	32/17*	39/20	97	7
Denmark	3	1	68	10	66	20
Finland	2	2	47	48	40	10
France	6	15	44	52	11	12
Germany	11	12	42	51	48	31
Greece	3	6	10	72	0.6	5
Ireland	3	–	53	–	49	8
Italy	3	7	40	45	0.2	6
Luxembourg	–	1	–	58	87	6
Netherlands	3	8	37	43	90	4
Norway	2	3	43	44	37	18
Portugal	3	1	50	50	13	11
Spain	2	3	34	48	3	18
Sweden	3	5	48	43	52	20
Switzerland	3	–	26	–	95	20
UK	2	5	45	42	10	20

* Flanders and Wallonia respectively.

Source: Based on data from the European Audiovisual Observatory, 1999

development is under way now. The number of channels the different cable networks supply ranges from 11 (Finland, and some networks in the other Scandinavian countries, Germany and Switzerland) to more than 40 (in Portugal, Luxembourg and some of the other Scandinavian networks). The last ten years have observed an increase of pay TV channels to around 300 (depending on definition). About one-third is freely available, one-fifth are premium channels and the rest are broadcast encrypted and often available in packages of thematic services for a subscription fee. The overall effect of this explosion of channels and viewing opportunities has been a sizeable decrease in the audience for the traditional national public channels. Where until the 1980s they usually had a more or less complete monopoly, we now see that only the Danish and Irish public channels have more than 50 per cent of the market share. In Greece, Switzerland and Belgium the public stations have severe difficulties holding on to their audiences who, with the remote control in hand, zap across the multiplicity of channels. The coming of digital TV will further affect their market share and will also increase the number of subscription or pay-per-view channels.

To distinguish between the public and the private and to describe the status of TV broadcasting in Europe – its similarities, disparities and changes in the different countries – it is useful to highlight some of the characteristics of both broadcasting systems. We will therefore look at the ways they are financed, to whom they are accountable, what their mission is and what the programmes look like. In reality the public–private dichotomy is, however, a continuum between public aims and private ambitions, between political beliefs and economic realities.

FINANCING

As we have seen, the public service model was dominant in Europe until the mid-1980s. Only Luxembourg's CLT (better known as RTL) was from its beginning in 1929 purely private. In 1954 a commercial Independent Television Authority was established in the UK next to and competing with the BBC and in Finland MTV was established as an independent private company which had to pay one-fifth of its earnings to the public YLE. Elsewhere in Western Europe the public TV channels had a monopoly and were financed mainly through licence fees. These fees are mostly collected by official authorities (only in the UK and Austria do the corporations collect them themselves) and in most countries Parliament decides on the amount and about the endowment that will be attributed to the public service corporation. Not in every country do the corporations get the full amount, which makes public service systems vulnerable to and dependent on political decision making. The same can be said for the situation in the Netherlands, where in 1999 the government abandoned the licence fee and now pays directly from taxation.

In most Western European countries licence fees for a colour TV set vary from 100 to 200 Euro. France's fee is among the lowest in Europe, with ± 100 Euro for a colour TV set. Four million households in this country are not required to pay, on account of their low income. This has resulted in insufficient funding so that public TV channels have become more and more dependent on TV advertising revenue. France is not alone in this. In order to increase their financial revenues, many of the public service TV systems introduced TV advertising on a limited and non-commercial basis: the money earned went into programming (see Table 1.2). The amount of advertising and insertions were legally restricted so that the print media, which are highly dependent on advertising revenue, would not suffer. In the UK, Norway, Denmark, Sweden and Belgium no advertising was allowed on public TV (in the French speaking part of Belgium TV advertising was introduced, in a limited way, in 1989 on the public TV RTBF).

Over time, public service systems have become more and more dependent on advertising revenue, as a rise in the licence fee was not considered viable in light of the growing number of commercial channels that were (relatively) freely available. Some countries even cut their fees. In Spain a fee never existed. After the Franco regime, the Spanish government decided that the PSB-system was to be financed by advertising revenue and small public support. This situation was unique in Europe and until today there is no licence fee in Spain.

TABLE 1.2 Public service TV revenues (%)

	Licence fee	Advertising/sponsoring
Austria	46	53
Belgium (W.)†	65	34
Belgium (Fl.)	69	31
Denmark	91	9
Finland	74	26
France	44	56
Germany	60	31
Greece	82	7
Ireland	35	65
Italy	56	40
Netherlands	69	22
Norway	97	3
Portugal	23	62
Spain	13	75
Sweden	94	6
Switzerland	71	28
UK	78	15*

* Mainly programme sales.
† W. = Walloonia
Fl. = Flanders

Source: European Audiovisual Observatory, 1999

With the success of new commercial TV stations from the mid-1980s, the advertising revenue of public channels in some countries fell sharply. In Germany for instance, ARD's advertising revenue decreased from 19 per cent in 1988 to 4.1 per cent in 1994. ZDF, the second public TV system, in 1988 still had 38.4 per cent and in 1994 only 15.8 per cent (Ros, 1998: 228). The same happened in many other countries and the loss of advertising caused many a PSB financial problems, prompting them to campaign for the removal of legal restrictions on TV advertising. At the same time, many PSB systems were allowed to carry sponsoring, even in those countries where advertising was forbidden.

The success of the first commercial stations has recently been affected by many newcomers who have intensified the competition for viewers and advertisers in a relatively inflexible advertising market. In the UK, ITV's advertising income dropped from 85 per cent in 1991 to 78 per cent in 1995; BSkyB has become an important competitor on the TV advertising market. In Spain the three new commercial stations provoked an acute crisis for the public TV (RTE). This led to a dramatic situation in the 1990s in which RTE accumulated debts, forcing government support. In fairly exceptional situations like that of Denmark, the new commercial stations were, from the point of audience share, less successful than public TV. The erosion of the advertising market in the digital age will undoubtedly place a further burden on the survival chances of many (public and private) channels. In a 500-channel world, 490 services will fight for ever smaller audience fragments (Jankowsky and Fuchs, 1995: 161). Indeed, many authors have their doubts whether an extension of the channel range will drastically alter viewers' habits. In most countries viewers are relatively loyal to the channels in their own language and the market quickly reaches saturation point in terms of segmentation (Achille and Miège, 1994: 43; De Bens, 1998: 33).

As the advertising market will not be large enough and audience fluctuation creates uncertainties for advertisers, viewers will have to pay for most *à la carte* services, notably sporting events, that accompany digital television. Some thematic channels offering movies, sports or news might be successful. Many pay TV channels in Europe, however, never reach their break-even point and demonstrate that viewers are not easily prepared to pay for TV services. Most of the movie channels in Europe broke down or were taken over by their more powerful rivals such as Canal Plus. This transnational pay channel, originally a movie channel, acquired the broadcast rights of important sports events. In 1996 the European Parliament amended the renewed directive, Television Without Frontiers, ensuring free access to television coverage of major sports events like the Olympic Games, world and European soccer championships. Pay TV channels like Canal Plus will be obliged to sell these broadcasts at a 'reasonable price' to national TV channels, an amendment multinational media tycoons are strongly objecting to. On the other hand, Canal Plus and Eurosport have pushed most of their competitors out of the market, only to illustrate that the thematic, narrowcast TV market is a high risk business.

It cannot be denied that in Europe public broadcasting systems are under heavy pressure. The European Commission has argued in the past that licence fees were to be interpreted as an unlawful state subsidy. This could threaten public service broadcasting. On the initiative of the Dutch government, with the support of Belgium, Ireland, Sweden, the European Broadcasting Union (EBU) and the European Parliament, a proposal was made to the EU Council of Ministers that licence fees for PSB be excluded from the definition of state subsidy. At the Amsterdam Summit meeting of 1997 a protocol to that effect was adopted.

ACCOUNTABILITY

Commercial broadcasters sometimes say that they produce real public TV, because they know and do what the public wants. To put it simply but not untruly, however, the commercial broadcaster is ultimately in the business of making money and thus accountable only to his shareholders. They judge his performance on the basis of audience-related cost–benefit analyses of the annual turnover. The bottom line of commercial accountability is whether the books say in hard cash what the broadcasters have promised their programmes will deliver in audience size. If the latter waver or retract, first the advertisers go, to be followed shortly by the programme and, sometimes, the programme manager and even the managing director.

Accountability in commercial broadcasting is a matter of 'deliverables': audiences and revenues. Accountability in public broadcasting is much more complex and based on the idea that asking money (licence fee) for public goods demands some form of responsiveness to the public or to its representatives in politics that oversee their financing and regulation. Looking at Europe, there are really two patterns or modes of accountability in public broadcasting discernible: political accountability and administrative accountability (cf. Mitchell and Blumler, 1994: 5–6, 207–227). It was and often still is mainly through political institutions like ministries, parliaments or one or more parties and sometimes social groups like labour unions that European public broadcasters are held accountable for their finances, policies and programming. Being public monopolies, such accountability was more or less self-evident. Even the commercial RTL in Luxembourg was (loosely) monitored by the Prime Minister's office. Moreover, in many instances the formal powers of the government or Parliament over television broadcasting are supplemented by varying measures of informal influence, not least over appointments (Mitchell and Blumler, 1994: 211). In that sense public broadcasting in Europe is still heavily politicized.

In the wake of neo-liberal policies, governments try to increase their distance from broadcasting by transferring supervision to more or less independent authorities. The appointment of the members of these bodies is still mainly a matter for the executive and the legislative, but a new non-governmental category of social groups is becoming involved in the nomination and sometimes appointment of the members of these regulatory bodies (Robillard, 1995). For some time now the UK has had its Broadcasting Standards Council, which considers complaints from viewers about programmes, and in France the main regulatory body CSA (Conseil Supérieur de l'Audiovisuel) holds frequent consultative meetings with viewers' organizations. Further ahead in constitutional arrangements for representation of viewer interests are Germany, which with its legalistic tradition has different *Räte* for the commercial and private sectors which all have representatives of cultural and other interests in society. Greece has an Assembly of Viewers and Listeners, which functions as a watchdog of the public broadcaster. Portugal has an opinion council with representatives from consumer, family and other associations, and even Luxembourg is planning a Conseil National des Programmes with a degree of representation for civil society (Robillard, 1995: 267–272).

Overseeing recent developments in Europe, Mitchell and Blumler conclude, however, that accountability to viewers has been marginalized. 'It has not so far been a central concept in the governance of European broadcasting systems – not in shaping their law and organization; not as a focus of public debate (though the UK is a marked exception here); and not as a high priority for the consumer movement' (1994: 231).

MISSION

Today, every organization is supposed to have a mission. Private broadcasters often remind critics that their social responsibility lies in providing programmes people like. But as commercial broadcasters are ultimately in the business of making money, they produce programmes to attract audiences that they can sell to advertisers. Again, the mission of public service broadcasting is a different and more complex one, and in fact consists of three, related elements: a cultural-pedagogic logic, its place in civil society, and its contribution to national social cohesion.

The *cultural-pedagogic logic* is part of the Enlightenment ideal of the welfare state and the assumed 'makeability' of society. Television programmes should thus be in the public interest and not necessarily what the public is interested in. They are to educate, to inform and to enrich the public culturally. Or as the British Annan Committee put it in 1977: 'to enlarge people's interest, to convey to them new choices and possibilities in life'. Television is also be enjoyed, of course, as long as its programmes are of high quality. As such, this logic has a relatively paternalistic view of television's role in society, based on a mixture of high hopes about the potential of the medium and fears about its potential incitement to consumerism if television is only treated as a pleasure machine. How differently from its predecessor did the British Peacock Committee put it ten years and a cultural change later: 'The fundamental aim . . . should in our view be to enlarge both the freedom of choice of the consumer and the opportunities available to programme makers to offer alternative wares to the public' (Peacock, 1986: 125).

Related to the cultural-pedagogic logic is the *function of broadcasting in civil society*, the roles media in general and public service broadcasting in particular are expected to perform for democracy. According to this view, in order to arrive at rational decision making an informed citizenry is necessary which can take stock of all opinions aired in society. That way they can make sense of that information and of themselves in relation to it, and thus be able to participate in and contribute to the functioning of democracy. The latter requires that the media – and for Europe particularly public service broadcasting – perform and provide a number of functions and services for the political system. In the words of Blumler and Gurevitch (1995: 97) these are:

- surveillance of the socio-political environment, reporting developments likely to impinge, positively or negatively, on the welfare of citizens;
- meaningful agenda setting, identifying the key issues of the day, including the forces that have formed and may resolve them;
- platforms for an intelligible and illuminating advocacy by politicians and spokespersons of other cause and interest groups;
- dialogue across a diverse range of views, as well as between power holders (actual and prospective) and mass publics;

- mechanisms for holding officials to account for how they have exercised power;
- incentives for citizens to learn, choose and become involved, rather than merely to follow the political process;
- a principled resistance to the efforts of forces outside the media to subvert their independence, integrity and ability to serve the audience;
- a sense of respect for the audience member, as potentially concerned and able to make sense of his or her political environment.

Finally, the mission refers to *social cohesion*, albeit in a complicated and sometimes conflicting form. Public broadcasting should both contribute to the dominant consensus in a society and support the process whereby alternative, minority identities and sets of values can be put forward (cf. McQuail, 1992: 263). In programme language this means: a combination of programmes for 'everyone', specific programmes for minorities, programmes that highlight and strengthen the national cultural heritage and programmes which recognize minority (ethnic, gender, class) cultural identities as valuable to society as a whole.

In combination with broadcasting's function for civil society, the idea is that knowledge is a prerequisite for participation, which in itself strengthens loyalty and stronger involvement. The basic premise of the cohesive and consensual function of public broadcasting is that the more individuals participate, the stronger their bond with the system and the more they identify with it, and the greater the social cohesion of the system will be. Openness of and access to the public broadcasting system ideally provides the prerequisites for a common frame of reference.

PROGRAMMES

'Selling audiences to advertisers' is how commercial broadcasters often describe the bottom line of their programme strategy. Their policy is aimed at two kinds of viewers: those that are commercially interesting by size and those that should be targeted for spending potential. Commercial broadcasters are well aware that the well-off are more (or at least also) interested in quality programmes like news, current affairs, culture and the arts, and that public broadcasters not only have a lead here, but that to provide these is also part of their mission. The commercial strategy is thus firstly aimed at audience size, which in programmatic terms means an emphasis on entertainment. But secondly, they feel they have to broadcast news and quality programmes in order to minimize the potential damage done by public competition for the higher income audience groups.

Public broadcasters, on the other hand, are confronted by private stations that are tied less by legal obligation to broadcast informative, educational, cultural as well as entertainment programmes; to give a diverse and balanced representation of social and political views in society; and to cater for minorities as well as the whole public. Moreover, their commercial competitors can go all out for the viewer and are thus bound to take a big chunk out of the advertising pie. Public broadcasters thus feel they have to compete and a commercialization of programme policy, though legally restricted, is a tempting option.

So, where commercial broadcasters are relatively bound by their goal of selling audiences to advertisers, public broadcasters are tied by public obligations and their non-commerciality. The money the latter make, they spend on programmes while, relatively speaking, private stations make programmes for money. One of the crucial questions here is whether the numerous new television channels in Europe have resulted in a change in the ratio of light, entertainment programming, compared to 'serious' informational genres; in a marginalization of less popular and informational programming (outside prime time); in an increase of the total amount of imported TV programmes (especially from the United States) because of the increase of TV hours to be filled; and in a growing convergence of public and private TV channels in style and ethos as well as in content, as different channels compete for the same household audiences at favourable peak viewing times.

In all, the picture of TV programming in Western Europe that emerges from not always comparable research is scattered and as yet not unequivocally supportive of a convergence hypothesis which claims that public TV will adopt commercial programming. Firstly, there is an increase of entertainment programming, mainly because of the increase in the number of commercial channels and also because public stations now broadcast longer hours than before. Competition has stimulated the increase of entertainment, especially fiction, on both public and private stations, especially during prime time. Even in Norway, where the public monopoly was only broken in 1992 and where the new commercial station is not so successful, public TV has increased the entertainment category. In Italy, France, Finland, Belgium and probably many other countries the entertainment category has slightly expanded and is scheduled especially during prime time (McQuail, 1998: 123; d'Haenens and Saeys, 1998; Euromedia Research Group, 1997, European Audiovisual Observatory, 1999).

Looking at the larger countries, there still is a marked difference between the two systems: entertainment is considerably more popular with commercial stations (see Table 1.3). In Germany trends between 1986 and 1997 show stability of programming in the public service channels: entertainment did not grow very much but scheduling is mainly in prime time. Krüger (1998: 326) stresses the fact that homogenization and convergence between the programme output of public and private TV stations increases during prime time.

Secondly, most public channels screen a higher percentage of information programmes than commercial stations. France tops the bill. Even if with some stations the information category has dropped, it still exceeds that of commercial stations, Italy being a notable exception. The arts

TABLE 1.3 TV programming in Western Europe in % (1997)

	Entertainment		Information		Arts		Sports	
	Public	**Private**	**Public**	**Private**	**Public**	**Private**	**Public**	**Private**
France	36	60	45	22	1	0.7	3	3
Germany	40	56	20	13	3	0.7	4	2.5
Italy	55	73	18	24	7	–	7	2
Spain	43	58	16	12	7	1	10	8
UK*	31	49	30	18	**	2	9	8

* Without BSkyB.

** No comparable data available.

Source: Based on data from the European Audiovisual Observatory, 1999

usually have a marginal position, while sports is still predominantly for the public stations. Pay TV is taking over here, however.

Although there is a difference between public and private stations, there is no confirmation of a structural convergence of the former with the latter in the style and format of informational programmes. Both commercial and public channels in Germany have increased their political information in the news since the mid-1980s; commercial competition in Denmark has led to more varied news from more sources; and Dutch news increased its number of national political items (Brants, 1998). Public TV in Spain, however, has seen a dramatic homogenization of programme supply. In spite of a discussion about the BBC 'dumbing down', media content in the UK still falls under strict programme obligations. Since the arrival of BSkyB in the early 1990s, which has no such obligations, ITV became 'a much more belligerently commercial network' (Tunstall, 1997: 252). However, on both BBC and ITV information programmes are important.

Thirdly, the main share (71 per cent) of imported fiction programming is of US origin. Of the total imported fiction (including feature films) on offer, however, this is never higher than 50 per cent (see Table 1.4). On the whole, private stations use considerably more imported fiction programmes than the public channels. Where one would expect larger countries to have a bigger budget for national programme production, there does not seem to be a link between country size or language (English, German, French) and percentage of imported fiction. Practically the only country making money out of its programme sales abroad is the UK, which accounts for 5 per cent of the fiction imported by TV channels in the European Union. While the import figure for US fiction is still slowly going up, that of the UK is going down.

Authors like Biltereyst (1995) claim that the omnipresence of American fiction on European channels stimulates convergence and undermines the cultural diversity of the European programming industry. He also points out, however, that viewers invariably prefer home-made fiction, which also yields the highest ratings. Moreover, the European Commission has put forward a binding directive (Television Without Frontiers) to counter US influence. Part of this is a quota system in which 'a majority proportion

TABLE 1.4 TV fiction import in Western Europe (in % of total broadcasting hours, 1997)

	Public		Private	
	Total	US	Total	US
Austria	44	29	–	–
Belgium	28	14	49	36
Denmark	23	13	61	46
Finland	27	13	36	27
France	24	11	44	30
Germany	31	9	60	48
Greece	23	4	30	22
Ireland	47	30	–	–
Italy	20	13	46	32
Netherlands	18	7	27	22
Norway	19	9	59	48
Portugal	31	15	65	39
Spain	25	15	43	33
Sweden	12	6	52	38
Switzerland	49.5	32	–	–
UK	20	16	26*	21

* Excluding BSkyB.

Source: based on data from European Audiovisual Observatory, 1999

of broadcasting needs to go to European works' (Art. 4 of Directive 89/552/EEC). According to the latest report of the Commission (1996), practically all channels comply with these rules, but as all programmes can be counted (except news, sports, games and advertising) the results are ambiguous.

The so-called Media-programme has been set up by the European Commission to subsidize and support cooperation, co-production and in general activities in support of the European audiovisual industry. In recent years, most European channels have made major financial efforts to produce more fiction. Because of the extension of broadcasting time, however, they are forced to rely on foreign imports to fill the many programming hours. The scenario is the same everywhere: American productions are cheaper than the European ones.

A CONCLUDING OVERVIEW

The West European broadcasting landscape has changed dramatically over the last ten or twenty years, though not everywhere as significantly as is sometimes claimed. Financially public broadcasting has suffered substantially. From a monopoly situation, with an income in most cases of both a licence fee and advertising, the public broadcasters now have to share that

System	1980	1990	1999
Public monopoly	Belgium, Denmark, Norway, Sweden		
Public monopoly/ Mixed revenue	Austria, Finland, France, Germany, Greece, Iceland, Ireland, Netherlands, Portugal, Switzerland	Austria, Denmark, Iceland, Ireland, Netherlands, Portugal, Switzerland	Austria, Ireland, Switzerland
Private monopoly/ advertising only	Luxembourg	Luxembourg	Luxembourg
Dual system	Italy, UK	Belgium, Finland, France, Germany, Greece, Italy, Norway, Spain, Sweden, UK	Belgium, Denmark, Finland, France, Germany, Greece, Iceland, Italy, Netherlands, Norway, Portugal, Spain, Sweden, UK

FIGURE 1.1 **Typology of national systems (1980/1990/1999) (Siune and Hulten, 1998: 27)**

last resource with an increasing number of private channels while the licence fee is not going up. With more broadcasters eating from the same cake, the slices become thinner and thinner.

From a programmatic point of view, entertainment programmes have increased with the advent of stations aiming at as large an audience as possible, and so has the import of American fiction. However, the total picture is more diverse and ambiguous than to warrant a claim of Americanization or 'a crisis in public communication' (Blumler and Gurevitch, 1995). The tight regulatory regime which typifies public broadcasting seems to have rubbed off, in a way, on the programmatic output of the private channels. In that sense, the simple dichotomy between, on the one hand, private stations with purely commercial aims and entertainment programming and, on the other, public channels with a cultural-pedagogic mission, ditto programming and public financing only, is too simple. If only when looking at the UK's ITV and Channel Four, Sweden's TV 4 and Finland's MTV 3, there is a 'third way' of private stations with a profit motive but also a more or less public obligation, set out by broadcasting law.

The change is most dramatic if we look at the system changes in the European countries (see Figure 1.1). From a public monopoly in the 1980s, in most cases with a mixture of licence fee and advertising, we now see an almost complete dual picture in Western Europe. The notable exception is Luxembourg, which with its population of just over 400,000 is really too small for its own public channel. For Austria, Ireland and Switzerland the clock is ticking away.

ACTIVITIES

1 Do you recognize the cultural and social goals defined by the Council of Europe, if you look at the public broadcaster in your own country?
2 Take a programme magazine and compare the programmes on offer of a private and a public channel over a period of a week. Categorize the programmes (news and public affairs, fiction, entertainment shows, sports, talk shows, etc.).

- What are the differences and similarities that you can find between the two kinds of channel?
- What conclusions do you draw from this?

Do the same, but now compare two countries. How do they compare on informational programmes, fiction, foreign import, etc.?
3 Tape the main news programme of the major public and private channels. Compare the topics covered, the order of topics, national versus international news, etc. Do the same, but now for two countries.

SUGGESTIONS FOR FURTHER READING

Euromedia Research Group (1997) *The Media in Western Europe*. London: Sage.

A regularly updated country by country study of the historical developments, present day situation and policies of the different media in different West European countries compiled by the Euro-Media Research Group. All studies follow the same format and give comparable statistics.

European Audiovisual Observatory (1999) *Statistical Yearbook '99. Film, Television, Video and New Media in Europe*. Strasbourg: Council of Europe.

All the statistics of the media, their finances, business, sales, content in 34 European countries, with short discussions of trends, cross-cultural comparisons, also with other parts of the world. A new edition every year.

McQuail, D. and Siune, K. (eds) (1998) *Media Policy. Convergence, Concentration and Commerce*. London: Sage.

A comparative analysis of developments, trends, economics and policies of press, broadcasting, new media, the Internet in Western Europe based on the country studies of the Euromedia Research Group.

CHAPTER 2

KEY TRENDS IN EUROPEAN TELEVISION

Peter Dahlgren

In the previous chapter Brants and De Bens presented an overview of television – both public service (PSB) and commercial – in Western Europe today. In this chapter we will be looking at some of the factors that have been shaping television in recent years and that are defining its future. Television does not operate in a vacuum. It is structured by policy decisions, and these in turn are influenced by a range of societal circumstances. We will thus look at the deregulation of broadcasting and the larger ideological changes of which it is a part, as well as some key social trends that have contributed to altering the circumstances of broadcasting. We'll also take a brief look at developments in the new television landscape at the turn of the century. We conclude with some lingering issues that continue to be discussed in regard to television's future.

DEREGULATION

Society is not a static entity; it is always in dynamic flux. An institution of such central importance as television obviously cannot remain frozen in time – it too must evolve. The question is in which directions. There are a variety of factors that help define the character of television in modern society, and one of the key elements is to be found in its regulation. Regulation has to do with the sets of laws and codes by which governments define how television is to operate. This in part relates to programming: regulation specifies in very general ways the character of the programming. For example, broadcasters are under obligation to provide certain categories of programming, such as news and current affairs, and often minimal amounts are specified. There is also a variety of restrictions, for example how much advertising (if any) may appear. Yet regulation also deals with an even more fundamental question, namely how broadcasting is to be financed.

In the first chapter we saw how the idea of public service television was institutionalized in almost all Western European countries after the Second World War. The basic structure that emerged was that PSB had a regulated monopoly. Where there were commercial television stations, chiefly in the UK, these were integrated within an overarching regulatory framework where public service ideals set limits to the free play of commercial activities. The private broadcasters had to operate in a regulatory environment that emphasized public service over profits.

The actual regulation set by governments is a result of complicated policy processes where a number of different interests try to influence what the regulation will look like. Among the actors who can have a stake in the shape of broadcast regulation are newspaper publishers, independent programme production companies, advertising companies, other financial interests, and political parties (for ideological reasons). Also, there is a growing number of actors in the area of newer media, such as cable-TV operators, satellite investors and commercial television entrepreneurs, not least transnational ones. The policy process can be understood as political negotiation, in which regulation is a compromise solution between competing interests.

Beginning in the early 1980s, the political climate that had prevailed for many years in regard to broadcasting began to change. We'll discuss why this was so in a moment. The regulatory compromises were no longer satisfying for many (newer) actors on the scene. What emerged was a development called 'deregulation': the regulatory framework that had defined and held public service in place began to erode.

The Danish media scholar Stig Hjarvard suggests that deregulation here has three elements. The first is a break-up of the monopolies of public service broadcasters, which resulted, among other things, in a competitive situation. Public service broadcasters were no longer the only players. A second element is the commercialization of broadcasting: the new actors in broadcasting were permitted to organize their activities according to market principles, with advertising as their source of income. Various arrangements for pay TV services are also a part of the commercial model: one subscribes to a channel (or 'package' of channels) or pays per programme viewed.

In keeping with this move to market mechanisms, many of the programme obligations associated with public service were greatly relaxed or removed entirely. The new commercial broadcasters had fewer restrictions placed on them in regard to programming. And enforcing the regulations that remained at times proved difficult. In practice, commercialization is a complex practice that cannot simply be deemed 'good' or 'bad' (cf. McQuail, 1998). The commercial model, however, does imply a different societal orientation, compared to PSB, as we will discuss below.

There was a third element of deregulation: transnationalization. While public service broadcasters were national in their operations, the new players were local, regional, national and transnational. Deregulation opened the gates to the transnationalization of television, but it could also be argued that deregulation in part was a response to growing transnational tendencies. For example, TV3, a commercial satellite channel, began in the late 1980s to transmit to the Scandinavian countries from London, but in the Scandinavian languages. In Sweden seeing advertising money being drawn out of the country in this way was an important factor in the establishment of TV4, the commercial terrestrial channel, in the early 1990s.

IDEOLOGICAL SHIFTS

The emergence of deregulation of broadcasting did not take place suddenly, nor was it isolated from other societal developments. One can understand deregulation as part of a larger shift in the political climate of western societies. In very simplified terms, the first three decades or so after the Second World War were characterized by the development of social welfare states within capitalist economies. The breadth and depth of the welfare provided to citizens varied between countries, but there was basically a consensus that society had a responsibility to guarantee a minimal level of well-being for its citizens, in terms of health services, social security, education, environment, and so on. The funding for this of course comes from taxes, on individual wage earners and on corporations. This can be seen as a form of 'regulation', not least of the mechanisms of market forces. Society was dependent on an expansive economy, but this expansion was to be steered and channelled for the public good, not just for the profits of a few.

For a variety of reasons, including global economic difficulties during the 1970s and inefficiencies and rising costs in some areas of the public sector, this consensus began to unravel. A strong, international neo-liberal political shift to the right developed. In the United States, the Reagan administration in the 1980s went far not only in deregulating broadcasting, but generally in removing many restrictions on market forces. In Britain, in the same period, the Thatcher government also proceeded to further unfetter the mechanisms of market. Many previously public bodies and services were sold off, privatized and operated for profit.

While not as pronounced as in the US and UK, similar patterns were witnessed in other Western European countries, with support from a variety of political parties, even social democrats in some cases. Social development was to proceed according to the dictates of the market, with a minimum of government involvement. According to this neo-liberal view, this political shift would enhance the freedom of the individual. At the same time, the gaps between rich and poor widened dramatically, and the influence of the corporate sector on political life expanded.

Broadcasting could hardly remain exempt from these developments. In Europe, Italy was among the first to dramatically deregulate (Humphreys,

1996: 178–180), beginning in the mid-1970s. By the time regulatory legislation caught up with the situation in the form of a new Broadcasting Act in 1990, it could do little more than legitimize and solidify a situation that has been profoundly altered by commercial mechanisms during the previous decade and a half. By contrast, legislation in Germany managed rather well to protect public service values in this period of commercial growth (Humphreys, 1996: 187).

A number of different 'actors' or 'players' strive to promote broadcasting systems in keeping with the principles of market forces (Humphreys, 1996: 176). Obviously advertisers, cable and satellite lobbies and the electronics industry all support such developments, since this opens up new possibilities for them. So too do governments, who wish to stimulate the economy, attract media investors, and develop new media technologies; they are increasingly willing to weaken their support for public service in order to attain larger economic benefits. Political parties on the right, with a neo-liberal agenda and a commitment to the interests of business, also support the 'marketization' of television. It should be noted here that the European Union, chiefly through its Commission, has also been playing an active role in promoting a television steered by market logic. In support of public service we naturally find the broadcasters themselves, but also a diverse coalition of citizen groups, political parties on the left, unions, and educators.

The arguments put forth in favour of the commercialization of broadcasting had several components, some of which struck at PSB's vulnerability at this time. It was argued that public service broadcasting was a stagnant, inefficient structure, and that competition would stimulate the television environment. And many of the TV institutions had become too bureaucratic and less creative. The proximity of public service to state power varied between countries, as we saw in the last chapter, but in many contexts the argument about state-influenced television hit home. The picture of an old-fashioned, paternalistic television often met with a positive political response. Perhaps most important was the claim (classic in the American context) that commercial broadcasting would better be able to give the public what it wanted, via cost-effective companies tuned to consumer demand. Certainly commercial television can manifest a dynamic quality many viewers have found lacking in public service.

One particular argument often put forth in support of commercial model of broadcasting is that it enhances diversity; broadcasters will 'give viewers what they want'. However, the general pattern, witnessed globally, is that commercial broadcasters tend to display considerably less diversity in their programming compared to PSB. This is because their economic logic aims for the 'great middle': commercial broadcasters are largely all competing for the same large audience, so the programming tends to follow rather confined patterns. We would stress, however, that commercial logic need not *per se* be antithetical to quality. Quality is an elusive concept, and there have been various efforts to define and even measure it (cf. Ishikawa, 1996), but what people define as 'good' programming will always be open to debate. Our point, however, is simply that a commercial model does not mean that there will be no good programmes, but that one should not expect as much diversity in the overall programming as found in PSB.

If we compare this last assertion with the Council of Europe's nine goals justifying public service structures (see Chapter 1), we see that the ideological framework is quite different in the case of commercial broadcasting. There is for example, no mention of any 'common reference point for all members of the public'. The 'mission' of commercial broadcasting, if we can use that term, does not take into account the three aspects central to public service: (see Chapter 1) there is no cultural-pedagogic logic, no reference to civil society, and no concern expressed for social cohesion. Deregulation and the larger ideological shifts of which it is a part raise important questions about the character of television and its place in society. We will return to these questions at the end of the chapter. Let us now look briefly at some of the major changes in society that have contributed to ushering in a new television age.

SOCIAL CHANGES

If deregulation as a policy direction is related to the larger changes in ideological climate, both are in turn inseparable from larger social developments. We will not attempt a far-reaching analysis of late modern society here, but only mention a few interrelated themes that are significant for understanding trends in television. The first has to do with cultural differentiation. This in part relates to the large immigrant populations in many Western European countries that have contributed to giving these societies a more pluralistic composition. Many countries, in short, have become multiethnic. Some, such as the Netherlands, have had long experience of immigration as part of their colonial legacy, while others, such as Sweden, have experienced relatively recent immigration via the labour market and refugee measures.

Yet cultural differentiation has emerged on many fronts, not least in the domain of consumption and leisure. The popular magazine market can serve as a mirror of this development. If one walks into a well-supplied newsagent's today one is struck by the vast array of categories among the magazines: computers, gardening, skateboarding, music, musical instruments, tattoos, cigar-smoking, fishing, antiques, skiing, UFOs, boating, romance fiction, science fiction, popular psychology, celebrities, etc., etc. And within each category are often many sub-categories, further defining and specifying interests.

What this suggests is a massive growth in the diversification of leisure and lifestyles. With the general growth in affluence of the populations of Western Europe (despite the economic difficulties) more people are in a position to engage in consumer-based leisure. As markets expand, more people feel that they have more choices they can make in this regard. Travel and tourism are also domains that have helped promote new ways of seeing the world and oneself. We can also note that a good deal of the civic involvement that engaged people in the past is not as strong today. Particularly among the young, participation in politics and membership in parties and other traditional institutions of civil society, such as church or neighbourhood associations, is often less strong. The cultural unity such involvement fostered has in part been replaced by diversified consumer leisure activities.

In short, the popular cultural landscape has become more differentiated; our social world a bit more pluralistic, and our identities – our sense of who we are and what we want – somewhat more heterogeneous. The cultural commonality of national populations – as manifested in everyday leisure activities and lifestyle identities – has declined (but by no means vanished). If we situate these developments in the context of television, it suggests that it is now more difficult to satisfy the interests of a large population with only one or two television channels, and that audiences will obviously be attracted to a wider channel choice. Yet this also implies that the audiences in a media landscape with more channels will be more fragmented, reducing the cultural commonality that prevailed under a one- or two-channel system.

THE EMERGING TELEVISION LANDSCAPE

The commercialization of television comes in part from domestic initiatives, in part from transnational activities. The economic and technological spheres have been undergoing extensive globalization in recent decades. Michael Tracey (1998: 46) observes that among the top 500 corporations in the US, half proclaim that they belong to no single nation. Within the communication field, Herman and McChesney (1997: 1) describe a very clear tendency:

> Since the early 1980s there has been a dramatic restructuring of national media industries, along with the emergence of a genuinely global commercial media market. The newly developing global media system is dominated by three or four dozen large transnational corporations (TNCs), with fewer than ten mostly US-based media conglomerates towering over the global market. In addition to the concentration of media power, the major feature of the global media order is its thoroughgoing commercialism, and an associated marked decline in the relative importance of public broadcasting and the applicability of public service standards. Such a concentration of media power in organizations dependent on advertising support and responsible primarily to shareholders is a clear and present danger to citizens' participation in public affairs, understanding of public issues, and thus to the effective working of democracy.

The welfare state, with its national boundaries and its economies traditionally shaped largely by national enterprise, has increasingly been confronted with economic actors – in the media as well as in other domains – for whom national borders have less meaning. The most obvious example are the transnational satellite channels, which readily cross national frontiers, but even national commercial TV channels often have foreign investors. This, together with fiscal limitations, ideological shift and social changes, has made it more difficult for governments to enact effective broadcasting policy with regulation aimed at public service.

At the beginning of the 1980s almost all television transmission was by terrestrial broadcasters and limited to a small number of public service channels. This changed dramatically as the decade wore on. Commercial stations were introduced, and new technologies appeared. While there are now terrestrial commercial broadcasters in most Western European countries, up to 90 per cent of households in some areas of Europe receive their television transmission via cable and/or satellite. Satellites help make more efficient use of the airwaves, a direction that is being further developed by the technologies of digitalization, as we will see in the next chapter. It is useful to understand that satellite transmissions can be of two basic types: direct-to-home (DTH; previously termed direct-broadcasting-satellite, DBS), where a receiver 'dish' is used, and satellite-cable system relay, which is by far the most common. Cable links relay the satellite signal to paying subscribers. Cable companies operate in specific, delimited areas, often competing with each other, offering somewhat different channel 'packages'. This situation, with commercial competitors operating both via terrestrial stations and cable-satellite relays, is far removed from that of the public service monopolies.

How has PSB responded to these developments? These broadcasters have over two decades been witnessing the loss of their monopoly, the introduction of competition, deregulation and an overall ideological shift in favour of market forces, processes of media globalization, and the increasing cultural diversification of the population. In countries like Germany and Sweden, the viewing of PSB declined by nearly a half in the first years of the 1990s. Hultén and Brants (1992) suggest that there are basically three possible strategic responses: adaptation, purification, and compensation. Adaptation implies abandoning the public service vision and simply trying to compete with the commercial broadcasters using a similar strategy. We saw in the previous chapter that this has not happened.

Purification is the mirror opposite: here PSB would simply ignore ratings and competition and pursue its own vision unaffected by competition. This too seems not to have been the route chosen. These two logical extremes indicate the difficulty of the option that PSB generally has pursued, namely compensation, that is, some kind of adjustment to the new realities. Compensation strategies vary greatly, but all are framed by the dilemmas of the extremes: simply to copy the programme strategies of commercial broadcasters would evoke the political question from viewers, 'Why should we pay a licence fee to get similar programming that we get from the commercial stations?' Alternatively, to go the purist route and aloofly ignore declining viewer ratings would prompt a different, but equally problematic question: 'Why should we all be paying a licence fee for programmes only watched by an (elite) minority?' PSB compensation strategies, in response to the new situation, must always avoid these two pitfalls.

Let us be clear and say that competition has not been simply a negative experience for PSB. It has stimulated and rejuvenated the creative capacities of these organizations. And as we observed in Chapter 1, the response has not dramatically altered the profile of PSB. There have been changes, most notably a clear drift to the more popular programming, and the relegating of programmes likely to draw small audiences to less convenient times. Important structural features of PSB, however, such as the commitment to diversity in programming, remain basically intact. Institutionally, PSB has restructured and streamlined its organization over the past years; PSB finances tend to be more stable today, even if they are still seen as too limited.

The overall television programming available in Western European audiences, of course, looks different today compared with 20 years ago. And audiences have responded accordingly; PSB generally is faced with declining ratings, as we take up in more detail in Chapter 4, though in many countries there now seems to be a new stability in regard to viewing patterns. But a smaller share of the audience is a constant dilemma PSB organizations face as they struggle with their compensation strategies. What vision of public service, what goals, should guide PSB's activities, not least in relation to its commercial competition? To what extent can it maintain mission? What, indeed, is or should be its mission in the context of a changing society and evolving media landscape?

If we pull together the trends we have observed in the discussion thus far, what can we expect of television's future, looking ahead in the short term? Combining the perspectives presented by Olof Hultén and Karen Siune (1998) with those of Denis McQuail (1998) and Michael Tracey (1998), we get the following picture:

- There will be more and more television available to viewers, although the fragmentation of audiences means that there are economic limits to how many channels will be viable in a competitive setting.
- Television will be increasingly 'popular', in the sense that it will be produced largely to please large audiences, rather than the tastes of any elite groups. Even if PSB does not reduce its diversity, the overall diversity of the television available within any given country will reduce.
- We can expect some increase in viewing time, though this will vary between countries, cultures and specific groups.
- Marginalization of the less popular cultural and informational programming will continue. This implies not least that programming for minorities will continue to be of low priority, as a result of unfavourable scheduling and lower budgets.

- Fragmentation of national audiences will continue with the increase of channels, though we can expect to see various 'regroupings' according to taste categories, interests and socio-economic level.
- Transnationalization will continue to be felt. Much programming will be domestically produced, but a good deal will originate from elsewhere. Viewing patterns will remain still quite nationalist, though less so among younger viewers.
- Commercial funding will increasingly replace the public funding of television. PSB will constitute a decreasing portion of the overall television available to viewers.
- The regulation of television content by governments will continue to diminish.
- The capacity and ambition of television to inform and educate will further decline, while infotainment will increase.
- The technical future of television lies in the increasing interface between this technology and the technologies of the computer and of telecommunication. The convergence of media technologies toward a single, digital standard (multimedia) is already being witnessed by the first steps toward digital television and the presence of television on Internet. We will pursue this theme in the next chapter.
- The future of public service broadcasting is unclear; it is a vision formulated and institutionalized under different historical circumstances than exist today. It must be revitalized if it is to offer a compelling direction for television's future in the next century.

LINGERING ISSUES: DEMOCRACY

In this chapter we have traced the key developments in television over the past two decades, and sketched a prognosis. The story we have presented has tried to capture a number of major transitions in progress. Today the continued tradition of public service in Western Europe cannot be taken for granted; it is in question. Indeed, its actual meaning in the present situation is part of the difficulty; in a commercial, competitive setting, its vision is not as clear as it was under monopoly conditions.

Television globally is understood as an entertainment medium, and no doubt it will continue to deliver ever more entertainment in the future. Certainly television can function as a 'pleasure machine'; nothing wrong in that, and in this regard commercial television clearly has the advantage over PSB. But there are also other considerations. Leaving aside difficult questions about evaluating the quality of programming in aesthetic terms, there are still issues that are problematic in the face of the expansion of market-driven model. Many of these issues cluster around the broad and crucial theme of democracy, as Herman and McChesney remarked in the long quote above.

PSB's focus on the social citizen is being replaced by an emphasis on the individual consumer. We are all to various degrees both consumers and citizens, and the two roles are not necessarily always in opposition. In our roles as consumers we act out of our individual motives via our commercial actions. In democracy, however, and in the public service mission, there is embedded the idea of universalism. Not only do all citizens have a right of access to broadcasting, but the programming should, as far as possible, be aimed at everyone, in the sense of striving to address the needs and interests of the many different groups which comprise society. The needs of a democratic society cannot be fully served if its major medium is organized exclusively along the principles of market forces (cf. Murdock, 1990). Graham and Davies (1997: 9), in their analysis of broadcasting policy, suggest that the market cannot take into account concerns with citizenship, culture and community.

It is important to bear in mind that democracy requires not only a formalized, institutional system, with legal rights, structures and procedures for representation, and so on. To survive and to thrive, democracy must also fulfil cultural and informational criteria. Television's role is central here. Values, norms, and common, shared knowledge and frames of reference are also necessary. This points to some minimal, shared public culture to which all citizens, regardless of their background, ethnicity, lifestyle and identity, can relate.

This common public culture must of course be diverse in its content and its forms of expression to give voice to the cultural differentiation we discussed above reflecting a broad panorama of daily life and experience. Television must make visible, give voice to, and legitimize various groups and divergent views. Yet, there must also be links to a shared public culture if society's democratic character is to be sustained. The nation state is in transition, yet it is still the basic entity for the organization of democratic life and it is still a prime focus for most people's identities. Television is inseparable from the national democratic project, but it must adapt as 'the nation' historically evolves. The nation is not only internally differentiated, but it is also porous in relation to global realities. For the sake of democracy, television has to address these developments.

PSB has found it difficult in practical terms both to foster a common culture and to address national audiences as they become more heterogeneous. Commercial broadcasting, on the other hand, has no commitments at all in this regard unless it coincides with profits. Herein lies the great challenge facing television: governments, together with the interested parties and actors – including the public – must formulate policies that regenerate a public service vision under the new societal circumstances and the new media landscape. At the same time, policies must also give ample room for the important functions that commercial broadcasting can serve, and yet keep it socially responsible. Further, the two domains need to be united in a policy framework such that both are viable and that the resulting television system enhances democracy. This is undeniably a tall order, but we can't settle for less: television is too important.

ACTIVITIES

1 The expression of the public service mission varies somewhat between countries. How does PSB in your country define its role? Contact the companies' information department and read what PSB says about itself. Do you feel that it lives up to its goals in the programming it offers?

2 Look (again) at the TV listings and see what programmes you think might be relevant for helping to promote the democratic character of society. News and current affairs programmes are obviously relevant, but consider what other kinds of programmes may be significant here. For example, do certain talk shows contribute to democracy? How?

3 Contact the governing body in your country that is responsible for broadcast regulation and ask for information about the basic regulatory process. Inquire also about changes in regulation over the past ten years. Try to analyse how these changes have impacted on television in your country.

4 Obtain the annual reports from PSB for the past few years. How has its basic financial situation evolved? Does it need more funding? In what areas of programming do you feel that additional funding could make a difference?

SUGGESTIONS FOR FURTHER READING

Barker, C. (1997) *Global Televison: An Introduction.* Oxford: Blackwell.

In this excellent and very accessible overview, the author situates television in the context of globalization, with particular focus on cultural identities and theories of postmodernism. Special attention is given to TV soaps and news programmes.

Carlsson, U. and Harrie, E. (eds) (1997) *Media Trends 1997 in Denmark, Finland, Iceland, Norway and Sweden.* Göteborg: Nordicom.

This useful volume pulls together thorough and current statistics on the media of Denmark, Finland, Iceland, Norway and Sweden, and includes a detailed chapter discussing developments in each country. An update of the statistics, with the inclusion of Estonia, Latvia and Lithuania – but without analytic chapters – is found in Carlsson, U. (ed.) (1999) *Nordic Baltic Media Statistics.* Göteborg: Nordicom.

Collins, R. (1999) *From Satellite to Single Market: New Communication Technology and European Public Service Television.* London: Routledge.

This book examines the interesting efforts to foster pan-European cultural identity via a public service satellite network. The network, backed by EU financing, eventually allied itself with the commercial Sky network, owned by Rupert Murdoch.

Hjarvard, S. and Trufte, T. (eds) (1999) *Audiovisual Media in Transition*. Copenhagen: Sekvens (Film and Media Studies Dept, University of Copenhagen).

Based on current research in Denmark, this is an outstanding and readable collection of articles on television as an institution and on programming and audiences. The final group of articles deals with computer media.

Ledbetter, J. (1998) *Made Possible By: The Death of Public Broadcasting in the United States*. London: Verso.

Public service broadcasting never was very strong in the US, compared to its commercial counterpart. This insightful book analyses the circumstances that have continued to erode its position.

CHAPTER 3

DIGITAL FUTURES: EUROPEAN TELEVISION IN THE AGE OF CONVERGENCE

Graham Murdock

AFTER ANALOGUE

> There is some fundamental change going on, and it raises difficult questions. How do we adapt to new media? We're searching, we're experimenting, and we have some fairly strong ideas – but no certainties. (Rupert Murdoch, head of News International, quoted in *Wired*, 2000: 253)

The major technologies that mapped out the media landscape of modernity – photography, cinema, the telephone, and radio and television – were based on analogue systems of coding and transmission. They produced continuous flows or fields of information with traceable relationships to the sights and sounds they recorded. When we take a photograph of friends at a party for example, and we hold the developed negative up to the light, we expect to see a recognizable picture of what was in front of the lens when we clicked the shutter: smiling faces, glasses and bottles, a table of food in the background. The information carried by analogue broadcasting is expressed through continuous variations in wave-like signals sent through the atmosphere using the transmission properties of the radio segment of the electromagnetic spectrum discovered by the German physicist Heinrich Hertz in 1887.

This age of analogue communications is now coming to an end. It is giving way to a new media landscape based on digital technologies. These translate all forms of information – speech, music, written text, tables of figures, still and moving images – into the universal language of computing and express them as an array of 0s and 1s. There is no negative for a digital photograph. There is only a chunk of digital data. There are no broadcasting waves in a digital transmission.There is only a stream of separate 0s and 1s. Analogue technologies expressed information in recognizable patterns – radio waves or fields of tone or colour. Digital technologies create an abstract 'world belonging exclusively to computers' (Feldman, 1997: 1).

It is already clear that this simple shift will have profound consequences for every aspect of communications, from the structure of the media industries to the routines and textures of everyday experience. To understand why, we need to grasp the importance of convergence.

In the analogue age each communications sector developed its own particular set of technologies which were often incompatible. There were some successful attempts to bring different media forms together. Newspapers printed photographs alongside text, cinema films, and later television broadcasts, carried synchronized sound. But there were formidable technical barriers to more wide ranging combinations. The telephone could not carry moving images, for example. Gramophone discs proved a little more flexible, but attempts to store video material in the grooves of vinyl records were short-lived. In addition to technical difficulties there were strong regulatory prohibitions on further convergence on the grounds that allowing companies with a dominant presence in one sector to move into another key market would create undue concentrations of power that might operate to limit diversity of expression. Telephone companies for example were barred from entering the broadcasting market. It is the relaxation of these traditional regulatory barriers to combination, as much as the technological logic of digitalization, that is propelling the current rapid movement towards convergence.

UNPACKING CONVERGENCE

> The key to the future of television is to stop thinking about television as television. (Nicholas Negroponte, founder of the Media Lab at MIT, 1995: 48)

Although 'convergence' is defined in a variety of ways in current debates it is possible to identify three major meanings:

- the convergence of cultural forms
- the convergence of communications systems, and
- the convergence of corporate ownership

Convergence 1: cultural forms

At the present time we are just at the very beginning of what many observers predict will be a far-reaching recomposition of cultural forms but we can glimpse some of the possibilities if we look at the current generation of CD-Roms and Internet websites. Not only do they bring all the major forms of expression together in one place for the first time, they allow users to move through the materials on offer in a range of ways. They are no longer readers following a set sequence but navigators mapping out personal routes.

Convergence 2: communication systems

Because digitalization translates everything into the same basic language of 0s and 1s, a number of commentators envisage the development of 'open' systems in which any form of information can be delivered to any group of customers over any of the major communications networks. This vision underpins the definition promoted by the European Commission's influential Green Paper on convergence which identifies it as 'the ability of different network platforms to carry essentially similar kinds of services' and the subsequent 'coming together' of the telephone, television and personal computer, to create new household devices with multiple functions (European Commission, 1997b: 7). There are considerable technical barriers to systems' convergence at present, but they are rapidly being overcome. Traditionally for example, telephone systems using copper wires have not had enough capacity to carry moving images, since these take up much more space than the human voice. The solution is to replace them with high capacity fibre optic systems which transmit digital pulses of light down hair-thin strands of glass. Although these broadband systems (as they are often called) have been installed in many recently built cable television systems, many older cable systems and much of the existing telephone network, especially the 'local loop' (the final stretch connecting individual homes to the trunk routes) still use the old wired systems. However, the recent development of ADSL technology (asymmetric digital subscriber loops) provides a convenient interim solution by boosting the capacity of existing systems sufficiently to allow them to transmit moving images to domestic subscribers. Britain's dominant satellite television operator, British Sky Broadcasting, has recently signed an agreement with the company operating the telephone system in Hull, in West Yorkshire, to test the potential of this technology as a way of distributing its digital television services. At the same time, the third generation of mobile telephones, now coming into use allow users to send and receive Internet data, e-mail and video images, while the development of 'streaming' technology allows broadcasts to be transmitted over the Internet and received on home computers. The BBC made its first foray into this uncharted arena in February 2000, when it broadcast a race meeting live from the course at Ascot.

Not surprisingly, the development of these new distribution channels has excited considerable interest among the major broadcasting companies, who see the chance to sell their services in a greatly expanded range of markets. As Tony Ball, the chief executive of British Sky Broadcasting recently announced, 'At Sky, we see convergence as a huge opportunity . . .

We are already a very powerful brand. In the future, Sky will sit happily whether it is on the PC, the mobile or on television' (Harding and Larsen, 2000: 23).

In moving into these new markets, however, broadcasting companies immediately run up against the entrenched power of the major operators in the fields of computing, telecommunications and the Internet. The solution has been to seek alliances. Consequently, we are currently witnessing the construction of an increasingly complex web of interconnections linking companies controlling key areas of content (such as film rights, sports rights, and original production) with players operating one or more of the six major distribution 'platforms' from which assaults on the emerging consumer markets for digital television services can be launched, either now or in the near future. These are: terrestrial systems (using land-based transmitters); satellite television systems; cable television systems; fixed line telephone systems; mobile telephone networks; and the Internet (a network of telecommunications networks), particularly the World Wide Web, the section of the Net that most people use.

Convergence 3: corporate ownership

So, by steadily rubbing away the established boundaries between different media sectors and bringing previously separate interests together, innovations in digital technology have led to an unprecedented wave of mergers, acquisitions and partnership agreements, as the major communications companies seek to extend their reach and position themselves to take full advantage of future moves towards systems convergence. The most significant instance to date is the January 2000 merger between America's major media conglomerate Time-Warner which has extensive interests in television (including the CNN news service and the Home Box Office film channel), and one of America's leading Internet companies, America On Line (AOL). However, smaller deals linking content providers and platform operators are now announced almost daily as major 'old' media players struggle to maintain their position. A few weeks after the Time/AOL tie-up was launched, Rupert Murdoch, head of one the world's leading media conglomerates, announced that he was offering a minority stake in Platco, his satellite television services subsidiary, to another leading Internet company, Yahoo! As he told a journalist, since the AOL/Time merger, 'There has been a greater sense of urgency. We do not need to be equal to them in size, but we do need to maximise' (Harding, 2000: 19).

This drive to 'maximize' is the key aspect of convergence since it is the emerging mega corporations that span content and distribution and combine established and emerging media under the same administrative umbrella, who are setting the pace for digitalization and writing the rules for the emerging communications marketplace. There is little doubt that 'in the European television of the future, these media giants will, sooner or later, dominate the field and the smaller and weaker players are likely to be eliminated' (Papathanassopoulos, 1998: 83). We will look at the pattern of interlocking relations now emerging in Europe in more detail later on in this chapter, but first we need to sketch in some of the essential background to these developments.

FROM MACHINES TO MARKETIZATION

A great deal of writing on digitalization, particularly in reports from corporations, governments and commercial consultancies, is based on a technological determinist view. It starts from the new machineries of communication and asks: what can they do? and how will they alter the ways we work and play? From this perspective digital technologies appear as the major and prime movers of change. Pronouncements in this vein usually promote a relentlessly upbeat view of the future, filled with promises of improvements and gains. They offer us a never-ending story of positive events and inventions that ignores the ways that technologies and their uses are themselves profoundly shaped by longer term shifts in underlying economic, political and social structures. Once we recognize this we are prompted to query many of the more optimistic claims being made and to ask whether digital technologies are more likely to reinforce or to challenge the prevailing distribution of power and advantage.

As we saw in the two previous chapters, over the last two decades the television system in Europe has moved from being centred around national public service systems to being increasingly dominated by commercial operators. This shift is part of a wider process of *marketization* through which private enterprise has become the dominant model of cultural activity and market criteria of success, such as market share and return on investment, have become the main yardsticks against which the performance of all cultural institutions, including those in the public sector, is judged. As a result, established ways of organizing and funding public service broadcasting, and traditional definitions of its mission, have come under more and more pressure. The digital 'revolution' in television is taking place within an economic and cultural arena that has already been comprehensively restructured by over 20 years of marketization. Consequently, to understand its likely impact and implications we need to explore the interplay of emerging technological possibilities, established economic logics, and shifting political perceptions.

Although we can identify a clear movement towards greater marketization in every European country and in the policy thinking of the European Commission, it is by no means a uniform process. Marketization is made up of five separate shifts, which may or may not occur together. They are: privatization; liberalization; the reorientation of regulation; corporatization; and commodification. Let's briefly look at what each involves.

Privatization is the sale of public assets to private investors. Examples include the French government's sale of the country's major public television channel, TF1, and the decsions by a number of European governments to sell shares in their country's publicly owned telecommunications operators (known as PTTs – Post, Telegraph and Telecommunications companies). Examples include British Telecom (BT) which has been fully privatized, Deutsch Telekom which sold 26 per cent of its shares in 1996, and France Telecom which sold a 20 per cent stake in 1997. This change in economic status, from public organization or utility to private or semi-private company, is accompanied by a shift in aims, from underwriting the public interest to delivering financial returns to shareholders.

Liberalization is the introduction of competition into markets previously served by a monopoly supplier or dominated by two (duopoly) or three large concerns. Examples include: the decisions taken by a number of European governments to break public service broadcasting's historic monopoly over national television services and license competing commercial cable and terrestrial channels; the British government's 1992 decision to allow cable companies to offer telephone services; and, most important of all, the European Commission ruling that national telecommunications markets throughout the EU, which had previously been the sole preserve of the PTTs, be opened to competition by 1 January 1998 (see Clegg and Kamall, 1998).

Although this decision opened previously closed markets to new entrants, the historic advantages enjoyed by the old PTTs have enabled them to hold on to their central position and provided a launching pad for expansion into new areas of activity, including digital television. France Telecom for example is a major shareholder in Britain's leading cable television operator, NTL, which offers subscribers a range of interactive services and BT is a partner in BSkyB's satellite-delivered home shopping and banking service, Open. In the future, however, they will face increasing competition from mobile telephone companies. The merger of the British firm Vodaphone and the German group Mannesmann at the beginning of 2000 for example, created a company that controls an estimated 13 per cent of the world's mobile telephone traffic, putting it in a very strong position in the emerging market for mobile access to Internet services. These new clusters of corporate power raise major questions for public regulation.

Reorienting regulation. Since the rise of the modern corporation at the end of the nineteenth century, governments have wrestled with the regulatory problem of reconciling the private interests of shareholders with the public interests of employees, consumers and citizens. Their interventions were based on the assumption that 'The purpose of economic and social life cannot be solely to play host to successful business, so that the maximisation of shareholder value and single-minded pursuit of economic efficiency become ends in themselves. Other human values . . . also require expression' – values of justice, equality, and dignity (Hutton, 2000: 23). The communication industries have always presented a special case since their products provide the basic information, knowledge and opportunities for debate that are generally considered essential for a fully functioning democracy. As a consequence, rules were devised to prevent any one company from dominating any major communication market and to restrict cross-media ownership, on the grounds that a plurality of different providers was more likely to ensure the diversity of information and debate that democratic life required. Under marketization these regulatory barriers to corporate expansion have been progressively weakened or removed. In his chapter, Peter Dahlgren characterizes this as a process of 'deregulation'. I am describing it here as a 're-gearing' to emphasize the shift in the basic rationale for intervention, from a defence of the public interest to a promotion of corporate interests and from cultural goals to economic priorities. The aim now is to foster corporate convergence in the interest of creating strong national and European companies that can compete effectively in international markets with the major American players. As a recent European Commission report argued, future regulatory action should 'seek to remove as far as possible barriers which prevent businesses from entering new markets or extending activities from one market to another' (European Commission, 1997a: 13). To this end, the competition directorate of the European Union has declared that it intends 'as a general rule' to take 'a positive attitude to cross border alliances' providing they involve companies whose activities are mainly concentrated in separate geographical markets (Pons, 1998: 4). Hence, the joint venture between two of Europe's major forces in the television industry, Bertelsmann of Germany and Audiofina (whose interests include the CLT group based in Luxembourg and a major stake in Canal+ in France), was approved, whilst Bertelsmann's proposed merger with the other dominant player in its home television market, Leo Kirch, was blocked. Cross-border alliances may still run up against entrenched national interests, however. As Pierre Lescure, the chairman of France's leading satellite television operator, Canal+ complained, after pressure within France had forced him to break off talks about closer links with Rupert Murdoch's media interests, 'The thing that gets in the way is the people who want to stay within the castle walls of France. I say that is ridiculous. We could do something magnificent at a European level' (quoted in *Economist*, 1999: 102).

By attempting to create 'something magnificant in Europe' by encouraging cross-border and cross-sector alliances, the emerging regulatory regime in Europe is supporting corporate demands for more freedom of action whilst retreating from the defence of the public interest as traditionally understood. This move reflects 'a growing feeling within policy-making circles that, once the technology is developed to enable normal market transactions for media products, the industry does not need special regulation' (Gibbons, 1998: 88). In the process, audiences are redefined as customers and their economic rights as consumers are given precedence over their cultural rights as citizens (Murdock, 1999). Addressing this problem and guaranteeing everyone access to the widest possible range of information, knowledge, representation and participation has been one of the major aims of public service broadcasting. But here again, marketization cuts across this historic commitment.

Corporatization involves governments urging, or requiring, public institutions to recreate themselves as market-oriented organizations. In the last few years for example, the BBC has responded to pressure from successive governments, by significantly increasing its commercial activities. Its commercial arm, BBC Worldwide, has signed partnership arrangements with the American owners of both the Discovery Channel and the cable and satellite programming group, Flextech, to develop new programmes and new subscription channels for the global market. It has also established a commercial Internet site, as a joint venture with ICL the Japanese owned computer company. This process looks set to accelerate in future. Announcing the new licence fee settlement in February 2000 (which fell some way short of the sum the BBC had argued it needed to fund its new digital services) the government was careful to stress that it expected the Corporation to make good the deficit through a combination of cost savings and significant increases in its earnings from commercial activities. One major consequence of this is to institutionalize a dual structure in which the BBC's public service activities, funded by the licence fee and open to everyone, jostle uneasily with the new commercial ventures which are only available to consumers willing and able to pay a subscription. This, in turn, is part of a wider shift in the economics of television.

Commodification. Unlike paperback novels or cinema seats, which could be sold to individuals, early television broadcasts were freely available to anyone who had a working receiving ariel. Consequently, the industry could not be financed by customer payments. It had to be supported either by public taxation (usually in the form of an annual licence fee) or by selling air-time to advertisers. People living in areas where off-air reception was difficult or impossible might pay a cable company a monthly fee to feed clear signals into their homes through their wired network but they were paying for the relay service, not for the programmes. At the same time, early broadcasting's technical inability to 'address' viewers individually and charge them directly for what they consumed was seen by many commentators as a virtue rather than a deficiency. It provided a solid material basis for the idea that broadcasting should be a universal medium that gave everyone the same level of service. As the BBC's first Director General, John Reith, argued in 1924, outlining his working philosophy of public service, and comparing it favourably with the railway system of the time which offered levels of service stratified by price: 'There need be no first and third class. There is nothing . . . which is exclusive to those who pay more, or who are considered in one way or another more worthy of attention' (Reith, 1924: 218).

Over the last two decades the universality of broadcasting has been steadily eroded by the growth of subscription services. Initially cable and satellite operators offered their customers a standard package of channels for a basic monthly fee, with additional charges for premium channels showing recent films or current sporting events. Now we are seeing the rapid rise of video-on-demand and other pay-per-view options, where viewers buy the right to watch a particular movie or a particular event. In the process, more and more television services are offered for sale at a price and available only to those who can afford to pay. This adds new forms of information and cultural exclusion to the familiar patterns of economic and social exclusion that low income households are already subject to.

By extending the options open to commercial companies and obliging public service broadcasters to adapt to a new marketplace not of their making, these five separate but interlinked aspects of marketization have comprehensively remodelled the economic and political environment in which contemporary television operates. This is the essential backdrop we need to bear in mind when considering the possible impacts of digitalization.

REVOLUTION OR BUSINESS AS USUAL?

> There is no digital television – there are only 10 or 15 new channels, and how they are transported to households is not important for viewers . . . They don't care if they get the programmes by digital or analogue or whatever means. (Helmut Toma, chief executive of CLT quoted in Papathanassopoulos, 1998: 80)

> It doesn't matter whether it's analogue or digital, it's all multichannel TV to us. (Adam Singer, chair of Flextech, quoted in Beavis, 1998: 21)

> For years now, we've called the television the 'box', and in the future it looks like that won't just be a nickname, but a proper technical term. For the glowing object in our living rooms in ten years' time won't just be a passive receiver of broadcasts, it will be a real box of tricks – a computer, videophone, radio, film archive, CD player, encyclopedia – even a secretary and babysitter. All rolled into one. (BBC promotion for its Futureworld exhibition, Middleton, 2000: 6)

As these statements make clear, European broadcasters currently disagree sharply on the likely impact of digitalization. Some see it mainly as a way of enhancing and extending what they do now and compare it with the earlier move from black-and-white to colour transmissions. Others are convinced that it paves for the way for a fundamental change in the range and nature of the services that television can offer. How credible you find each of these positions depends largely on which aspects of digitalization you choose to focus on. We can usefully begin by separating two major movements:

- *Replacement*: the uneven transition from analogue to digital forms of production and transmission that is currently taking place in the three established television 'platforms', terrestrial, satellite, and cable, at different speeds in different European countries;

- *Convergence*: the rapid growth of new broadcasting platforms based on wired and mobile telephone networks and the Internet, together with the development of systems convergence and multifunction television sets.

The first process is mainly propelled by government ambitions to reassign the spectrum space released by the cancellation of analogue transmissions to other communication uses. It is already clear that this will generate very substantial sums that can be used to boost public spending. In April 2000 the British government auctioned five national licences for sections of the radio spectrum capable of supporting third generation mobile telephone services. The results far exceeded the original projections and the bidding eventually raised $35 billion. This unanticipated windfall has prompted other European governments, who had originally intended to give spectrum space away free or to charge only a nominal fee, to move towards an auction system. It has also increased pressure for an early switch to digital television transmission. The British government envisages discontinuing terrestrial analogue services some time between 2006 and 2010 and auctioning the spare spectrum to mobile telephone operators. In preparation for this day the major broadcasters are currently launching new digital services alongside their established analogue transmissions in an effort to persuade viewers to invest in digital reception technology. At the present time, however, digital television sets are still relatively expensive, so companies are promoting their new services by offering set-top boxes that convert digital signals for display on analogue sets, in the hope that viewers will get used to living in a digital environment and be persuaded to replace their old sets with digital ones, sooner rather than later.

Alongside this process of replacement we are also seeing the first moves in what many commentators predict will be the rapid convergence of broadcasting, telephone and computing systems. Take the Internet, for example. For most of its brief life, the Net has been seen as having nothing much to do with broadcasting. Over the last two years this perception has changed dramatically as leading companies operating in computing, broadcasting and the Net itself have simultaneously recognized its huge future potential as a broadcasting medium. They envisage it moving from a 'pull' technology, where each individual user searches for what they want and drags it down into their home computer, to a 'push' technology where users are offered pre-designed packages of content, including television programming, together with carefully organized opportunities for interactivity centred on home shopping and other forms of electronic commerce. Originally commentators assumed that most people would obtain these services using a personal computer, since PCs have so far been the main point of access to the Internet. With recent moves to integrate limited internet capacity into interactive television services, however, more and more observers think that the new generation of television sets will provide the major link between viewers and content providers, and an increasing number agree with the prediction of Ron Sommer, the chief executive of

Deutsche Telekom, who argues that 'customers will no longer be satisfied with phone services, internet providers or interactive television that all have to be acquired and operated separately . . . [they] will expect to have all of these applications combined in one personalized service package' (quoted in Anders, 1999: 51).

Separating these two broad currents of change – replacement and convergence – is a useful first step in clarifying current debates around digital television, but to go further we need to identify the basic dimensions of these transitions a little more carefully. There are five major aspects:

enhancement
compression
consolidation
interactivity
access

ENHANCEMENT: MELTING SNOW

Unlike analogue waves, digital broadcasting signals are not subject to interference from atmospheric conditions. This guarantees that the picture will never again be obscured by 'snow' and that images will never again distort or break up. To capitalize on this clarity digital set manufacturers are aiming to offer pin-sharp high definition pictures (achieved by more or less doubling the number of lines on the screen from the present 625 to 1,125), hi-fi quality sound, and a widescreen viewing space based on a 16: 9 ratio that is closer to the cinema screen or the football pitch than the familiar square box in the corner. There are also plans to replace the present cathode ray tube technology, with its awkward bump at the back of the set, with flat screen technologies that allow sets to be hung on the wall. Digital compression technologies can also deliver three-dimensional pictures, but there are no firm plans to do so in Europe at present. Watching standard television programming under these conditions will arguably be more pleasurable, but it will remain essentially the same experience.

COMPRESSION: CHANNEL ABUNDANCE

Because digital signals take up far less capacity than analogue transmissions, many more channels can be accommodated in the same space, whether it is the spectrum used for terrestrial and satellite transmissions or the underground ducts that carry hair-thin fibre optic links instead of the old, bulky, copper wires. This has led enthusiasts to argue that the signal compression made possible by digital technologies is progressively putting an end to scarcity and opening up an era of abundance in broadcasting' (Chalaby and Segell, 1999: 354). This enlarged capacity can be employed in a variety of ways. It can be used to offer near-video-on-demand services, for example. These are based on transmitting say a feature film on a number of channels simultaneously, starting at 15 minute intervals, so that viewers can watch it more or less when they wish, rather than waiting for it to appear in a scheduled slot at a time that may well be inconvenient. More importantly, compression also increases opportunities to develop channels directed at specific, specialized markets. As the director of programmes for a recently launched British cable and satellite channel aimed at young people put it, 'television is not just about boxes and decoders, television is about . . . taking people where they want to be, when they want to go there, with people they want to be with' (Kilgarriff, 2000: 8).

This vision immediately raises two questions. Firstly, in an increasingly commercialized television environment it is clear that not all minorities are equal. There is likely to be a number of channels aimed at young people because of their high levels of disposable income. Similarly, a swathe of channels will follow in the wake of the Travel Channel, the Auction Channel, and France's Fashion TV, serving particular areas of consumer activity. As one industry insider notes, 'These channels spell lucrative ad revenues for operators' because their viewers 'have greater spending power potential' than audiences for mainstream general channels. 'It's an attractive proposition' (Sutherland, 1999: 54). In contrast, poorer segments of the audience, such as those with disabilities, who are rather less 'attractive' as potential customers are rather less likely to be less well served, if they are served at all.

Secondly, the channel abundance produced by digital compression allows programmers to divide the desirable sectors of the consumer market into thinner and thinner slices, and to target say participants in extreme sports (like bungee jumping) or supporters of Manchester United (both of whom already have their own channels) rather than sports fans in general. This strategy makes good sense commercially but it carries significant social costs. By reinforcing the fragmentation and dispersal of the television audience set in motion by the first wave of multichannel television it prompts us to ask: what is likely to happen to the quality of communal life if the shared symbolic spaces that national broadcasting has traditionally provided through its coverage of great civic and sporting occasions are only available in the future on specialized subscription channels?

The atomization of television experience is taken a stage further by the institutionalization of personalized viewing regimes, sometimes called 'Me TV'. The TiVo system recently introduced on BSkyB's satellite services, for example, allows viewers to instruct a set-top box to search out and record their favourite kinds of programmes whenever and wherever they are being shown and to download them on to a hard disc capable of storing up to 30 hours of material. As a consquence people might develop a customized viewing regime which had little or nothing in common with the choices of the people they generally talk to, leaving them with no shared mediated experiences to trade in everyday conversations. Enthusiasts of individual choice see this as a major, and welcome, break with the past. Sceptics argue that since it continues and intensifies the individualization of television viewing that began with the growth of multi-set households and the rise of video recording it suggests that 'Life in the digital world won't really be very different from life in the analogue world after all' (Allen, 1998: 70).

To the extent that they extend processes that pre-date the shift from analogue to digital technologies, both enhancement and compression appear primarily as forces ensuring continuity. However, if we look at the way digitalization is altering patterns of corporate control within the media industries the argument that business in the new television environment will continue much as usual becomes more problematic.

CONSOLIDATION: OLD AND NEW MEDIA MOGULS

The established broadcasting industry's transition to digital is being led by companies who already occupy key positions in the terrestrial, satellite and cable sectors. There are two main reasons for this. Firstly, because the costs of 'going digital' are very substantial only companies with 'deep pockets' and well established customer bases can afford to absorb the considerable start-up costs and early operating losses. Secondly, the advantages that 'first movers' enjoy in an emerging market are cumulative. Early entrants have a better chance of securing a central position and of shaping the way the market is organized, making it increasingly difficult, and costly, for late arrivals to establish themselves.

By extending the scope of the television marketplace and opening it up to leading players in the computing, telecommunications and Internet industries, digitalization is also shifting the locus of corporate control, away from companies based in broadcasting and towards businesses coming in from outside. A number of these entrants are North American corporations taking advantage of the newly liberalized marketplace and the more sympathetic regulatory environments. If we look at Europe now we can already see the outlines of the new corporate map these two processes are creating.

Commercial digital television was first introduced into the European marketplace in 1996, when, within months of each other, three major pay-TV operators launched digital services. Telepiu started its Italian digital service DStv in January, Canal Plus launched Canal Satellite Numérique (CSN) in France in April, and the Leo Kirch Group in Germany introduced its digital satellite package, DF1, in July. This last decision followed the collapse of attempts to form a more broadly based German consortium to develop digital services. In 1994 Kirch had arranged to form a joint venture with Deutsche Telekom (then still a publically owned PTT) and the other major force in German commercial television, Bertelsmann.When this was ruled to be anti-competitive by the European Commission, two of the original partners attempted to set up a more broadly based cooperative venture which included all the public and private organizations operating in the German television market. However, Kirch refused to join and insisted on using its own set-top box rather than the one proposed by the new consortium. The alliance fell apart and Kirch was left to launch its DF1 service uncontested.

Since then, both the major broadcasting companies involved in these failed efforts have been incorporated into European-wide partnerships. The CLT-Ufa consortium (formed in 1997) and currently the dominant presence in European commercial television is a joint venture between Bertelsmann and Audiofina, the holding company controlled by the Belgian financier, Albert Frère. The other major shareholder in Audiofina is Vivendi the French utilities and communications group which also has a controlling 49 per cent interest in Canal Plus, which has recently made a number of significant acquisitions of its own outside France, including the Dutch pay-TV operator, Nethold, in 1996 and a 90 per cent stake in Telepiu (now renamed Tele+).Vivendi is also a major shareholder in Rupert Murdoch's BSkyB, which in turn has a 24 per cent stake in the Kirch Group's pay-TV subsidiary and a 35 per cent stake in Stream, Telepiu's major rival in the Italian market for digital television services. In June 2000, in its most audacious move yet, Vivendi acquired the North American Seagram group whose interests include the Universal Pictures Hollywood studio and Universal's major stakes in the music industry, thereby ensuring a major supply of content for both its pay-TV channels and its Vizzavi internet portal (launched in partnership with the leading mobile telephone operator, Vodaphone-Air Touch).

Some commentators see this emerging pattern of interlocking interests as signalling a shift from competition to 'co-opetition', based on increased co-operation between competing companies (Harding, 2000: 30). As this unfolding network also makes clear, 'it is industrial alliances, rather than public institutions, that are driving the next generation of TV technology – a process that runs counter to [the] European tradition' of state-directed change (Kleinsteuber, 1997: 94). Figure 3.1 shows a simplified map of the current pattern of interlocks.

Although BSkyB is a central player in this emerging European network of broadcasting interests the pattern of interconnections in Britain also illustrates very clearly the other main trend in the general movement towards corporate consolidation: the entry of major American computer and telecommunications companies into the European television market-place.

Digital pay-TV requires two key devices to be installed in set-top boxes or integrated sets: conditional access systems (CADs) which unscramble encrypted signals and manage subscriptions to the service, and electronic

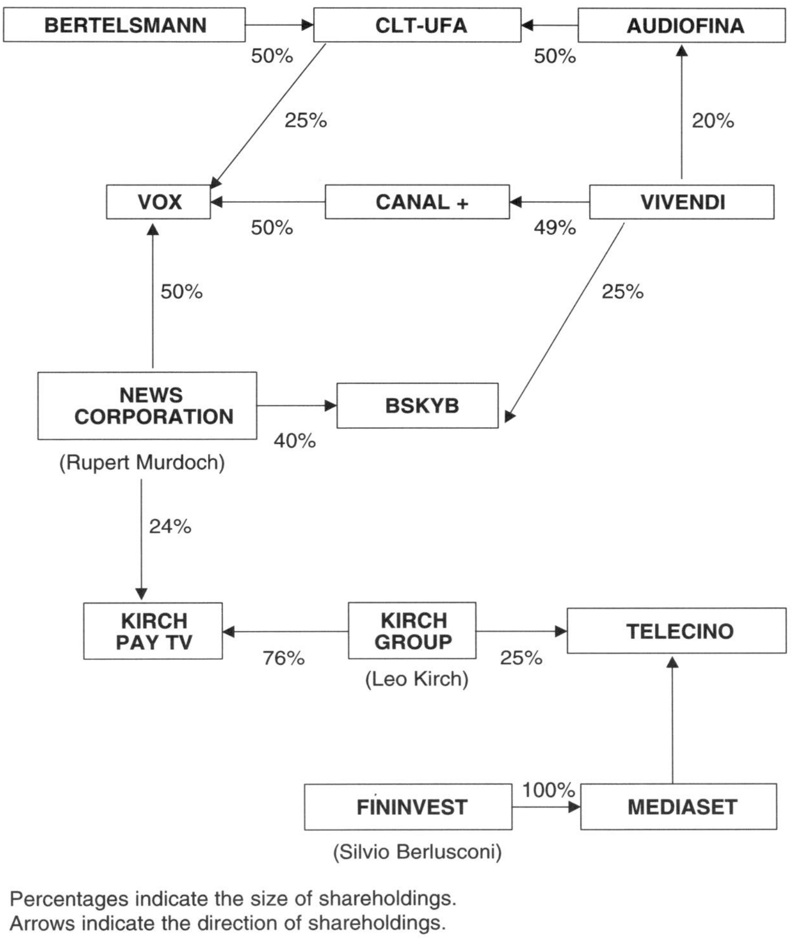

FIGURE 3.1 Corporate interconnecting in the European commercial television industry (as of January 2000)

programme guides (EPGs) which help viewers to navigate their way through the multiple channels on offer. Both of these 'intelligent' devices open up lucrative new markets for computer software companies, who are also very aware of the need to prepare for the predicted migration of popular Internet access from PCs to interactive television and mobile phones, by making sure that their Internet browsers and gateways (or portals) are incorporated into the next generation of broadcasting platforms. These opportunities have prompted the major software companies, led by Bill Gates's Microsoft, to form alliances and acquire stakes in a range of digital television platforms, particularly cable and telecommunications systems, whose two-way capacity places them at the hub of interactive services. As Microsoft's head of television operations in Europe explained, 'The reason we invested

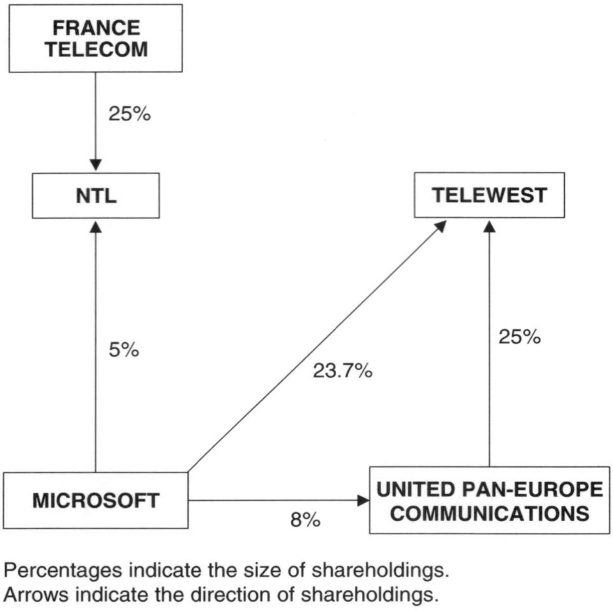

FIGURE 3.2 Patterns of ownership in the British cable television industry (as of August 2000)

in cable in Europe is because we want to make sure that our financial partner becomes a business partner and uses our technology' (Rose, 2000: 249). The major telecommunications operators (including the newly liberalized and privatized European PTTs) are also looking to expand their business by playing a central role in developing interactive television services. As noted earlier, BT is a major investor (along with BSkyB) in Open's British portfolio of home shopping and home banking services, and in 2001 (when a long-standing ban is finally removed) it will be free to offer television entertainment over its own networks. However, it will be entering a market already dominated by two powerful cable consortia – NTL and Telewest.

Although digital cable television was only launched in Britain in 1999, almost a year after Sky launched its satellite service, and OnDigital (the consortium controlled by the two largest players in the British analogue commercial market, Carlton and Granada) introduced its terrestrial service, it is widely thought to be in the best position to develop the interactive services which most commentators now see as digital television's principle selling point. The present pattern of control in this sector is outlined in Figure 3.2.

This shows that the key players are the world's leading computer software company, Microsoft, and one of the the world's largest telecommunications groups, France Telecom, ranked sixth (by revenues). We need to keep these patterns of interlocking corporate interests firmly in mind when we turn to debates on the liberatory potential of interactivity.

INTERACTIVITY: SMOKE AND MIRRORS

> We're transforming the face of TV with a host of interactive and enhanced services, from interactive shopping and banking services, to televoting and the chance to control a camera angle on a football match, or even your favourite drama. (recruitment advertisement for NTL, February 2000)

Linked to a cable or telephone system, digital television offers viewers the chance to talk back to their set. This is being hailed as a genuinely revolutionary advance on the present one-way, top-down, structure of analogue broadcasting, one which transfers power decisively from producers to consumers. At the present time, interactive capacity is being used in four main ways.

Firstly, viewers are being offered more control over the timing and presentation of what they watch. Full video-on-demand systems enable people to call up a film or programme from a central store whenever they wish, while services such as the one introduced on Sky's Sports Extra channel allow them to customize the programmes they watch by choosing from a range of camera angles and calling up instant replays of the action. Similarly, by streaming its coverage of Formula One motor racing across seven channels, each providing a different camera angle, Canal Plus viewers can see the action from a variety of vantage points, including the pit lane and the inside of one of the cars. As Vic Wakeling, Sky Sport's managing director was keen to emphasize, 'The digital revolution is not just about more channels. It's about having a different way of . . . choosing how you want to watch television' (Chaudhary, 1999: 3).

Secondly, through Internet sites linked to programmes, interactvity extends the active life of a transmission, encouraging viewers to find out more about the subject, to e-mail their comments to programme makers, and to use message boards to exchange views and information with other viewers.

Thirdly, interactivity allows viewers to move from being spectators to participants. Currently they can join in with a quiz show, register their opinions on the issues being discussed on screen through push-button opinion polls, and link up with other subscribers to play video games.

Fourthly, interactivity allows broadcasters to develop electronic commerce services such as home banking and home shopping. This is the area that has attracted most interest in the industry and led many commentators to predict that once integrated digital sets become standard household fixtures, interactive services will overtake the delivery of programming as broadcasters' prime source of revenue. In presenting this scenario as ushering in an era of unparalleled consumer convenience and choice, however, enthusiasts of e-commerce conveniently forget the difficult issues of surveillance, privacy and power that it raises. Interactivity will strengthen the power potential control of advertisers and marketing interests in two significant ways.

When viewers click on a product icon on the screen they are ushered into a selling environment offering sophisticated product demonstrations and opportunities to interact with the goods. TPS, the main rival to Canal Plus's digital satellite platform in France, has a shopping mall sponsored by the toy maker Lego, where viewers can play on-screen games featuring the products as well as browsing through an electronic catalogue. By making virtual shopping more entertaining and involving it is hoped to increase sales by cultivating a warmer, more intimate, relation to the goods on display. These innovations blur the line that regulators have traditionally drawn between advertising and programming. As one television executive noted, with enthusiasm, digital productions will follow Internet sites by building 'community of interest packaging surrounding particular genres' and using this to generate 'affinity selling' and enhanced 'opportunities to purchase' (Walmsley, 1999: 29).

All information sent with a purchase order can be collected and stored. This opens the way for marketing personnel to construct thick descriptions of particular individuals which can be used to target them more precisely. As the market researcher John Clemens has noted, 'Demand represented by consumers will provide detailed personalized information stating what they want (or needs or interests they would like to have satisfied) in a form that can be used by suppliers' (Clemens, 1996: 6).

The promoters of commercialized interactive television are careful to present it as an endless vista of new ways of welcoming television into our lives and to emphasize that in this new digital kingdom the consumer is king. However, it might be more accurate to think of the digital screen as a one-way mirror concealing an unseen army of watchers logging every click of our remote control buttons, whose presence is comprehensively obscured by the smoke of positive publicity. True, the old set menus offered by traditional broadcasting are being replaced by extensive *à la carte* menus which encourage people to order from a much longer list of dishes and to consume them in any order they choose. But the menu is still devised by the restaurant owner and his or her star chefs. It is, in a favourite industry phrase, a 'walled garden' not the open countryside, and as with gardens in a privately owned château or castle, there is an admission charge for visitors.

ACCESS: PRICES AND EXCLUSIONS

Once television services become commodities sold at a price, people's access to the cultural and information resources they offer depends directly on their ability to pay. As a result, 'We may see the emergence of the information-rich and the information poor – an underprivileged knowledge underclass, denied access to the quality of information, insight and entertainment enjoyed by the richer members of the community' (Birt, 1999: 10). There are four aspects to this emerging pattern of exclusion.

Available evidence reveals a very strong relationship between income and entry into new communications markets. In Britain for example, only 8 per cent of the poorest fifth of households have a home computer and only 3 per cent have a mobile phone (two devices which are now being promoted as additional delivery platforms for television services). In contrast, the top 20 per cent of households are seven times more likely to have a computer and ten times more likely to have a mobile phone (Golding and Murdock, 2000). Nor will this gap necessarily close over time. The price of these devices may come down but the cost of using them is likely to remain relatively high. Computer software needs to be regularly updated and 'on-line' connection charges have to be paid for. This is also true of digital television. Even if the basic cost of a digital set is brought within the reach of poorer families, the subscription charges for premium channels and interactive services are likely to exclude them.

As well as sharp inequalities of access *within* societies, there are marked divisions *between* European countries. If we again take home computers as an indicator, we find that whereas in the affluent countries of the north (Denmark, The Netherlands, Sweden, Finland and Germany) 20 per cent or more of the population currently have access, in the countries of the south, Italy, Spain and Portugal, the figure drops to below 10 per cent (*Economist*, 2000a: 38).

The pattern for access to the Internet is almost identical, which is not surprising since PC's remain (for the moment) the main point of entry into the Net. In the Spring of 1999 the cross-national Eurobarometer survey found that 39 per cent of the population of Northern Europe had access to the Internet as against only 8 per cent in Southern Europe. As with all averages, these statistics conceal even starker differences between individual countries: 61 per cent of Sweden and 44 per cent of Danes claimed to be on-line for example as against only 5 per cent of Portuguese and 7 per cent of Greeks (Norris, 2000: 5). This digital divide between Northern and Southern Europe is only partly explained by differences in economic structure and average incomes. There are also cultural factors.

Having access to the Internet does not necessarily mean that someone will be able to make full use of its potential. The global reach of English, and more particularly American-English, has long been a focus of concern in Europe, with critics condemning popular American films and television programmes as agents of cultural imperialism. As long as broadcasting was a national enterprise the amount of American material appearing on television screens could be limited by quotas on imported programming. Integrating Internet access into digital sets makes policing cultural borders much more difficult. In 1999, more than three-quarters (78.3 per cent) of all Internet pages were presented in English. The corresponding figure for the three other major European languages – French, German and Spanish – added together was 5.9 per cent (*Economist*, 2000b: 53). This suggests that full participation in one of the major arenas opened up by interactive television will require a reasonable degree of fluency in English, reinforcing the advantages already enjoyed by the more educated sections of the population and excluding those with minimal schooling.

The problem of access, however, is not simply a matter of how many people are excluded from full participation in the new digital television environment. It is also a question of what they will be left with. In order to sell their new services, digital entrepreneurs have to offer people something they can't get from free-to-air channels. They key is programming, which is why the leading companies in the emerging marketplace have been battling to secure the exclusive rights to recent feature films and major sporting events together with the back catalogues of leading film studios and television production organizations and first options on new productions. Once these key areas of programming are bought up by subscription channels they are no longer available on free-to-air services, or available only some time after their first showing. Public channels become 'secondary' markets. As a result, the poor are disadvantaged twice over: barred from access to the new subscription service by the high price of entry and left with radically thinned out 'free' services. This is the major reason why public service broadcasting is not only relevant in a digital age, but arguably more relevant than ever. Without its commitment to universality, we will be left with deep and enduring inequalities of access to information, knowledge and representation. If allowed to proceed unchecked this break with the historic promise that every citizen has an equal right to the cultural resources required for full citizenship, is likely to have serious consequences for the integrity of democracy and for the vision of shared fate and the common good on which it rests. This is why the future of public service broadcasting remains such a central issue.

REMAKING PUBLIC BROADCASTING: COMMERCIAL VENTURES OR COMMON NETWORKS?

As the shift to digital television gathers momentum in Europe, public service broadcasters must prepare to enter the post-analogue age. A number have already developed new free-to-air channels. In 1998 and 1999 the Italian public service network RAI launched three digital satellite services, RAI Sports, RAI All News, and RAI Educational. But the most ambitious response to date has come from the BBC. In addition to launching a series of free terrestrial digital channels it has developed a free internet site offering viewers opportunities to explore the subjects dealt with in programmes in more depth, and has plans for a new children's channel and several additional educational channels linked to the school curriculum. However, the BBC also illustrates the mounting problems and difficult choices that public service broadcasters face in the digital age.

Its licence fee income falls some way short of the sum needed to finance its full development programme for digital services and it is under mounting pressure to make up the deficit by expanding its commercial activities. However, the more successful it is in this the stronger the case for privatization since, critics argue, why continue to give it a unique public subsidy (in the form of the licence fee) when its entrepreneurial activities suggest that it can compete effectively in the new marketplace without it? As a British House of Commons committee of inquiry noted, 'the greater the BBC's commercial sector the more its claim to be funded by the licence may be called into question' (House of Commons, 1998: para. 93).

This move towards privatization by attrition received strong support from the draft proposals published by the European Commission's competition directorate in 1998, which recommended that state-aided PBS organizations should be barred from using this subsidy to make programmes that were already being provided by commercial operators (see Murdock and Golding, 1999: 122–125). Since this definition covers all the most popular programme genres its application would produce an immediate decline in audience share, making the case for retaining the licence fee politically untenable. The alternative route to privatization is to argue that in an increasingly multichannel system public broadcasting is itself now a niche market (based on offering what the mainstream market cannot or will not provide), and that as such it should be opened to competition. As the first draft of the European Commission's Green Paper on convergence argued, since 'Fair and open markets are . . . the best way of ensuring that public interest objectives are achieved' (1997a: 10) any organization should be free to 'bid to undertake public interest obligations' and invite viewers to subscribe to its services (ibid.: 21). If this provision is implemented it will mark the final break with public broadcasting's historic commitment to universal access.

In responding to these attacks, public broadcasting organizations tend to insist on their unique national histories and status. Their overview of the battlefield is based on an analogue map which shows other public cultural organizations as separate divisions or brigades. In contrast, a digital map would emphasize the lines of communications, supply and support running between them. As we have seen, the major commercial players on this digital field are increasingly interlocked and interconnected in European and global alliances. To match this powerful new configuration public broadcasters need to see themselves not as free-standing pillars of cultural enterprise but as nodes in a network of public institutions which embraces museums, libraries, galleries, schools and universities. Digital technologies offer an unparalleled chance to pool the cultural and knowledge resources held in each of these domains and to create a new public network, a digital cultural commons, operating across borders, accessible to everyone, at the cutting edge of experiments in new ways of combining and presenting material, and hospitable to a wide range of contributions from users and participants. Rising to this challenge is the central task facing public broadcasting and public culture more generally in today's Europe.

ACTIVITIES

Since the situation sketched in this chapter is unfolding on a daily basis, the first step towards forming a considered view on its possible impact is to keep abreast of what is happening now and what is being planned. You can usefully begin by looking at the situation in your own country and asking the following questions:

1 Which private companies are currently offering digital channels on the three main television platforms – terrestrial networks, cable systems, and satellite systems? How many are general mixed programming channels and how many are niche channels? Which interests and markets do the niche channels cater for? Which social groups or interests do they ignore? Are there channels for the elderly, the disabled or ethnic minorities, for example?
2 How much does it cost to access commercial digital channels? What is the current cost of an integrated digital television set or a set-top box that will convert digital signals for viewing on an analogue set? How much does it cost to subscribe to the full range of channels offered by each company? How much does it cost to spend an hour 'on-line' (connected to an Internet site produced by a television organization, for example)? What other equipment is needed to do this? What is the average monthly household income? Who cannot afford to gain access?
3 What interactive services are on offer? What kinds of interactivity do they promote?
4 How are advertisers using digital television? What kinds of advertising and promotional material are being produced? How does this differ from conventional television advertising? What kinds of home shopping and electronic commerce services are being offered?
5 What free digital services are public broadcasting organizations offering? To what extent do they differ from those offered by commercial companies, in terms of what they cover and how they present it?
6 What commercial digital services are public broadcasting organizations involved in, as partners in joint ventures, members of consortia, or sole providers?
7 How are broadcasters – both public and private – responding to the

rapid growth of the Internet? Have they launched their own Internet sites? If so, what are they using them for – promotion, supplementary material, interaction with viewers?

8 How are national governments and the European Commission proposing to regulate the emerging digital television marketplace?

SUGGESTIONS FOR FURTHER READING

Steemers, J. (ed.) (1998) *Changing Channels: The Prospects for Television in a Digital World*. Luton: University of Luton Press.

A wide ranging and informative collection of articles on recent developments in digital television and the issues they raise.

Levy, D.A. (1999) *Europe's Digital Revolution: Broadcasting Regulation, the EU and the National State*. London: Routledge.

A useful introduction to the development of European regulatory thinking on digital television.

The following readily available newspapers and magazines are useful sources for tracking new developments and initiations: *Cable and Satellite Europe*; *The Economist*; *The Financial Times*; *Le Monde diplomatique*; *Wired*. There is also a great deal of useful information on the Internet. Use one of the main search engines (like Alta Vista) that employs key words to begin searching for material on relevant companies and topics. The major broadcasting organizations all have their own sites, as do the relevant directorates within the European Commission and most relevant national ministries and regulatory bodies. These sites often contain archives of press releases, speeches and reports that can be downloaded free of charge.

II

TELEVISION TRENDS: ORGANIZATION AND REPRESENTATION

INTRODUCTION

Graham Murdock

The chapters in Part I detailed the rapid transition that television in Europe has undergone over the last decade or so. We saw how the familiar landscape of restricted competition dominated by national public service organizations has been replaced by a much more open environment increasingly commanded by transnational commercial operators. This movement accelerated in the 1980s and 1990s with the arrival of multichannel cable and satellite services and the launch of new advertising-supported terrestial channels and, as we saw in Chapter 3, is now being given a further push by the convergences set in motion by the shift to digital technologies. As a consequence, audiences are more likely to be addressed as consumers making choices in the marketplace rather than as citizens with rights and responsibilities within political and moral communities.

Many observers have seen this shift as accelerating the 'Americanization' of European culture. However, as Taisto Hujanen points out in Chapter 4, this is a more deep seated and subtle process than it might look at first sight. It is not simply that more American programmes are now being shown on European screens. It is also that broadcasting executives are looking to America for guidance on how to operate effectively in a competitive and commercialized environment.

Traditionally, public service television based its operating philosophy on programme making. It set out to make productions that provided a broad range of cultural resources for citizenship. The key words were diversity, quality and innovation. In contrast, the core strategies of American commercial television centred on programming. The aim was to assemble a schedule that would entice people to tune in and keep them watching in sufficient numbers to maximize the price that the channel could charge advertisers for a promotional spot or sponsorship opportunity. Public broadcasters saw their relations to their audiences as a matter of quality as much as quantity. They were interested in indicators of appreciation (how much audiences liked and valued a programme) as well as in raw ratings points (the average percentage of the population viewing). For commercial programmers in contrast, it was size not satisfaction that counted. As long as too many people did not switch over, the value of the programmes was secondary.

As Taisto Hujanen points out, there are a number of well established devices for cementing viewers' loyalty to the channel. Two of the best known are serialization – favouring programme forms which require people to watch the next episode or edition if they want to follow the story; and stripping – showing episodes of the same show at the same time each night. Because these strategies use up original material quickly it is imperative to make maximum use of programme resources. This can be done by regularly repeating and rerunning shows, by launching spin-offs featuring characters or personalities who are already well known from other shows, and by developing hybrid programme forms such as docu-soaps, that combine familiar elements from different popular genres, in this case soap operas and fly-on-the-wall documentaries. The aim of these ploys is to maximize novelty whilst minimizing the risks of low ratings. The comforts of familiarity replace the shock of the new. This makes sound economic sense but it poses serious threats to the values of programme diversity, aesthetic innovation and service to citizenship that public broadcasters have traditionally laid so much store by.

As Taisto Hujanen shows in his analysis of the Nordic countries, despite mounting competitive pressures, these values still enjoy widespread support within public broadcasting organizations, including the hybrid organizations that are funded by advertising but remain regulated by public service obligations. This suggests that announcements of the death of public broadcasting's core ethos may be premature. Yet the continuing proliferation of channels, the intensification of competition, and the arrival in the television marketplace of powerful new players from the computing and telecommunications industries, poses a permanent threat to public broadcasting's survival as a central cultural institution. But the pattern of change currently unfolding in Europe is not simply a matter of commerce. It is also a question of political communities and cultural identities.

It is tempting to characterize the process we now see occurring as an instance of the 'cultural imperialism' whereby programmes, styles and ways of working made in the USA, or in other major English speaking markets, increasingly dominate European commercial television, pushing more nationally inflected material and sensibilities to the margins. But as Albert Moran argues in Chapter 5, this is too simple. He traces the European career of the hit Australian soap opera, *The Restless Years*, made by one of the country's leading television production companies, Grundy (since acquired by Pearson, the British-based international media conglomerate). Although the early episodes of the versions produced in Holland and Germany worked with the original characters and the Australian scripts, he shows how this space was used to develop a dense network of specifically local associations which rooted the narrative very firmly in the here-and-now of national conditions.

The resilience of local structures of feeling is also confirmed by Aurélie Laborde and Michel Perrot in their case study of one instance of cross-border collaboration in programme production – current affairs – the magazine *Eurosud (EuroSouth)*. This project was intended as an intervention in a Europe seen not as a 'common market' but as an emerging sphere of plural publics rooted in shared histories and conditions.

Eurosud was launched jointly by three regional public service broadcasting organizations: the Bordeaux divisions of the French regional network, France 3; TVE Bilbao in the Basque region of Spain; and RTP Porto in northern Portugal. The project was not a co-production in the full sense. There were no pooled finances and no written contract. Rather it was a collaboration, financed internally within each organization and based on verbal agreements reached at regular joint editorial meetings. It was launched in 1988 in an atmosphere of optimism. Spain and Portugal had just joined the European Community (in 1986) and recently made the transition from dictatorship to democracy. European membership seemed to mark a new era of change and opportunity. *Eurosud* was conceived as a space in which these changes could be explored against the backdrop of the long-standing affinities in the three regions' economies and cultures. As Laborde and Perrot show, however, in common with almost all European joint ventures in programme making, the project was marked by permanent tensions between local sensibilities and cross-border ambitions.

Collaboration depended on not offending partners. This meant that the participating journalists continually exercised self-censorship in proposing themes for programmes and avoided issues that might provoke arguments. Awkward questions about child labour in Portugal or the terrorist activities of the Basque separatist group, ETA, remained firmly off the agenda. Instead, the programmes focused on non-controversial aspects of change – the rise of white collar work or partnerships between firms and universities – interspersed with slices of everyday life and leisure – football fandom, religion, female body builders, cooking – and examinations of well publicized general social problems such as unemployment, crime or road deaths. This relatively cautious, uncontroversial, agenda was reinforced by an emphasis on human interest and lived experience rather than analysis and explanation. Similarly, the original idea of getting each reporting team to make a film in one of the other participating countries was dropped as too expensive and replaced by domestically made items. The result was a juxtaposition of national productions rather than a collision of 'crossed looks' which explored similarities and differences in an innovative way. Hence, despite its best intentions, the programme failed to break out of the frameworks established by national ways of looking.

Their resilience is forcefully demonstrated by the first table in Winfried Schulz's chapter, which shows the highest-rating television programme in each European country in 1997. It confirms that national audiences generally gravitate towards images that reinforce their sense of themselves and their distinctive qualities. Hence the Danes watched handball, the Swedes, cross-country skiing, the British, the funeral of Diana, Princess of

Wales, and the Irish, who are famous for breaking into song at the drop of a hat, the Eurovision Song Contest, for which they were the hosts that year.

Eurosud was conceived as a modest intervention in the wider enterprise of rubbing away these imaginary borders and building a transnational public sphere within Europe. At one level it was a success. Despite its shoestring funding it sustained itself for six years and produced 42 editions, most of them half-hour programmes. But it also points up the problems of developing common projects guided by public service principles in a televisual environment increasingly dominated by the logic of sales and the ascendancy of American programme forms.

Eurosud was discontinued in 1996, just when this new environment was beginning to consolidate itself. Its producers were fortunate in not having to worry too much about audience size. Indeed, as Laborde and Perrot point out, they displayed little interest in who was watching or what sense they made of what they saw.

As Winifried Schulz demonstrates in Chapter 7, this is a luxury that broadcasters can no longer afford. Increased competition and the resulting fragmentation of audiences has brought home to everyone the importance of knowing as much as possible about your audiences. For commercial broadcasters it is an economic necessity. For public broadcasters it is an essential weapon in making the case for continued public subsidy. Because commercial broadcasters and advertisers are primarily interested in 'ratings', an immense amount of money has been spent in perfecting measurement technologies that ensure that these are as accurate as possible. In contrast, the case for public broadcasting can best be made on the basis of estimates of reach – which measure the percentage of the population that tunes into a particular channel over a given period (usually a week) – supplemented by research on appreciation and interpretation. If a public broadcasting organization can demonstrate high levels of reach it can plausibly argue that it is fulfilling its role of providing something for everyone over the average week, and is therefore deserving of continued support from the public purse. Moreover, if it can go on to show that people positively value the programmes they do choose to watch, it can reasonably claim to be fulfilling its role of providing quality.

The Irish writer, Oscar Wilde, berated the cynics of his day for knowing the price of everything but the value of nothing. Whether this will turn out to be a valid judgement on the commercialized, multichannel television system currently emerging in Europe will partly depend on how far public broadcasters are able to develop new points of contact with audiences. As Graham Murdock argued in Chapter 3, the Internet offers opportunities for new kinds of connections, but also a whole series of new challenges.

CHAPTER 4

PROGRAMMING AND CHANNEL COMPETITION IN EUROPEAN TELEVISION

Taisto Hujanen

PROGRAMMING IS CHOICES OF VALUES AND POLICY; FORMS, CONTENTS AND AUDIENCES

Can no television channel afford to broadcast a religious service on Sundays? That question was asked a week before Easter 1999 by a columnist from *Aamulehti*, the main regional newspaper in Tampere, the home city of my university. He was told by broadcasters that using outside broadcast units for direct transmissions on Sundays was too expensive. How then, he insists, can television channels afford to relay figure skating championships and ice hockey play-offs? He concludes that what is at stake here is a matter of priorities rather than costs.

In Finland there are, for the moment, four national broadcast television channels, two public service (YLE1 and YLE2) and two commercial (MTV3 and TV4). As elsewhere in Nordic countries and Europe, these channels now compete with a growing number of cable and satellite services. In terms of viewing time, however, they continue to dominate. In Finland, cable and satellite offer programming mainly in foreign languages, and their share of viewing time remains as low as 5 per cent (1997). Even so, their entry to the marketplace has changed the terms of competition in important ways. Before the present competitive structure of television emerged, the Finnish national broadcasting company YLE could 'afford' regular televised religious services on Sundays. At that time, prior to the 1980s, there was also an illuminating division of labour between the public YLE and its commercial partner in the Finnish television duopoly. The commercial company MTV (now MTV3), which operated within both of YLE's channels, concentrated on popular drama and entertainment, and was not allowed to carry religious and political programming or news. National rituals, be they religious, political or social like sports, belonged firmly to the sphere of the national broadcasting company.

In the early 1980s, the public television YLE formally adopted the notion of public service to distinguish itself from commercial television. Today, after almost two decades of growing commercial competition, YLE's two channels still account for nearly half of all television viewing time in Finland. At the same time, as the example of religious services shows, the official formulations and practices of public service have been renegotiated. A similar competitive situation has developed in all Nordic countries of Europe since the late 1980s (see Appendix 4.1, p. 82). Sweden was among the last countries in Europe to introduce a commercial broadcast television channel, TV4 in 1992. This long rearguard action against commercialism and the discontent it generated among viewers, explains, at least in part, why cable and satellite services have achieved a considerable share of the total viewing time in all other Nordic countries except Finland (25 per cent in Sweden in 1997).

If we return to the case of religious programming, we see that despite basic structural similarities in the television systems of Nordic countries, national differences still play a role. Week 48 (23–29 November) of 1998 serves here as a sample case to exemplify the similarities and differences of programming in Nordic television. On Sunday, 29 November, the Finnish YLE2 and the Swedish SVT2, both of them second channels operated by public service broadcasters, were the only channels to broadcast a direct religious service. NRK1, the first channel of the Norwegian public service broadcaster which normally transmits religious services, substituted *Sunday Sports*, with a direct transmission of cross-country skiing, a world-cup relay competition in northern Finland. That Sunday NRK1 had, in fact, a block of three direct sports transmissions, covering nearly all the daytime slots from 9.45 a.m. to 4 p.m. In contrast, the Finnish YLE2 packaged three religious programmes for the morning, starting with a Finnish language religious service at 10 a.m., continuing with a religious magazine at 11.30 a.m. and then a Swedish language religious service at noon. So on that Sunday, even Finland's 6 per cent minority of Swedish speaking people was offered a live religious service.

As the case of NRK1 shows, religion and sports are often alternative options for broadcasters on Sundays. Again the Finnish YLE2 makes a case for comparison. On the previous Sunday, 22 November, it transmitted no religious services but offered instead a direct transmission of world-cup cross-country skiing. Such a choice illuminates how the programming preferences of broadcasters have changed over time. Despite the fact that 85 per cent of Finland's population belong to the Lutheran state church, only 6 per cent of the TV audience watched the religious ceremony on Sunday, 29 November 1998. In the case of the Norwegian NRK1 which aired a live religious service a week later, the audience was even less, 3 per cent. The respective figures for live sports transmissions were 9 per cent for the Finnish YLE2 (on Sunday, 22 November) and as high as 17 per cent for the Norwegian NRK1 (on Sunday, 29 November).

The *Aamulehti* columnist arguing in favour of live religion on TV dared to question the future of cross-country skiing, the most traditional Nordic

Box 4.1

In May 1995, Finland beat Sweden in the finals of the ice hockey World Championship and won the championship for the first time. The victory over the team Finns love to hate (in Finland called 'the beloved enemy') was celebrated enthusiastically in restaurants and in the streets: behaviour atypical in Finnish tradition. That event symbolized the popularity of new collective sports over the old individual ones like cross-country skiing and light athletics. This match was transmitted by YLE2 and was the most popular programme of the year. It had a record

audience of 2.9 million, corresponding to a rating of 50 per cent. Similar ratings for sports events are common in other Nordic countries, although soccer seems to be most often the number one sport. In addition to Finland, Sweden is a country where ice hockey succeeds in reaching high ratings – 26.3 per cent for Sweden against Canada in the Winter Olympics 1998. In Norway, cross-country skiing is a national success story and was followed by 49 per cent in its own Winter Olympics 1994. But in the same year, a World Cup soccer game between Norway and Mexico achieved an even higher rating: 55 per cent of the population. Denmark played Brazil in the World Cup for soccer in 1998, and it was the most popular TV programme in Denmark that year with a rating of 48 per cent; followed by the World Championship final in handball between Denmark and Norway, with a rating of 47 per cent.

sport in Finland. There are reasons for such a doubt. As the above comparative figures from Finland and Norway show, it seems that the TV audience for cross-country skiing today is even bigger and more enthusiastic in Norway than in Finland (for the most popular TV sports in the Nordic countries, see Box 4.1). However, in comparison with religion, sports remain an important part of media rituals, though it is questionable how far one can still call sports national rituals. But as Box 4.1 demonstrates, at least the major sports events on TV continue to offer an experience shared by a vast number of people. As to religion, the Finnish example suggests that religion may now be more important as a media ritual than a live one. Among the members of the Finnish Lutheran church, only 2 per cent go to church on Sundays which is far less than the per centage watching religion on TV (6 per cent on YLE2, Sunday, 29 November 1998).

In his search for arguments in support of more live transmission of religion on TV, the columnist of *Aamulehti* refers to an opinion poll which showed that half of the Finnish people believe in angels. This argument is defensible in terms of the pluralism of programming. In principle, television should serve people who believe in angels. In today's secularized society, however, it is questionable how many of those Finns would elect to watch a religious ceremony on television. Probably, most would opt to watch sports on the other channel, if these were the only two choices. However, if more than two options were available, men and women would most likely select differently. In today's multichannel environment, sport is more than ever a male-dominated genre.

Programming is about a series of choices which are dependent not only on broadcasters and their audiences but also on the society and culture as a whole. Programming choices form a hierarchy in which values and policy precede the choice of forms and contents. What then is the position of audience(s) in this hierarchy? Are audiences a point of departure or an end for programming? Of course, for commercial broadcasters attracting audiences is basic to their ideology. On the other side, European public service broadcasters have been often blamed for their paternalism, for looking at audiences from above, and using them as objects of education. In a multichannel environment, in the middle of intensifying competition, these traditional differences tend to diminish and all broadcasters are compelled to pay more attention to their audiences.

CONTRASTING TRADITIONS

Religious services or sports, news and documentary or drama, serious or light, domestic or foreign, European or American, all these are examples of choices which are incorporated in the concept of programming. As Raymond Williams (1974) demonstrates in his classic book on television, 'the work of programming' has been an element of broadcasting since the early beginning (1974: 88). Accordingly, problems of *mix* and *proportion* became predominant in broadcasting policy. Mix refers to the composition of daily and weekly programme schedules, proportional to the overall structure of programme output classified in terms of basic categories. Two classifications are important in broadcasting policy debates. The first sorts

Box 4.2

In 1992 the Finnish commercial television company MTV (today MTV3) bought the rights to a well-known American daytime soap, *The Bold and the Beautiful*. In Finnish television, it serves as an example of an exceptionally strong lead-off programme in prime time. Its early time slot of 5.35–6.25 p.m. restructured the whole audience for TV in the early evening and, in fact, resulted in an earlier start for prime time

in Finnish television. Transmitted Monday to Friday, it introduced the American way of stripping popular programmes for all weekdays. Today, MTV3 also has a domestic soap which is stripped for all weekdays based, however, on an imported format. In only its second year (1993), *The Bold and the Beautiful* attracted 1 million viewers, which corresponds to a rating of 25 per cent. In the autumn of 1995, the start of *The Bold and the Beautiful* was transferred to 6.05 p.m. Since the autumn of 1998, its time slot has been shortened to half an hour and it starts even later, at 6.30 p.m. The average rating still remains at 20 per cent.

programmes into genres, like fact and fiction, information and entertainment, serious/popular drama, or categories like news and current affairs, documentary, drama series/serials, movies, sports, personal interest, talk shows, children's programmes, religion, etc. The second identifies items by their geographic origin using categories like domestic or foreign, European or American.

Williams's conceptualization of programming was based on the contrast between the European tradition of broadcasting and the American commercial model, which he observed in detail during a year spent teaching in the United States. In his typology of programming, the European public service tradition was named Type A, favouring news and public affairs, features and documentaries, arts and music, plays, and children's programmes. The commercial tradition he called Type B and was characterized by programme types like drama series and serials, movies and general entertainment (1974: 84–86). As Hellman (1999: 306) concludes, several later national and cross-national studies have confirmed the validity of that basic typology. Williams's approach of contrasting the two traditions of broadcasting also produced the concept of *flow* which is now one of the most debated aspects of television (for examples on this see Ang, 1985; Ellis, 1992; Jensen, 1994; Ridell, 1996; Corner, 1999). Flow is a conceptualization of Williams's experience of American television as a continuous melange of different elements in which advertising was mixed with programmes, programmes with other programmes, channels with other channels. He contrasted this with the programme-based aesthetics of the European tradition.[1]

In the later discussion of flow, viewers' experience is often analytically separated from other constructions like that of broadcasters themselves. The remote control console is now often seen as a symbol of viewers' active role in producing their own flow. As to the role of broadcasters, one should emphasize that flow is – to cite the above phrase of Williams – a result of the conscious 'work of programming'. Looking back, it is now clear that in a highly competitive environment, like American network television, the daily and weekly mix of programmes was (and is) of high strategic value. Indeed, one can say that programming as 'flow' was a response to intensifying channel competition. It was developed in order to keep the viewer watching one's channel as long as possible. To build up a succesful mix of programmes, scheduling and ratings analysis (see Schulz, Chapter 7) were considered as key assets, along with marketing in terms of programme and channel promotion.

Programming as a strategic tool for broadcasters is of growing importance in the context of today's European television, as well. Channel competition is now an everyday reality for European broadcasters. As the Nordic television scene demonstrates (Appendix 4.1), new private and semi-public operators have come on stream as well as more national and international cable and satellite services. At the same time, the former national broadcasters have turned from state bureaucracies to cultural industries with changes in organization and economic logic. The ongoing transformation to digital television will further accelerate these changes.

Having set the scene we can now explore the cultural transformation of European television in more detail from the point of view of programming. The case of Nordic countries is used here as an example of contemporary European television, but comparative conclusions in relation to other European countries will be made whenever possible. The basic aim is to test the hypothesis that European television is becoming Americanized, as a result of increased commercialization and channel competition, and the adoption of measures and practices of programming which are typical of the American commercial model (for documentation of this in Nordic countries, see Søndergaard, 1994; Syvertsen, 1996; Hellman, 1999; Lähteenmäki, 1999; Ytreberg, 1999). We begin by defining the American practice of programming. On the basis of that definition, the development of European television is then considered, with particular attention to similarities and differences between public service and commercial television.

DIMENSIONS OF PROGRAMMING

The strategic importance of programming in the American television system is demonstrated by the fact that there is a vast professional literature available on the subject (as examples, see Carrol and Davis, 1993; Eastman, 1993; Vane and Gross, 1994; Pringle et al., 1995). We will be using one of these sources, Susan Tyler Eastman's (1993) well known analysis of broadcast/cable programming strategies and practices, to highlight the basic features of the American conception of programming. She understands programming as a strategic tool/practice of broadcasting management which can be divided into three dimensions, *evaluation*, *selection* and *scheduling* (1993: 19). She summarizes her view of programming and programming skills as follows:

> Programming can be defined as the strategic use of programs arranged in schedules or tiers to attract target audiences. Programmers need the knowledge and skills to define such audiences and to select, acquire, and place programs that will attract them. In carrying out these tasks, programmers use strategies based on the inherent characteristics of radio and television, whether delivered by broadcast signals, cable signals, or other means. These strategies cluster around the concept of *compatibility, habit formation, audience flow, program conservation, and wide audience reach*. From these broad concepts follow specific strategies, such as day-parting, stripping, counterprogramming, and rerunning. Programmers evaluate the probable success of untried programs in terms of the types of appeals they have for audiences, expecting succesful mass audience programs to contain elements of conflict, comedy, sex, information, and human interest, plus a number of secondary qualities. (1993: 38; emphasis added)

This summary should not be understood as a scientific theory of programming but as a concrete explication of the American professional experience of succesful/effective programming. The emphasized list of concepts, in particular, generalizes from the American model (1993: 9–18).

A closer look is therefore needed to highlight the particularities of the American experience.

Compatibility refers to time-budgeting as an aspect of programme scheduling. The principle is to make the programming compatible, as Eastman formulates it, with what people do throughout the daily cycle of their lives (1993: 10). The idea of *prime time* coinciding with people's evening leisure time, is the best known example. But time-budgeting is also incorporated in a range of other programme categories like daytime soap operas, morning or evening news, late night shows, and morning/breakfast television. Other major time-budgeting dimensions are the weekday/weekend division and seasonal variations of programming. This sort of compatibility is a part of the European broadcasting tradition, as well. For example, in Nordic countries time-budgeting has been a regular element of audience research since the 1960s (for the development of broadcasting research in Nordic countries, see Carlsson, 1997). But there is an important difference between the two traditions concerning the interpretation and use of available information. The idea of prime time illustrates the point. For American broadcasters, prime time was the time to offer what most people wanted to see. For the European broadcasters, it represented an opportunity to transmit what was considered socially and politically most relevant. Naturally this opposition exaggerates the daily practices of European broadcasters, but in broad lines it demonstrates very well the normative approach to audience which Ien Ang (1991) argues characterizes public service.

Habit formation refers to standardization of programme schedules in terms of transmission time and contents. Ideally, Eastman concludes, habit formation calls for *stripping* programmes, that is, scheduling them Monday through Friday at the same time each day (1993: 11). News is the most typical example of such stripping. In the American television daytime soap operas are another example. In practice, habit formation is more often based on weekly cycles than on day-to-day stripping. In fact, one could say that *serialization* is the most widely applied form of habit formation. Serialization is a result of the industrial nature of American television and is one of the most effective tools of scheduling. It represents a *horizontal* measure of scheduling distinct from *vertical* measures which point to the next aspect of Eastman's summary, the control of audience flow.

With regard to habit formation, European television is again both similar and different. Television news is the most obvious instance of similarity. For example in Finland, the early findings of broadcasting research demonstrated that viewing news is in many respect ritualistic.[2] The news constituted a national ritual which formed one of the basic institutions of the so-called paleo-television, the golden era of national public service television. Religious services also belonged to the national rituals of paleo-television. But the European tradition differs from the American with respect to habit formation. In particular, the aesthetic tradition of European television prefers arts and high culture over the popular. In Williams's framework (outlined above), flow and serialization symbolized industrial

Box 4.3

Prime Time Scheduling Strategies (Eastman, 1993)

Blocking: Block programming refers to placing a new programme within a set of similar older programmes to fill an entire evening or a part of an evening.
Bridging: Bridging has two forms. One is the regular use of long-form programmes that start during the access hour and continue into prime time, thus running past the broadcast channels' lead-offs and interrupting their strategy when viewers later switch channels. The second form involves starting and ending programmes at odd times, thus causing them to run past the starting and stopping points for shows on other channels.
Counterprogramming: Scheduling programmes to pull viewers away from competitors by offering something with completely different appeal to the other shows. According to Eastman, most other strategies are intended to hold viewers who are already watching (flow strategies); counterprogramming interrupts flow to gain different viewers. Consider scheduling news against news, as an example of counterprogramming with a similar appeal.
Hammocking: Refers to moving an established series to the next later half-hour slot and inserting a promising new programme in the vacated slot. In this way, the new programme can take advantage of audience flow from the lead-in programme to the rescheduled familiar lead-out show, automatically providing viewers for the intervening programme.
Lead-in: The lead-in strategy places a strong series before a weaker or new series to jump-start it. This is called the inheritance effect, i.e. the strong lead-in carries part of its audience over to the next programme.
Lead-off: Refers to the strategy of beginning an evening with an especially strong programme. It is assumed that the first prime-time show sets the tone for the entire evening.
Stripping: Means scheduling programmes Monday through Friday (or like news, daily) at the same time each day.
Stunting: Includes scheduling specials, adding guest stars to regular series, having unusual series promotion, shifting a half-hour series to long form, and otherwise altering the regular programme schedule at the last minute.
Tent-poling: Is an alternative to the hammock. Instead of splitting up successful time blocks to insert an unproven show, each channel focuses on a central, strong 9 p.m. show on weak evenings, hoping to use that show to anchor the ones before and after it.

mass culture which was to be considered qualitatively different from the programme-based aesthetics of European television.

Control of audience flow refers to ordering the daily mix of programming in ways that maximize (1) the number of people who flow through to the next programme on the channel, and (2) the number who flow in from rival channels, at the same time minimizing (3) the number that flow away to competing channels or activities (Eastman, 1993: 12). Naturally, people's initial decision as to whether to watch in general, what and on which channel is also related to the daily mix of programming. Current practices for the control of audience flow are the result of the competitive nature of

American television. The most refined measures of control have been developed in order to match the competition in prime time, the decisive area of programming for the economic success of commercial television networks. Eastman lists eight scheduling strategies which dominate prime time: lead-off, lead-in, hammocking, blocking, tent-poling, bridging, counter-programming, and stunting (1993: 135–138). Stripping could be added to this list, as well as checkerboarding (on these two see Carroll and Davis, 1993: 308).

Control of audience flow is one aspect of American television which clearly represents the differences of the two models. A similar conclusion can be made with respect to the general role and strategic importance of prime time. In many European television systems, channel competition is still quite a recent phenomenon. In public service monopolies there was no need to match the competition. In Nordic public television companies for example, scheduling was based around programme coordination. In case of parallel public service channels as in Finland (since 1965) and in Sweden (since 1969), coordination was needed to avoid simultanous transmission of similar programme contents and genres. The aim was to offer two channels that complemented each other. In the sphere of production, parallel channels were gradually encouraged to compete. In Sweden parallel news organizations were created for the two public channels, for example. But in scheduling, coordination remained the principle. However, in the relationship with its commercial rivals, European public service television is now adopting a more competitive approach to scheduling especially in prime time. In Finland, a recent example of this more 'aggressive' attitude is offered by YLE2 which in January 2000 started transmitting a dating game programme parallel to a similar (and older) programme on the commercial MTV3 channel.

Programme conservation is an aspect of Eastman's summary which refers directly to the requirements of commercial broadcasting's economy. She points out that 'radio and television notoriously consume program materials faster than other media – an inevitable consequence of their being on round the clock' (1993: 13). Further on, she comes to the following conclusion:

> A major aspect of the programmer's job consists, then, in devising ingenious ways *to get the maximum mileage out of each program item*, to develop formats that require as little new material as possible for the next episode in a series, to invent clever excuses for repeating old programs over and over. (1993: 14; emphasis added)

Serialization is one of the traditional measures of programme conservation. But as the above citation from Eastman shows, *format development* and *repetition* (reruns) are also a part of the programmer's tool kit. Even in American broadcast television, however, round the clock transmissions are a relatively recent phenomenon, resulting from the challenge of cable and satellite services. A tremendous increase in programme hours has taken place without a matching increase in production resources. Against that background, it is easy to understand why many American television analysts unanimously point to the increased importance of programming as a response to intensified channel competition (Andersen, 1995; Caldwell, 1995; Feuer, 1995). Caldwell concludes that the economic crisis of network television has led to a clear-cut division of programming between what he calls 'boutique' programming and 'low-cost' programming (1995: 105–245). In the latter type of programming, in which Caldwell includes categories like 'Trash TV' and 'Tabloid TV', the refined technology of computer-based editing has opened up new opportunities for programme conservation, including the more effective use of archived materials, versioning, updating and repeating. Various forms of so-called 'reality television' also demonstrate the possibilities for programme conservation offered by the new technology. Similarly, the development and sales of formats is now a business which is of growing importance not only for American television but also for other major television markets (Moran, 1998).

With regard to the economic basis of programme conservation, the European tradition is significantly different. The difference is between business and public spending. At the same time that observers were pointing to the economic problems of American network television in the 1980s, European broadcasters, scholars and media politicians were claiming that there was a crisis in public service broadcasting. This crisis was not only a matter of ideology and identity. It was also an economic crisis. The standard accusation was that public service broadcasters were economically inefficient and were wasting public resources. As in the public sector in general, public service broadcasting organizations responded by adopting a more businesslike and industrial orientation in budgeting and administration (Achille and Miège, 1994). As in America, a huge increase of programme output occurred in Europe. For example, the recent Nordic media statistics (1999) show that the weekly transmission time of all main television channels expanded considerably in the 1990s, with the increase in commercial channels being slightly more than in public channels. The coincidence of a stagnating or declining economy and growing output is now part of the experience of present-day European broadcasters, as well.

The last concept on Eastman's list, *wide audience reach*, refers to the aspect of programming which professionals and critics alike call 'the numbers game' (1993: 14). However, although ratings analysis and audience and marketing research are important tools for evaluating viewing figures, programmers also apply rules of thumb to estimate the likely appeal of untried programmes. Eastman highlights how wide audience reach is understood in terms of prime time:

> Prime-time network television traditionally strives to woo the largest possible audience (overall or within a demographic group) *for its advertisers*, not necessarily the satisfied audience. Many programmers believe that prime-time series that generate strong reactions among viewers may split the audience into two groups: those that love and those that hate a show, and that a show that generates only moderate liking, but is hated by no one, may get the biggest audiences. (1993: 119; emphasis added)

This approach to prime time is known as the principle of *least objectionable programming* (LOP). Eastman concludes, however, that 'the least objectionable program theory becomes progressively untenable as viewing options increase' (1993: 120). The new approach of prime-time programming is characterized as follows:

> Under conditions of vastly increased program supply, prime-time programmers face the difficult task of satisfying advertisers' demands for large, well-identified audiences, and viewers' demands for programs they really want to see. These conditions have forced the broadcast networks into *increased targeting of specific audience segments.* (1993: 120; emphasis added)

So American network television tries to satisfy two parallel audiences: advertisers and viewers. In fact, it is often said that the main product of American television, the commodity it trades in, is audiences, not programmes. For American television then audience is traditionally more than a partner; it is an ideology. The commercial programming slogan of *giving the audience what it wants*, is the keystone of this ideology. The central role of audience(s) is also expressed in Eastman's overall definition of programming, as having in the last instance 'to attract target audiences' (1993: 38).

Audience orientation is historically one of the major differences between the two television models. Critics of the European tradition have pointed out that the public service philosophy underestimated or even neglected the audience's point of view. Applying Ang's notion of 'normative audience' (see above), one can say that for European broadcasters the audience was a qualitative category whose needs the programming was to serve. Paternalism, looking down on people from above, is one of the terms that has been used to describe the audience orientation of public service broadcasting institutions. The value basis of the European programming tradition is formulated in the slogan *something for everyone*, which can be understood as an expression of value *pluralism*. In a way, pluralism was also a measure of wide audience reach. But the point is that this goal was evaluated on the basis of total programming output and less in terms of individual programmes.

In the present competitive environment of television in Europe, the numbers game has become an everyday one for programmers. In order to keep their role as generalists who offer a universal service of contents and genres, public service broadcasters are now forced to play this game. This means that in their tool kit for programming, audience research and market analysis are now key assets. One part of the numbers game is expressed by the statistics in Appendix 4.1, demonstrating the market shares of various television channels in Nordic countries. In Finland, in the early 1990s, the public service broadcaster YLE set itself the goal of maintaining a 50 per cent market share in the competition for daily viewing time. That share was considered critical for the political legitimation of its operations. This, in turn, acknowledged that the legitimation of public service broadcasting was no longer based on politics alone, but also on its success in the market.

Box 4.4

In the autumn of 1997 the Swedish public service broadcaster SVT launched a programme series entitled *Expedition Robinson*. It applied the so-called 'reality TV' format and was based on the experiences of a group of 16 volunteers who spent two months together with a camera crew on a desert island. The group was divided into two teams which competed to be the most skilful 'Robinsons'. After each competition, the losing team was forced to send one member off the island. The

programme became very popular and achieved an average rating of 16.7 per cent in its first season; by the final episode, aired in December 1998, the rating had risen to 30.4 per cent. The programme created a heated discussion on how public service broadcasters should respond to increasing channel competition. For example, the ethics of the game were seen as cruel and unsuitable. Prior to the airing of the programme, one of the ousted team members committed suicide (but for reasons not related to the show), and this added to the dramatic impact of the series.

AMERICANIZATION OR NOT?

How can we interpret these new developments in programming traditions and practices? Is European television now more similar to the American commercial model? Are the two models converging? Thinking about forms and dimensions of convergence, it is important to remember that although economy and even technology may change overnight, cultural, social and political shifts are seldom so rapid. A Finnish scholar, who recently published a major study on the changing broadcasting markets and television programming in Finland (Hellman, 1999), makes this point when evaluating his research findings. He wondered why the range and diversity of television programming in both public service and commercial channels were still high in Finland compared to other countries. His conclusion was that, because of the country's dintinct historical experience, for Finnish people the idea of a TV channel includes diversity of contents and a wide range of programming in terms of genre. So if there is convergence, it takes place in both directions, from commercial to public and from public to commercial.

Finland is an interesting case of convergence, because from the viewer's point of view the old structure of television had already in a way converged. The reason is that in the era of duopoly commercial television was transmitted in blocks within the public channels. So from the viewer's point of view, Williams's Type A and Type B programming always appeared side by side. Similarly, convergence has been an aspect of the old television culture in all those European countries in which advertising was allowed on television before expansion of channel competition in the 1980s. As examples one could refer to the British TV duopoly of BBC and ITV or the German networks ARD and ZDF. Both ITV and the German networks represent forms of television which are often called hybrid. In textual theory, hybrid refers to a mixture of qualitatively different forms which, put together, construct something new. As a characterization of television channels, hybrid means a mixture of public service and private/commercial elements. In this sense most of today's European television channels are hybrids. Therefore, it might be better to use the phrase more narrowly, as a description of television channels which are funded (at least in part) by advertising but whose operations are regulated by public service obligations.

Appendix 4.1 demonstrates that in Nordic countries the so-called hybrid channels are today the main competitors of the old public service broadcasters. These channels include TV2 in Denmark, MTV3 in Finland, TV2 in Norway, and TV4 in Sweden. The public service channels consist respectively of DR1 and 2, YLE1 and 2, NRK1 and 2, and SVT1 and 2. A distinction between public and private channels can also be applied to the hybrids, as shown in Table 4.1. In Danish TV2 represents the public/hybrid category; the rest of the hybrids belong to the private/hybrid type. Except for Norway's NRK1, the hybrid channels are now the most popular individual television channels in Nordic countries. In terms of market share, the public service channels have lost most viewers in Denmark. In other countries the market is still more or less balanced between traditional public service and commercial television, although the market share of the public service channels is slightly below the 50 per cent level.

Table 4.1 summarizes data on the programme contents of different kinds of television channels in Nordic countries in the period 1988–95. It demonstrates that despite convergence one can still see clear differences in the overall programming profiles of public service television as against other forms of television. The traditional emphasis on information is still

TABLE 4.1 Programme content in television by channel type in the Nordic countries, 1988–95 (%)

Channel type	Share of information	Share of fiction	Share of entertainment	Share of other categories
Public, non-commercial	41	23	12	24
Public, hybrid	35	34	13	18
Private, hybrid	32	37	18	13
Private, commercial/satellite/cable	16	55	9	20
Mean	32	36	12	19

'Other categories' includes, for example, sports, children's programming, local programming.

Source: Hellman, 1999: 309

stronger in public channels, be they non-commercial or hybrid, while the share of fiction is clearly lower. Public channels also offer more specific categories of programming, like children's programmes and local programming. Purely private commercial channels and satellite/cable services have a distinct profile of their own. They concentrate heavily on fiction and certain niches like sports.

The above data can be compared with an earlier analysis of De Bens et al. (1992) which covered 53 Western European television channels in 14 countries. Their research was based on a simple dichotomous distinction between public and commercial broadcasters and did not include Hellman's category of hybrid channels. By using the distinction between serious and popular programmes, the data show even stronger differences between public and commercial channels than Hellman's later conclusions. Especially in prime time, the commercial broadcasters concentrated almost exclusively on popular programmes (86 per cent of programmes) while the public broadcasters had a considerable share (38 per cent) of serious programmes even in prime time. It is worth noticing, however, that popular programmes accounted for the majority of the output of both public and commercial television: 57 per cent in public channels and 74 per cent in commercial channels.

The problem with the above figures is that they are, at least in part, outdated. Looking at the generic mixture of today's television, it is often impossible to make clear-cut distinctions between such traditional textual categories as fact and fiction, serious and light, information and entertainment. Consequently, relying heavily on traditional programme statistics in the analysis may be misleading. To get a fuller picture of programming trends, one should complement them with more focused analyses of specific programmes and genres. The coincidence of a stagnating television economy and a rapid expansion of time slots to fill has created a situation in which broadcasters are continually forced to rearticulate their old categories of programming and create new ones which often combine or mix aspects of old genres or programming traditions. A recent example of the changing genetic mixture of television is the 'docusoap', a trend in programming which refers to a new kind of real-life documentary series which make use of the typical narrative conventions of the soap opera. At the moment (January 2000), the Finnish YLE is transmitting one of the British BBC's best known docusoaps, *Airport*. A few domestic productions are already available and more will come. A Finnish researcher (Solla, 1999), discussing the trend, concludes that the introduction of docusoaps at the BBC was based on a careful analysis of programme schedules (remember the aspect of 'evaluation' in Eastman's concept of programming). The analysis suggested that there might be a substantial audience for a more dramatized form of documentary series; an audience which was younger and more female than for documentaries in general. One lesson from this example is that the BBC schedulers had a clear view of the time slot and the audience for docusoaps, before any episode of the series was produced.

The introduction of docusoaps illustrates major organizational change which is now taking place in European television. Following the model of American network television, even European public service institutions are now becoming programming organizations. The increased use of independents for production is part of this change, but even more important is the fact that the traditional relationship between programming and production is being turned upside down. As the above example of docusoaps demonstrates, ideas for programmes now are often generated by the logic of the schedule and by the programmers who are responsible for the schedules. One might describe the change as follows: earlier on everything started with a programme for which the schedulers tried to find a time slot and an audience. Today, there is first the time slot and the audience as defined by the schedulers. After that, the commissioning editors try to find a producer for a programme which fits the prescribed orientation. All these changes contribute to make programming into the power centre of today's television.

The idea of 'commissioning' programmes is central to the new managerial sysystem of broadcasting. Following the example of the BBC it is often referred to as 'producer choice' and is, in one way or another, applied by both Finnish public television channels as well as most other Nordic public service channels. As the term itself demonstrates, 'producer choice' is a measure to organized the selection aspect of programming, the acquisition of programmes. It means in practice that all decisions on production are based on 'commissions' which programmers negotiate with internal producers or with independents. Bargaining on commissions takes place in the so called 'internal market' which highlights the dominantly economic logic of the new managerial practices. The application of 'producer choice' is strongly centralized and, for example, in Finnish YLE1 only two persons take care of commissioning, one for fact and one for fiction. 'Producer choice' is submitted to the scheduling process, in other words, the formal decision on commissions wait until the decision on schedules has been made. As applied in the Finnish YLE, commissioning editors are consulted in all key phases of the scheduling process, and they participate in negotiations on schedules with production departments.

NOTES

1 Corner (1999: 62) points out when discussing Williams's concept of flow that Williams reports the experience of a cultural outsider. According to Corner, his personal encounter offers a way into analysis but it does not document the televisual experience of the American viewer precisely because of its lack of familiarity with the new conventions.

2 Nordenstreng (1972: 391), discussing the findings of early audience research in the late 1960s, points out that for many Finns following the news is a mere ritual, a way of dividing up the daily rhythm, and a manifestation of alienation. He cites a research report concluding that many people follow the news because in this way they gain a point of contact with the outside world – a fixed point of life – while remaining indifferent to the actual content of the news.

ACTIVITIES

1 How would you classify the TV channels available in your own environment? Apply the public service/commercial categorization and identify also the hybrid forms. Which is your favourite channel and why? What other sorts of channels are available? How do they they differ from broadcast TV channels?

2 What are the most popular TV programmes in your country? Are the popular programmes similar on all channels? Are they domestic or foreign? What are your own programme preferences? Are there any programmes which are particularly important for certain target audiences? Do you ever feel guilty about watching television?

3 Study the weekly schedules of TV channels. Pay particular attention to counterprogramming between the channels. What do the other channels transmit, when one channel airs a popular news magazine? How do the channels in general respond to the most popular programmes of other channels? Give examples of how channels try to control their audience flow into prime time and out of prime time (lead-in, lead-off).

4 Study separately the weekly schedules of public service channels. Would you classify those channels as generalists or specialists? In other words, do they try to cover a wide range of contents and genres or do they specialize in a certain kind of limited service? What does public service mean in programming terms on these channels?

5 Estimate how much the programming on different channels is serialized. What kinds of individual or single programmes are offered? What do the channels transmit outside prime time (late night and night, morning, daytime, afternoon, early evening)?

APPENDIX 4.1

TABLE 4.2 Main TV channels in the Nordic countries, their means of distribution and market shares of the total viewing time (%)[1]

Country	Channel	Distribution[2]	Market share/Year							
			1990	1991	1992	1993	1994	1995	1996	1997
Denmark	**DR1**	B/C	45	39	35	32	30	28	27	28
	DR2	B/C	–	–	–	–	–	–	0	1
	TV2	B/C	47	45	40	42	41	42	42	39
	TV3[3]	S/C	–	10	7	8	10	11	13	12
	TvDanmark	B/C/S	–	–	–	–	–	–	–	6
	Local TV[4]	B/C	–	–	5	5	6	6	5	1
	Other	C/S	–	–	13	13	13	14	14	12
Finland	**TV1 (YLE)**	B/C	33	33	30	24	25	25	25	24
	TV2 (YLE)	B/C	21	19	19	21	19	20	21	22
	FST1&2[5]	B/C	3	3	2	1	2	2	2	2
	MTV1&2[6]	B/C	26	23	20	–	–	–	–	–
	TV3/MTV3	B/C	13	16	24	47	46	46	44	44
	Nelonen (Channel Four)	B/C	–	–	–	–	–	–	–	2
	PTV	C	1	1	1	1	2	2	2	–
	Other	B/S/C	3	5	4	6	6	5	6	6
Norway	**NRK1**	B/C	79	59	62	53	48	43	43	41
	NRK2	B/C	–	–	–	–	–	–	1	2
	TV2	B/C	–	–	5	20	26	31	32	31
	TV3	S/C	5	14	8	6	6	6	6	6
	TVNorge	S/C	6	12	8	9	8	8	7	8
	Other	B/C/S	9	15	17	12	12	12	10	11
Sweden	**SVT1**	B/C	37	34	32	30	27	25	24	22
	SVT2	B/C	46	44	39	26	27	26	25	26
	TV3	S/C	5	14	10	9	9	9	9	10
	TV4	B/C	–	5	17	23	26	28	28	27
	Kanal5	S/C	1	3	2	3	3	4	6	6
	Other	B/S/C	11	0	0	9	8	8	9	9

1 Emboldened channels represent the traditional public service broadcasters.
2 B = broadcast channel, C = cable, S = satellite.
3 Including TV3+ since 1996.
4 Local TV was mostly Kanal 2 (Copenhagen) until 1996. From 1997 Kanal 2 has been part of TvDanmark.
5 YLE's service in Swedish in the channels of TV1 and TV2.
6 The commercial MTV Company operated until 1992 within the channels of TV1 and TV2. Since 1993 it has operated the former third channel.

Sources: Hellman and Sauri, 1997; *Nordic Baltic Media Statistics 1998*, 1999

SUGGESTIONS FOR FURTHER READING

Corner, J. (1999) *Critical Ideas in Television Studies*. Oxford: Clarendon Press.

Eastman, S.T. (1993) *Broadcast/Cable Programming*. Belmont, CA: Wadsworth.

Tracey, M. (1998) *The Decline and Fall of Public Broadcasting*. Oxford: Oxford University Press.

Williams, R. (1974) *Television: Technology and Cultural Form*. London: Fontana/Collins.

CHAPTER 5

POPULAR DRAMA: TRAVELLING TEMPLATES AND NATIONAL FICTIONS

Albert Moran

The Restless Years began transmission in Australia late in 1977. Made by one of the country's major production houses, the Grundy Organization, it proved immensely popular and ran for 781 half-hour episodes. It employed the conventions of soap opera to tell the story of a group of young people, leaving school and negotiating the uncertainties of work, family, intimate relations and rapid social change. The title evoked both the restlessness of youth as a time of life and the wider dislocations set in motion by economic and political change. Following its domestic success, Grundy entered into co-venture agreements in both the Netherlands and Germany to produce national adaptations.

Retitled *Goede Tijden, Slechte Tijden* (Good Times, Bad Times), it began transmission in the Netherlands in 1990. Two years later, a version using the same title, *Gute Zeiten, Schlechte Zeiten*, was launched on RTL, one of Germany's leading commercial channels. Both adaptations started out using the original Australian scripts, with very minor modifications. These versions ran for 460 episodes in Dutch and 230 episodes in German, before local writers were employed to develop original story-lines. *Goede Tijden, Slechte Tijden* was the first locally produced daily soap opera not just on Dutch television, but on European television as a whole, and it quickly acquired a substantial audience. *Gute Zeiten, Schlechte Zeiten* was also the first domestically produced daily serial on German television, and while it took longer to build a following, it eventually became a cult programme.

It is tempting to interpret these successes as instances of the cultural imperialism whereby Anglo-American programming comes to play a central role in the imaginary landscapes offered by European television, squeezing out more nationally specific visions. A pessimistic reading would see the rapidly expanding trade in programme ideas and formats as an extension of this process, a way of evading restrictions on the amount of 'foreign' programming that can be shown, by providing templates for productions that will be counted as 'domestic'. As we shall see, however, while Grundy's original conception clearly defined a number of key features of the serial, such as the initial story-line and the central characters, it did not determine how it looked and sounded or how it connected with core elements of popular culture in Holland and Germany. In both versions the accents and locations combined with the dense thicket of cultural associations carried by the characters and settings to produce fictional worlds that evoked specifically national forms of knowledge, experience and identity. But let's begin by looking briefly at how this process of 'nationalization' worked in the original Australian version.

THE RESTLESS YEARS AND AUSTRALIAN IDENTITY

The Restless Years was produced at the studios of Sydney's Channel 10 and its imaginary community is set in affluent enclaves close to the water, typical of Sydney harbour or the Northern beach suburbs. Some broader, more working class accents are in evidence from time to time although their paucity highlights a social absence in the serial. Similarly there is a noticeable absence of ethnic accents and appearances among the characters.

On the other hand though, the serial is not a saga of the rich and powerful. It is concerned with the affluent but not with the wealthy. Where earlier Australian series located social problems in the poorer working class suburbs of both Sydney and Melbourne, the Grundy serials – at times hesitantly, at times in a contradictory fashion – found these in more affluent surroundings (Moran, 1985). The affluence of many of the characters is thin. The school the students leave at the beginning is co-educational, located in relatively modern redbrick buildings, a free, public rather than a more expensive private school.

The Restless Years is also grounded in its Australian audience's experience of rapid change in the late 1970s. That social context is mobilized at a series of levels and through a dense network of detail. The students' nickname for Miss MacKenzie, the former high school teacher for example, is Big Mac. McDonald's, the fast food chain, opened its first store in Australia in Sydney in 1971 and, by 1977, when *The Restless Years* began on air, burgers and fries had become part of Australian popular culture. Another, older point of cultural resonance is provided by the figure of the Ocker, a term referring to a socially and often comically clumsy type. This person's poor manners, lack of breeding and social graces were seen to be an outcome of both their social position as working class and also of Australia's geographical distance from metropolitan Britain and the civilizing effects of its culture (Oxley, 1979). While the figure of the Ocker was by mid-century seen as something of an anachronism, the type was powerfully revalorized by the emergence of Australian television comedian Paul Hogan. He had a popular television show in the 1970s, and later achieved international success with the film *Crocodile Dundee*. Consequently the working class figures of Raeleen, Sharmaine and, to a lesser extent, Hoggo in *The Restless Years* have to be seen against Hogan's embodiment of the type. The mixed social and cultural references of the Ocker figure also underlines a more general issue about the intertextual knowledges that are mobilized by soap opera audiences.

The figure of Miss MacKenzie and the school should be set in the context of the other two Grundy serials, *Class of 74/75* and the contemporaneous *Glenview High*. The latter is particularly relevant to this serial, as it had a woman, Margaret Gibson as head of the Sydney high school represented in the programme (Kingsley, 1989; Moran, 1993). In addition, although none of the large cast of the serial had star status, several had familiar personas so far as the Australian viewing public in the late 1970s was concerned. The ABC serial *Certain Women* produced between 1973 and 1977 had indelibly stamped the image of actress June Salter as a middle-aged career woman who had never married and had a family, a persona continued in her role as Miss MacKenzie in *The Restless Years*. Similarly Joy Chambers, who appeared more infrequently as the devious Rita Merrick, was known particularly to viewers in her home city of Brisbane both as a television personality and actress and also as wife to the owner of the Grundy Organization (Beck, 1984).

Although the serial did not claim to be social realist, it constantly touches on social themes and issues. They include: parentless, children; adultery; marriage breakdowns; alcoholism; social loneliness; health problems; youth homelessness; unscrupulous recruitment of teenage prostitutes; teenage pregnancy and forced marriage; and backyard abortion. In other words the title of the serial can also be seen to be 'about' the dislocation and disharmony brought about by the social and economic policies of government and commercial institutions.

The key social problem that is repeatedly touched on, from the first episode to the last, is unemployment, especially youth unemployment. Between 1974 and 1978 youth unemployment jumped from 9 per cent to 22 per cent. From 1975 to at least 1978, the Australian media as well as the federal government pursued a campaign of scapegoating and punishing those who were on unemployment relief (Windshuttle, 1979: 38–79). These 'dole bludgers', especially the young, were seen as involved in various forms of 'dole rip-offs', from drawing more relief than they were entitled to, to making no effort to find paid employment. The thrust of such a campaign was, in effect, to suggest that much of the high volume of figures for Australian unemployment was, in fact, due to individual laziness and greed. It suggested that jobs were really there, provided one looked hard enough and that those who were unemployed were morally delinquent, if not criminal. While this discourse was prevalent in the popular media, including tabloid afternoon newspapers and talk-back radio, it was subjected to contestation elsewhere, in some of the quality newspapers, in radio and television documentaries, in several of ABC television's social problem drama series such as *Beat of the City*, *Pig in a Poke* and *Spring and Fall* and the feature film *Mouth to Mouth*. In its own way, *The Restless Years* can be seen as intervening in the 'dole bludger' debate. However, because the producers of this serial were never imbued with social realist ambitions for their stories this intervention is occasional and frequently inconclusive. Nevertheless this context provides the Australian backdrop for the serial.

DUTCH IDENTITY AND *GOEDE TIJDEN, SLECHTE TIJDEN*

Goede Tijden, Slechte Tijden was not only the first domestically produced daily drama serial on Dutch television, but it has remained the most popular. The programme has been of immense significance for Dutch broadcasting not only in economic but also in cultural terms. The popular success first of imported soaps such as *Dallas* and then of domestically produced serials such as *Goede Tijden, Slechte Tijden* has broken the stranglehold of public service 'quality' drama as the only legitimate form of fiction on Dutch television (Ang, 1991; Madsen, 1994). Madsen, a long-time producer of *Goede Tijden*, has written:

> A more general reason why a daily soap serial on Dutch television is important is that the audience is accustomed to the Dutch language as a language for fiction. Why is it that they say that it is bad acting when they hear 'ik hou van je' instead of 'I love you'? We are convinced that it is a necessity to make television drama in your own culture, your own language. (1994: 52)

The Dutch spoken by the characters in *Goede Tijden, Slechte Tijden* attempts to overcome regional variations and is best described as an accent found in the Randstad region, especially around Hilversum where the Dutch television industry is located.

If *Goede Tijden, Slechte Tijden* deliberately avoids specification of region, so too it elides place. Although other Dutch soap operas have deliberately represented cities such as Rotterdam in *Het Oude Noorden* and Amsterdam in *Vrouwenvleugel*, the intention of this serial – like another produced some years earlier, *Spijkerhoek* – is to construct the stories as taking place in a moderately large, but unspecified Dutch city. The characters speak a 'national' Dutch language and live in a 'national' place registered through a plethora of physical objects, social behaviours and routines drawn from everyday life in the Netherlands. Some examples make the point. An incidental item present in many scenes was flowers; as one of my interpreters Madelaine, explained: 'you see a lot of flowers in houses, on tables in Holland. The flowers are there all through the year – different types of flowers. You bring them when you go out or visit someone. You bring flowers or when it's someone's birthday.'

A basket containing fruit such as apples, bananas and oranges is also quite common. Sometimes elements of Dutch topography are drawn into the dramatic action. For example, in episodes broadcast in late 1996, Roos, Arnie Alberts's wife, is upset at his disappearance and narrowly avoids crashing her car into a 'sloot', a type of mini-canal. The most stereotypical Dutch figure in the serial is Govert Harmsen, a walking repository of cultural practices that are traditional in the Netherlands, a caricature of certain kinds of national behaviours and attitudes. At one stage, he is seen collecting tea labels in an envelope, a thousand of which will make him eligible for a gift. Thrift is his password.

Harmsen rides a bicycle and takes no chances with the weather, wearing an overcoat and a deerstalker hat, and with an umbrella tied over his shoulder. Indoors he always stays warm wearing under his jacket either a knitted cardigan or a camel's hair waistcoat. He holds to traditional Dutch cooking, including pea soup. His kitchen contains a picture of Queen Beatrix, a painting of a windmill, a copper plate with a Dutch scene and a woven cloth hanging. However, if Harmsen represents a particular Dutch cultural identity which the young recognized but did not subscribe to, we must look elsewhere to understand the kind of Dutch identity that *Goede Tijden, Slechte Tijden* offered them.

Marketing and promotion play their part in helping to construct the serial as an ongoing part of Dutch culture, especially but not exclusively youth culture. The Dutch telecommunications provider has a telephone hot line devoted to the programme, which updates stories for callers. The programme features heavily in teen magazines and television magazines. Stickers and wall posters can be had from these and other sources. In addition *Goede Tijden, Slechte Tijden* marshals generic and intertextual knowledges of other soaps and other programmes on Dutch television, as well as other kinds of cultural consumption available as part of Dutch youth culture. The programme, referred to in the Netherlands either as *Goede Tijden* or *GTST*, but never by its full title, forms part of a larger soap opera culture that includes the subtitled US import *The Bold and the Beautiful*, which plays earlier each evening on the same network. More importantly, this soap culture also includes several domestically produced serials such as *Onderweg Naar Morgen* and two recently defunct weekly serials *Spijkerhoek* and *Vrouwenvleugel*. In 1997, this body was swollen by the advent of yet another daily soap, *Gold Coast*. Seen in the context of this larger Dutch soap culture *Goede Tijden, Slechte Tijden* becomes a temporary stage for various Dutch actors and performers who have appeared and will appear in some of these other soaps.

Nor are the Dutch intertextual references limited to this genre of television. *GTST* is part of a Dutch youth culture that also includes pop music, film, theatre, clothing and fashion. Reinout Oerlemans, who played Arnie in the serial for over six years, has his own show, *Postcard Lottery*, while Tim Immers who plays Mark has a television music show, *Rabo Top40*. These Dutch stars turn up on panels in game shows on Dutch television. Babette van Veen and Guusje Nederhorst (Linda and Roos in the show) had their own show, *CallTv*, which included segments where viewers could ring them live on camera and talk to them. In addition, Linda/Babette is known to many in the Dutch audience as the real-life daughter of a famous father, the Dutch singer Herman van Veen. Linda/

Babette and Roos/Guusje together with Katja Schuurman (who plays Jessica Harmsen), have had a big hit song. Indeed, Katja Schuurman is currently the most popular star in the Netherlands and is much sought after for TV commercials. One of the original cast, Anthonie Kamerling, who played Peter Kelder, left the serial several years ago and now works in films and theatre. The styles and fashions of clothing worn by characters in the programme are those accessible to the youth audience watching the serial. Among the brands of clothes worn are Naf Naf, Esprit and Benetton, international brands and styles that help to confirm the characters as Dutch members of a cosmopolitan consumer culture.

In addition to this dense network of Dutch references, *Goede Tijden, Slechte Tijden* frequently develops story-lines that construct the Netherlands and the Dutch in relation to exotic or threatening 'others'. For example, Annette van Thijn was killed by terrorists in the Middle East, while in late 1996 Arnie disappeared while on a plane trip over Venezuela. His parents, Laura and Robert, made a trip to Venezuela to search tropical beaches for some sign, but in vain. However, Laura came to believe that he was still alive and consulted John Serrei. The latter is an exotic-looking, apparent expert on the jungles and indigenous peoples of the region where Arnie disappeared. The study where Laura visits him is bathed in shadows and adorned with native masks, strange wall hangings and exotic palms and other tropical plants. A drum throbs away on the soundtrack during their conversations.

The Netherlands presented in the serial is by no means impervious to migrants and visitors, however. Their presence helps make the point that the society of *Goede Tijden, Slechte Tijden* is an increasingly multicultural one. One set of story-lines involved complex ideological issues concerning an outsider's decision to remain settled in the Netherlands. Fatima is from Turkey and, at one stage, was under pressure from her brother not to have a Dutch boyfriend and to return to her homeland. However, the seriality of *Goede Tijden, Slechte Tijden* also allowed other ideological issues and ideas to be explored and yet remain narratively unresolved. Fatima is a dress designer, although she finds that because of a contract she signed with Frits van Houten, she is not allowed to put her name on the label of her designs. Instead, Frits passes these off as those of Linda Dekker. Fatima is physically intimidated by Frits and forced to hand over her designs. The matter is concluded when Linda learns of the situation but this does not resolve the more general issues of economic and often physical exploitation that face the new settler.

GERMAN IDENTITY AND *GUTE ZEITEN, SCHLECHTE ZEITEN*

Like its counterpart in the Netherlands, *Gute Zeiten, Schlechte Zeiten* was the first domestically produced daily soap on German television. The serial was slow to build an audience but, by 1994, had become the second most popular soap opera on German television, outstripped only by the public broadcaster ARD's *Lindenstrasse*. However given that the latter is broadcast only once a week, *Gute Zeiten, Schlechte Zeiten* has a much higher cumulative audience. Influenced by its enormous success, Grundy/UFA received commissions for three further daily soaps.

Except for occasional moments in *Gute Zeiten* when the characters use a word or phrase from another language, usually English, or a background song is in English, all dialogue in the serial is in German. In noting this, one is noticing the capacity of the programme to speak in a familiar way to audiences not only in Germany, but also in Austria, parts of Switzerland and France, and Liechtenstein. But, given the very different religious, historical, political and geographic backgrounds of these regions, as well as the intranational differences between states and regions within the German federation, there is inevitably a politics of dialect and accent at work in the programme's Germanness.

Unlike the public broadcaster ARD, which is committed to a regionalist view of the German nation state, RTL – the commercial broadcaster which commissions *Gute Zeiten, Schlechte Zeiten* – is oriented towards a national market for its advertising (Hofmann 1992). In addition, given the integration of East and West Germany that began in 1989, a multicultural approach could have the potential to draw politics into the fictional world of the serial. And finally, there was the example of the programme's two predecessors, *The Restless Years* and, especially, *Goede Tijden, Slechte Tijden*, neither of which had foregrounded regional accents within their fictional national setting. In the German version of the format then, the continuing characters mostly speak Hochdeutsch, a German dialect which initially emerged from Hanover but which is now an (accentless) state-German.

The extensive use of Hochdeutsch offers a further clue to the geographical location of the serial. Although produced in Berlin, there is in the programme a deliberate de-Berlinization of the text. The initials on car number plates in the serial are ET, designating a fictional region that could be anywhere in the country (although the programme's producers and writers jokingly see these initials as standing for Entenhausen, the German name for Duck Town in Walt Disney's comics).

If place is anonymous, accent suggests that the soap is set in a large urban centre or city where regional accents are mostly absent. The *mise-en-scène* of apartment blocks, the outside of restaurants and bars, mansions and office buildings as well as residential streets, gardens and parks confirms this metropolitan impression. Thus the permanent characters constitute a small segment of contemporary, cosmopolitan Germany. This is further solidified in *Gute Zeiten, Schlechte Zeiten* by the frequent invocation of a Germany set within an imaginary international geographic order.

Manjou Gunakar Neria, for example, is an Indian girl, who, at one stage, seemed set to have to return to India with her businessman father. Her Indianness (evident in her skin and hair colour, hair style and clothes and exotic looks) as opposed to the Germanness of the other characters (white skin, often blond hair, familiar hair styles and woollen and linen clothes) is sometimes used as a means of subtly exploring the complex issue of what it is to be a social outsider. Take, for example, the story of the young schoolteacher Mr Killian. Manjou's class, especially her three blonde girlfriends, came to suspect that he was homosexual and infected with AIDS. Manjou, however, was, initially, less condemnatory, both because of Killian's personal kindness to her and also because she was aware of the prejudice of her companions. In the event, however, she joins them in their discriminatory behaviour. When she and they drive the innocent schoolteacher from the school, the programme is able to examine some of the costs that outsiders pay for social belonging.

Time also plays its part in the depiction of this contemporary, cosmopolitan and anonymous Germany. The serial is set in the present and its scheduled broadcast has been arranged so that the calendrical time of national anniversaries, holidays and celebration is generally observed. There is therefore a broader congruence between the fictional time inhabited by the characters and the seasonal time inhabited by the programme's audience. Thus when it is winter in Germany, the characters are wearing warm coats in outside scenes while in late summer and early autumn, shorts, T-shirts, short skirts and ice-cold drinks are the order of the day. Beyond the crucial detail of language and the more incidental detail of place and time, *Gute Zeiten, Schlechte Zeiten* develops its Germanness through the social and generic knowledges that it mobilizes in its viewers.

Take, for example, the criss-crossing narratives to do with both the opulent Zimmerman family – Beatrice, Mattias and Tina – and also with the two half-brothers – wealthy Joe Gerner and aspirant Patrick Graff. Most of these plots centred on bitter, inter-family rivalry, on power politics and sexual intrigue, thereby conjuring up an image of a group that is intensely materialistic, competitive and rapacious.

Since the unification of the two states of East and West Germany (or colonization of the German Democratic Republic by the FRG), this domestic image of (west) Germany as rapacious, wolfish, free market capitalism has been intensely revalorized. While the programme does not contain contrasted images of east and west Germans, as in other recent domestic productions, this embodiment of the intensely competitive and uncaring forces of the free market does have a particular resonance in the light of recent German political and social history. In other words, even if *Gute Zeiten, Schlechte Zeiten* makes no overt reference to recent events in Germany, the imagery of free market capitalism contained in the programme links with this larger network of media representations and a tangled matrix of social, political and economic issues.

The narratives of domestic, sexual and business intrigues among members of rich and powerful families have another, equally strong, background in two highly successful American soaps: *Dallas* and *Dynasty* (Hofman, 1988). *Dallas* began on ARD in June 1980, 'domesticated' by being shown without commercials. Dubbed into German, it proved to be immensely popular. This revalorization of melodrama in a popular television genre was taken up in home-grown series such as *Die Schwarzwaldklinik* (the Black Forest Clinic) and *Lindenstrasse* (Linden Street), both of which – especially the former – owed a direct debt to the American prime time soap operas (Hofmann, 1988; Kreutzner and Seiter, 1995). Equally though, there are other generic references at work in *Gute Zeiten, Schlechte Zeiten* that mobilize the cultural capital that some segments of the German audiences will bring to its viewing. Take, for example, the character of the medical practitioner Dr Michael Gundlach. Although the figure of the doctor in this serial has its counterpart in Dr Bruce Russell in *The Restless Years*, Gundlach must also be contextualized within a tradition of German representations of the medical doctor. In *Die Schwarzwaldklinik*, the most immediate predecessor, Professor Brinkmann runs the clinic of the title, whose staff comprises himself, his son and a nurse who becomes his wife as the series unfolds.

Michael Gundlach, by contrast with Brinkmann, lives his life in a certain amount of domestic and professional chaos. Although he aspires to an authority commensurate with his social position as a healer of society's illnesses (frequently, for example, being brusque and rude to his assistant Elke Opitz) he is far from being able to control the direction and circumstances of his life. His wife Iris has died and he is caring for their adopted son Dominic. In 1994, there were at least two story-lines that saw his character foundering in various difficulties, unable to fully control his personal affairs. In the first, Gundlach as a single father was at the mercy of the child welfare agency and repeatedly close to losing his child to a state home for children without two parents. Later this was further complicated by Gundlach's abortive affair with a call girl, Ursula Berger. At first attracted emotionally to Ursula, only to be rebuffed, he is then insensitive to the real affection that she develops. The relationship fails because he insists that it is a business transaction between client and call girl. This not only destroys his chance of personal happiness but also reopens his difficulties with the child welfare authorities. Altogether then, Gundlach is a much more interesting and ordinary, everyday figure and can be read as a critique of the godlike Brinkmann in *Die Schwarzwaldklinik*.

To summarize the argument, one might say that *The Restless Years*, *Goede Tijden, Slechte Tijden* and *Gute Zeiten, Schlechte Zeiten* are national not because they mirror their respective societies as though the latter were single, homogeneous wholes. Rather, they stand in a complex relationship to the social order, both receiving but also constructing the representations through which citizens might articulate themselves. The Australianness, Dutchness and Germanness of these artifacts are always both obvious and banal, yet subtle and elusive, conservative and petrified yet progressive and challenging. Although seemingly trivial and everyday, they form or can form part of a much larger repertoire of images and practices generated in the media, popular culture, education, religion and elsewhere, out of which social groups can fashion various identities, including national identities.

ACTIVITIES

1 Which drama serials are shown on TV in your country? Which are imported and which are domestically produced? Where do the imported soaps come from? Which are the three most popular ones?
2 How frequently are drama serials broadcast? On which channels?
3 Compare an imported soap with a domestically produced one.

- What is the setting? A particular region, city, village, not defined?
- What kind of language is spoken (no particular accent, dialects)?
- What kinds of characters appear? Which world is represented (business, leisure, labour, school/college, media)? Do the characters belong to a particular social class?
- What kinds of topics are discussed?

Discuss what you have found out about domestically produced soaps in your country in relation to the last paragraph of this chapter.

SUGGESTIONS FOR FURTHER READING

Moran, A. (1998) *Copycat TV: Globalisation Program Formats and Cultural Identity*. Luton: University of Luton Press.

A well researched introduction to the growing trade in programme formats, concentrating particularly on the adaptation of American and Australian popular drama formats in European markets.

Skovmand, M. (1992) 'Barbarous TV international: syndicated *Wheels of Fortune*', in M. Skovmand and K.C. Schroder (eds), *Media Cultures: Reappraising Transnational Media*. London: Routledge, pp. 84–103.

An analysis of the European 'career' of one of the most successful American game show formats.

CHAPTER 6

PROGRAMME MAKING ACROSS BORDERS: THE *EUROSUD* NEWS MAGAZINE

Aurélie Laborde and Michel Perrot

Television in today's Europe is still mainly a national entity. Whatever it borrows from other countries, in Europe or further afield, each country has its own distinctive televisual identity embedded in its organization, its functioning and its programmes. Consequently, most of the attempts to describe television in Europe are condemned to being a juxtaposition of monographs.

As Philippe Viallon has shown in his study of French and German news magazines, the differences concern not only the language and the duration of the programme, but also the way the same technology and sometimes the same images are used. German TV news programmes are mainly referential whereas French TV news programmes are mainly phatic. These differences suit the mentalities of each country and are part of the confirmation of its cultural identity. They are further illustrated by Sari Näsi's chapter on the news coverage of the French road blocks in the final section of this book.

When there are European co-productions aimed at several national markets, analysts often reproach them for their patchwork character, and their desire to be an average product designed to please everybody, an outcome which has led to many of them being dismissed as 'Euro-puddings' – soggy, bland and with no particular taste. The compromises are sometimes so extensive that nobody likes the finished programme and it cannot even be broadcast, a highly paradoxical outcome given that the major aim behind collaborations is often to make savings in production costs.

Most European audiovisual collaborations deal with drama. This is not surprising. Fiction is the most exportable production and the most suitable for repeats, and therefore the most profitable for co-producers. News is very much the poor relation in the televisual politics of collaboration. News programmes do not get much financial support, firstly because national habits are a strong determinant of viewing in this field, and secondly because news touches political and social sensitivities and identities.

It is therefore particularly interesting to study one of the rare collaborations in the field of actuality programming, a news magazine, called *Eurosud* (*Eurosouth*) which was set in a range of locations and made by the TV stations of several European countries. In many ways this case provides an 'ideal' cultural laboratory in which to examine the concrete difficulties and achievements of cross-border collaboration.

In 1986 after two years of preliminary contact, the management of France 3 in Aquitaine (in south-west France) appealed to their European neighbours to collaborate in the creation of a joint news programme. It gathered together in a joint project the editorial departments of France 3 in Bordeaux, TVE Bilbao (from the Spanish Basque country), and RTP Porto (from Portugal). On 15 March 1988 the first edition of *Eurosud* magazine appeared. Its theme was 'communication'. From 1988 to 1990, it was broadcast four times a year and lasted just under an hour. In 1990 France 3, based in Poitou Charentes, joined the three editorial departments already associated. That same year a new strategy was suggested: a monthly programme lasting 30 minutes. In France, *Eurosud* was broadcast nationally. Altogether, the production of *Eurosud* lasted six years and ended on 18 June 1994 after 42 episodes.

Eurosud was a collaborative effort. A co-production proper requires the parties to put together a common pool of money, with a view to making a unique product. It is based on financial agreements and a contractual relationship between the partners. In contrast, collaboration does not necessitate either the signing of a convention or the amalgamation of finances, nor does it have the legal status of a co-production. In the case of collaboration, we speak of a partnership convention, and not of a co-production contract. Collaborations are essentially made by sharing the products and know-how of public channels, and thus form a moral contract. Several news programmes have been made through collaboration but very few by co-production. European co-productions are mostly made by independent European producers though they can also be made by national television channels.

In 1988 for example, the DAVID group (who were developing an audiovisual identity in Europe) gathered together a dozen European public TV stations. Most of the time, however, cooperation between channels happens in the 'sub-regions' of Europe. These initiatives tend to be based on the 'natural' links and solidarities generated by geographical, cultural or linguistic proximity. Dutch and Flemish television stations regularly work together, for instance.

In the domain of actuality broadcasting these collaborations are less common. News is a very strongly marked audiovisual form both culturally and nationally. Because it cannot logically be broadcast several times, it is more difficult to recoup the money spent on it. In contrast a magazine programme is made up of individual reports. This sets it apart from the usual time scale of 'news' and allows for multibroadcasting. To aid mobility these programmes generally have a cultural theme. Nevertheless, problems arise because they are produced by channels which operate within

Box 6.1

Examples of transnational news magazines co-produced by regional stations of France 3

EURO 3: a monthly magazine of 26 minutes
France 3 Nord Pas de Calais
RTBF of Charleroi
German WDR
ITV British network

DIAGONAL (1997): a monthly magazine of 26 minutes
France 3 Lorraine Champagne Ardenne
RTBF (Namur)
Television from Sarre

TRIANGLE (1994): 6 minutes twice a week
France 3 Alsace
SWF (Baden Baden)
Swiss television
ADRS

ALICE (1986): a monthly magazine of 26 minutes
France 3 Midi Pyrenees
RTBF
WDR
TSI
RAI
TV5 on ASTRA

different national audiovisual cultures and under different laws which go to the very heart of each country.

Eurosud was not an isolated case. Between 1988 and 1991 five transnational programmes made through collaboration appeared in France. At the beginning of 1991, 13 programmes of this kind were being transmitted in Europe uniting around 60 regional TV stations in 22 states. Today (as Box 6.1 shows) France, due to its geographical position and the willingness of the regional stations within the France 3 network, takes part in numerous co-productions.

The EC has no specific policy with regard to transnational news magazine programmes. They are produced without any link to its institutional planning and rely heavily on the enthusiasm of individuals. Some do obtain European financial backing but they are few and far between. The means of production remain modest and the audience figures achieved are almost always kept confidential.

Transnational magazine programmes adopt different formulas. One particularly interesting device is the principle of 'crossed looks' whereby the journalists of one country deal with a subject relating to a different country. Most of the time though the programmes juxtapose various nationally produced segments. This formula is often regarded as being less ambitious because allowing each country to use its own footage does not really require the making of a common but unique programme. At the same time it respects cultural identities, and avoids the paradox of having 'patchwork' programmes which in the hope of pleasing everyone, please no one.

It was in the context of the CIRCOM that the *Eurosud* partners and the representatives of other transnational programmes first met. CIRCOM (the International Research Cooperative in Communication) is a forum for meetings, ideas and brain-storming aimed at establishing joint projects between European regional television stations. CIRCOM, founded in 1983 in Lille, gathers together 38 countries and 376 TV stations. It goes far beyond the EC borders and has recently been turning its attention towards Eastern European countries. Without always being in at the origin of a project, CIRCOM often enables an initial meeting and a first exchange between regional TV channels.

THEORY, METHODOLOGY AND TECHNIQUES OF RESEARCH

In this chapter we wish to explore the concrete reality of European television, to show how it functions on the ground, in everyday practice. Many studies have been conducted on its institutional, juridical and economical dimensions, but works that deal with the reality of joint work are rare. We want to study television at a microsociological or anthropological level (Winkin, 1996), within a perspective of intercultural communication. What kind of television programmes do we create when we work together? How does the group of producers work? What image do they have of their partners? What images do the producers have of their audiences? But we should not forget that the idea of intercultural communication is far from neutral. It willingly incites ideological debate, inspired most of the time by humanistic ethics which urge an ideal of dialogue, a respect for all things different, a mutual understanding. This ideal commands wide support but does it really help us to understand problems which intercultural communication poses? (Ladmiral and Lipiansky, 1989: 13).

One way of getting away from this a priori ideology is to study a programme that has already been discontinued. This allowed us to trace *Eurosud*'s whole development and to put it in its proper context. On the other hand this choice obviously deprived us of direct observation and limited us to documents and testimonies. We quickly discovered that the memories of such a programme are extremely short-lived and the available documentation relatively thin. There were very few memos on its working procedures produced by those involved in its creation and broadcast.

Contact was essentially made through oral means, by phone and at meetings. Even the recordings of the programmes themselves were only partly accessible and in order to assemble just a simple list of the subjects dealt with, we had to search through a range of promotional leaflets, newspaper cuttings and television magazines.

This is quite paradoxical when you think that one of the operation's objectives when it started out was to show images and testimonies of 'Europe' at work in the regions. Even when the journalists we approached willingly agreed to answer our questions they emphasized the difficulty they had in remembering what they considered as ancient history.[1]

We will see later that the people who took part in this programme often changed greatly over the six years. In France, it was not even possible to compile a comprehensive list of those who had worked on it and therefore impossible to conduct interviews. Despite great efforts, it was also impossible to find the Portuguese personnel who had been involved, which limited the range of our conclusions. It would seem appropriate to draw another lesson from this experience as regards intercultural work: we could not expect all cultures to react in the same way. Although we knew this, we forgot it during our research. Taking into account others' attitudes, even when we know them, needs to be done each time. This research brought us another surprise: the total lack of any attempt to assess the programme's impact on audiences, a subject we will come back to when we describe the intuitive work of journalists.

Even if this omission can be explained by economic factors, that is to say the lack of financial resources in the regional stations and the voluntary nature of the experience, we should nevertheless emphasize the general characteristic of this phenomenon. The quantitative dimensions of audience reactions are sometimes measured but the qualitative aspect is hardly ever taken into account. From our viewpoint it is also important to note that the interviews were conducted by a French woman. This may have influenced the answers: if not the content, then at least the form or the insistence on certain points.

THE CONTEXT OF THE PROGRAMME

In 1986, at the time of the first contacts between the three partners, the ideas of Europe and of European collaboration were emerging as major themes in political debate. The notion that Europe would be able to build from the regions upwards, especially when they bordered each other, was also starting to gain currency. That same year, Portugal and Spain joined the EC and it became clear that the geographical proximity of the Basque country, Aquitaine and northern Portugal meant that these spaces could be used as areas of transit between the three countries, enabling economic, cultural and human exchanges. The natural conditions shared by the three regions (the vineyards, the sea and the forests) enabled them to create a synergy of agricultural and industrial sector activities. Finally, many people from these countries moved to live in neighbouring countries. Observers therefore started to think about the possible audience for cross-cultural news among the publics of these bordering regions. In 1986 the Council of Europe spoke of 'interregional and transnational cooperation'. *Eurosud* made this idea a reality.

According to the initial presentational brochure of the programme: '*Eurosud* will be a body enabling an exchange of ideas, a forum able to create industrial and cultural initiatives, and begin global reflection about this changing market.' These three regions already took part in common programmes, notably in the fields of transport by road and train, and in higher education and research. But there were other, more particular, factors that helped to explain the commitment of France 3 Aquitaine, TVE Bilbao, and RTP Porto to joint projects. In 1986 the regional stations of France 3 had already collaborated on programmes, essentially in France. In France at that time, the willingness to work on a South Atlantic axis was very marked. In the Spanish Basque country, terrorist attacks carried out by the ETA had created conflictual relations with France. To resume links between the two countries was a major challenge. However, TVE of Bilbao was in direct competition with Madrid television, and this new alliance could be an interesting asset. During the first discussions concerning *Eurosud*, Portugal was preparing for its entry into the EC. European projects and collaborations were therefore given precedence.

THE TURNING POINT FOR THE BROADCASTING SCENE

As Box 6.2 shows when the *Eurosud* magazine was created, competition in the television markets of the three countries was weak. By 1994, when the programme stopped being produced, the situation had changed greatly. The overall number of programmes available to the Spanish, the French and the Portuguese had increased considerably due to the growth of broadcasting by cable and satellite (companies). In France, commercial channels appeared in 1985, ending the monopoly previously exercised by the public service system. In 1986, the French people could watch six channels. In contrast, in Portugal in 1988, at the time of *Eurosud*'s first broadcast, RTP's monopoly had not yet ended and its two channels (RTP1 and RTP2) remained the only ones broadcast until 1990. At that time, a great part of the programming schedule was still made up of Brazilian television films of poor quality. The evolution of Portuguese TV broadcasting happened quickly after the country joined the EC. In Spain, private

Box 6.2

National and regional television

Spain

Apart from the two public national channels (TV1 and TV2) which produce regional programmes, the autonomous regions most marked by the nationalistic movement had their own television stations, before national legislation formerly allowed them: ETB was created in 1983, TV3 for Catalonia in 1984, TVG for Galicia in 1985, ETB2 in 1986, Channel 33, and Catalonia's second channel in 1989. Basque television stations ETB1 and ETB2 were created in 1983 and 1986 respectively.

Portugal

The Portuguese public channels RTP1 and RTP2 were created in 1958 and 1959. The country does not have regional television stations except RTP Madeira and RTP Azores. This lack of regional television seems to go with the delay in the political regionalization of the country.

France

France 3, the French regional channel, makes some regional broadcasting 'windows' available in its national programming schedule. Twelve regional centres of France 3 possess means of production and important infrastructures.

There are also some national programme production teams which were decentralized into regional stations, such as the editorial departments of France 3, in Nancy and Toulouse.

TV stations were not authorized until 1988. So, in 1988, Portuguese and Spanish TV stations were still largely dependent on the governments of these countries. Even today, in Spain, there is no authority in charge of the audiovisual sector's regulation. The Prime Minister's departments assume responsibility over the public service. Different managements are thus short-lived.

We should also repeat that the status of these departments in their respective countries was and still is different. France 3 Aquitaine produces regional programmes, so the *Eurosud* programme was made to be broadcast regionally. In contrast, RTP Porto in Portugal is not a regional TV station. Rather, it is a decentralized unit producing for Portuguese national television. In Spain, TVE Bilbao is a regional office of the national public station, RTVE. It produces regional programmes but also national and international ones. The Spanish RTVE station has faced serious financial problems since the beginning of the 1990s because of tough competition. Its finances come only from advertising.

We should also emphasize the initial differences between the three countries as regards technical equipment. At the beginning of the programme's life, the French already worked using Betacom whereas the Spanish and especially the Portuguese only got access to this system as the joint project went on.

CHARACTERISTICS OF THE PROGRAMME

There was no explicit contract between the original three partners. It was a collaborative commitment between public channels. The only firm organizational constraints were a monthly meeting of editorial staff as well as the obligation not to change the images provided by other countries. The monthly meetings took place alternately in each country and were generally held in French, which was the shared language spoken by the majority of those involved.

Each of the partner countries, in taking part in this collaboration, became a member of a 'club' which allowed them to use the others' products as they wished. The name of the magazine was *Eurosud* or *Eurosul* or *Eurosur*, according to the country where it was broadcast. The editorial staffs used different programming techniques and set the programmes out differently in every country. The programme functioned using the principle of a common set of images, supplied by those involved. After the editorial staffs had met, each country produced a segment on the theme chosen jointly. These were then taken on and adapted to the different televisual habits and cultures of each country. Between 1988 and 1990, *Eurosud* operated as a quarterly programme of about 50 minutes. After 1990, the formula changed and the programme became a monthly magazine of 30 minutes. This shift enabled the rhythm to become more lively and allowed greater viewer participation. The editors had initially chosen the principle of having 'crossed looks' in the reports, for example the Spanish filmed in France, and vice versa. However, this technique, with its high travelling expenses, was soon discontinued and the editors confined themselves to making material in their own regions. France 3 Aquitaine broadcast to five regions within France: Dordogne, Gironde, Landes, Lot and Garonne and Atlantic Pyrenees, to a total of 2.7 million inhabitants at that time. From 1990 onwards, some *Eurosud* editions were broadcast to the whole of France. TVE Bilbao broadcast in the three provinces of the Basque country: Viscaya, Guipuzcoa and Alava, to nearly 2.1 million inhabitants. RTP Porto covered the whole of Portugal, that is to say an audience of 10.3 million in 1988. Once the Spanish and the Portuguese were able to use satellites, they broadcast these programmes to all their linguistic communities, which was potentially a considerable audience.

Under this collaboration, the partners' undertook to take charge of producing one of the reports and to receive the others' reports in exchange, for free. However, for each edition along with the reports' production costs there were also translation and titling costs. Most of the people who took part in the projects also stressed the cost of the monthly meetings, which was considerable as the partners were geographically dispersed. Today telephone conferencing has reduced this expense. Despite the strong European ambitions of the three countries, the *Eurosud* programme was only modestly backed by the managements of the different channels. Nor was it subsidized, either by government organizations or European authorities. In 1989 a French edition of *Eurosud* cost 220,000 francs. It was hard for the regional station of France 3 to finance this. Indeed, France 3 Aquitaine had to take money away from other budgets and it was mainly its partnership with Caisse d'Epargne Aquitaine Nord which enabled the first editions to be broadcast. In the other countries, budgeting problems were also omnipresent. Despite its own difficulties, France 3 Aquitaine also financed half of the Spanish production expenses for the programme during its last year of broadcasting, since TVE Bilbao could not meet the costs.

THEMES REACHED BY CONSENSUS

The chosen themes were reached by consensus and avoided subjects that might disturb one of the countries. Effectively, no topic which could provoke memories of a possible conflict between the three countries could be used. For example no ETA attacks were mentioned. Except for the programme concerning the controversy over fishing, in which an editor from Bilbao and one from Poitou Charentes talk about problems between the French Navy and Spanish fishermen, the programme's subjects were always chosen to avoid a comparison or a clash between the countries. Every country dealt with its own problems and the viewer had to make comparisons.

As Box 6.3 shows the themes were extremely general. The desire to satisfy all parties could be the reason why the problem subjects selected were so vague. Also because the countries involved, whilst being close, remained stubbornly different, especially at the time when *Eurosud* was broadcast, very specialized sets of problems may not have found a place in each region's broadcast.

The themes were chosen from among the common points of interest in the regions involved. A certain number of problems were common to the four regions: their Atlantic frontiers, their forests and vineyards, their Southern culture and an economy largely based on tourism and agriculture. These aspects were all treated by *Eurosud* programmes with editions on viticulture, tourism, fishing and changes in the rural landscape. However, of the 42 themes discussed, only a dozen concerned specific problems directly. The other subjects were national themes, which were considered on a regional level.

Box 6.3

42 magazines

1. 'La communication' (Communication)
2. 'La viticulture' (Viticulture)
3. 'Vie économique et vie des régions' (Economic and regional life)
4. 'Les collectivités locales' (Public organizations)
5. 'Le tourisme' (Tourism)
6. 'Les migrants ou la vie des autres' (Expatriation, integration)
7. 'Douaniers sans frontière' (Custom officers without frontier)
8. 'Fous de foot' (Mad about football)
9. 'Diplôme cherche emploi' (Graduate looking for a job)
10. 'Mourir sur l'asphalte' (Death on the road)
11. '*Eurosud* special grands voiliers' (yachts)
12. 'L'été de mes 16 ans' (The summer when I was 16)
13. 'L'Europe bleue agitée' (Fishermen)
14. 'L'Europe des cols blancs' (White-collar Europe)
15. «L'Université partenaire» (University–firm partnership)
16. «Les hommes de l'ordre» (Crime)
17. «Les tickets de l'espoir» (Game)
18. «Le premier acte» (Young creators)
19. «Il était . . . la foi» (Religions)
20. «Le Papy boom» (The grandpa boom)
21. «Les nuits blanches» (The night owls)
22. «Les maîtres d'école» (Education and reform of the headmasters)
23. «Succès de femmes» (Women's success)
24. «Les ports de l'Atlantique» (Atlantic harbours)
25. «Misère, mode de vie» (Misery: a way of life)
26. «La couette en solo» (Bachelors)
27. «Les intermittents de l'émotion» (Artists)
28. «Handicap: la vie à côté» (Disabled people: life at the edge)
29. «L'espoir en jachère» (Fallow hope)
30. «Adieu les mains sales» (Farewell, blue collars)
31. «Profession: élu politique» (Political representatives)
32. «Les néo-couples» (The new couples)
33. «Les femmes de muscle» (Women with muscles)
34. «Menace sur la sécu» (Social insurance)
35. «Edition spéciale à Porto « le grand marché européen» (The great European market)
36. «Le surendettement des ménages» (Excessive debt of households)
37. «L'opéra bouffe» (Cuisine)
38. «Médecins sans diplôme» (Doctors without a diploma)
39. «Les vacances autrement» (Holidays otherwise)
40. «Service militaire» (Military service)
41. «Breuvages sacrés» (Sacred beverages)
42. «Lieu d'isolement» (Life on an island)

THEMES CONCERNING THE EC'S CONSTRUCTION AND ITS RESULTS

Contrary to what we might have thought, in the 42 themes tackled by the programme the word 'Europe' appeared only three times. Only one theme directly concerned this subject: 'the great European market'. Two other subjects directly dealt with European laws concerning commercial fishing. As for 'European white-collar workers', the theme was European in name only and was handled in a regional manner.

We can, however, find recurrent themes in the programmes. The tourism angle was dealt with in several different ways: the economy, daily life. Many programmes also considered the financial problems of people in the regions. Two programmes dealt with women. One was called 'Women's success' and the other 'Women with muscles'. When reading the programmes' themes one gets the impression that everyone made an effort to consider subjects likely to interest each of the three countries and that the economic point of view was the most common.

The chosen themes quickly took on the usual aspects of regional television. During the first two years under the 'old formula' (of the 50-minute slot) the themes were more general, and technical. The programmes gave an overall view of the subjects. From 1990 (when the format was changed to a 30-minute slot) the themes started to be illustrated by interviews and reports about life in the regions. The programme took on the same method of processing news as regional television. *Eurosud* established a dominant frame, set the tone from the beginning and kept it on till the end.

The problematics of the programmes laid particular stress on the phenomena of change and evolution. Consequently most issues were handled in a 'what is going to happen' way and analysed emerging customs and trends as if the arrival of Europe prefigured the beginning of a new world: *Fallow hope* (*L'espoir en jachère*), *Farewell, blue collars* (*Adieu les mains sales*), *The new couples* (*Les néo-couples*), *The grandpa boom* (*Le Papy boom*), *Customs officers without frontier* (*Douaniers sans frontière*).

On the other hand these reports did not lack a nostalgic dimension. The programme's focuses were generally traditionalist and popular; with such strong themes as youth, religion, the army, the earth and popular sport. This orientation reflected the nature of regional television as being generally close to traditional values. Each of the editors dealt with the subject from a different point of view. The agreed formula remained purely advisory and did not insist on a comparison or a parallel between the reports. This sometimes led the reports to get lost in trivial detail. There was apparently no discussion concerning specific ways of tackling the subjects, as if this was too complex. Analysis of choices made by different editorial staff concerned with the same theme does not give the impression that they had culturally different outlooks, but rather that their choices were the product of circumstances. We were not able to identify processing methods typical of one particular country or another.

Two types of programme followed each other in *Eurosud*'s history, with the journalists not seeming to master this change. The first type wanted to be explanatory and used voice-overs, whereas the second type wanted to show what was going on behind the scenes but in a limited way, and through one or two characters. This second method, more common from 1990 onward, corresponded to the fact that the partners initially wished to differentiate themselves from TV news or national news programmes which largely dealt with problems in a general way, and rarely showed men and women as individuals. In contrast the other transnational programme involving France and Spain, *Pyrénées-Pirineos*, did not have a chosen theme for its broadcasts. Each of them dealt with whatever subject they wished without any concern for overall coherence. Since 1990 audio-visual production rules have changed. This way of making programmes was acceptable at that time, however.

The presentation of the programme was specific to each region. The French version of *Eurosud* generally had very diverse modes of presentation: in the open air or in a studio, with or without guests, the presentation of all the reports at the same time or at the beginning of each programme, debates at the end of the programme or after each report, or with one or two presenters. In Spain the programme was generally presented by a female announcer, not necessarily by the journalist. As for translation, the four editing staffs adopted the same principles: subtitled interviews, and translated voice-over comments. All those involved remarked on the fact that the tasks, financial as well as organizational, were heavy. The most important problem concerned the simultaneous translation of the voice-over, which had to be carried out, in France's case in a studio in Paris.

JOURNALISTS: AN AVOIDING STRATEGY

Journalists of the three, then four regions, did not work together on the reports, but they gathered once a month for an editing conference in one of the regions. The reports integrated a block of common video footage and the journalists were free to do what they wanted in their programme according to the presentation they chose. The people we interviewed generally tended to 'overpersonalize' the creation and development of the programme and avoid a more sociological analysis. For the same reasons, we can see an overvaluation of techniques, used by the programme's representatives as an explanation for most of the troubles or complications they encountered. The people we spoke to saw the others involved as friends, but as friends unlike themselves. These differences mostly concern the training they had had and therefore their way of working. There is naturally an imbalance in favour of those who express themselves fluently. On another level this confirms the uneven technical abilities of the different

Box 6.4

The Euro-pudding

Everywhere in Europe, national programmes have the greatest number of viewers. Despite a tendency to standardize, the signs of identity are always present, allowing the viewer to guess at once where the programme comes from. Co-productions sometimes aim at an 'average taste' by mixing ingredients appropriate to each participating country: this is the Euro-pudding.

Is it true that communication leads to homogeneity of cultures and that homogeneity leads to death? Or on the contrary might we think that the differences between cultures that are in contact move and change but do not disappear?

countries, which may be obstacles to the communication and the construction of an homogeneous finished product. These were particularly noticeable at the onset of the programme's life. The journalists we interviewed insisted on changing the programming tools, which led to modifications in the form of the broadcast. We generally noticed a homogenization in the form and the content as the programme went along, moving it closer to the category of the 'Euro-pudding' (outlined in Box 6.4).

In 1988, when the programme started, the journalists from Aquitaine generally imagined that their Spanish and Portuguese neighbours were 'behind' in comparison with the French. One French participant said: 'The Portuguese at that time offered the equivalent of 1970s French television.' People also spoke of 'folklore' or 'exoticism' when they wanted to describe the nature of Portuguese reports at that time. French paternalism towards its European neighbours appeared very clearly. The French, whilst recognizing the merits of their associates, established themselves as the driving and the formative force behind the project. We should, however, recall that the interviews were conducted by a French woman and not a Spanish or a Portuguese woman, which could equally lead to this type of conclusion.

As for human relations at work, the journalists frequently refer to problems of misunderstanding between the countries. They take the discord between the countries and the excessive sensitivity of others for granted, without ever questioning it. This attitude seemed to be general since the different editing staff talked in the same terms when they spoke of other joint ventures. In discussions, two contradictory parameters in the relations between the journalists involved in *Eurosud* were evident. All the people interviewed spoke of feelings both of complicity and of lack of understanding. The strategy, whether it was a conscious one or not, which allowed these two states to co-exist, could be called, an 'avoiding strategy': they prioritized friendly contacts without reporting on a number of elements which could have turned out to be conflictual. We can speak of the strategy of those involved insofar as most declared that they had learnt to work together. The journalists talked easily about good relations with their foreign colleagues. They all seemed to have retained pleasant memories of this experience. Maybe the bad experiences were forgotten over the years, but it is certainly more than this.

Maybe it was the feeling of being part of something important that they made their own through this joint project. We heard such words and phrases as mates, pleasant recollections, old *Eurosud* solidarity, or: 'we started as colleagues and ended up as friends'. There was a real insistence on this point. They mentioned with pleasure how friendly the editing meetings were, which took place every month. These meetings involved journeys and often celebrations (dinners, visits) and were a major part of the whole experience.

However, the *Eurosud* producers also spoke of misunderstandings. The word 'conflict' was never used and was completely rejected when we suggested it. The misunderstandings mentioned were firstly on a relationship level and were attributed to different cultures and also to the personalities involved. Thus, the calmness of some people was mentioned, which suggested that others were more excitable. However, the major misunderstanding was seen to arise from the different technical level of the participants.

In 1988, when *Eurosud* was created, the Spanish, the Portuguese and the French possessed very different audiovisual facilities. As a consequence, the differences between the finished products, in both form and content, were very marked. This variation created a strain which lasted for the duration of the joint project and it is still considered the most important cause of tension in the history of *Eurosud*. The people interviewed also recalled taboo subjects. They were generally topics which went right to the very heart of the countries and that the channels did not wish to export (child labour in Portugal, for instance).

Finally, priorities in the domain of news varied according to the cultures. At times the preference of some people for some subjects turned out to be incomprehensible to others, who could see no link with their public's expectations. A programme about pets, for instance, was proposed in an editing conference and attracted no interest from either the Spanish or the Portuguese. The Portuguese refused it, as it would have appeared totally inappropriate in their country. This need to take other people into account can be found, in a more or less direct way, in all the accounts of those interviewed. It is seen as a constraint, an indispensable effort: 'We have to deal with it.' This 'avoiding strategy', dedicated to keeping good relations within the group, could be seen as abstaining, or as the acceptance of the other parties involved and their production teams. This last point was sometimes accepted only with difficulty: 'We cannot impose our individual requirements on our co-producers who are just like us. Their suggestions and judgements are just as worthy as ours.'

This strategy was very evident in the way the group functioned. The themes were chosen together after everyone had suggested an idea and it was the group as a whole that determined the final choice. Almost all the chosen themes were kept, in either the long or short term. Everyone was free then to choose their own way of tackling the theme in their own report. The programme's organization meant that points of conflict were systematically avoided.

AN ABSENT PUBLIC

The journalists interviewed claimed not to be aware of audience size. Estimates of viewing figures were initially based on guesstimates by France 3 Aquitaine concerning the three neighbouring countries. There was no systematic audience analysis. At that time, this type of survey did not exist in Spain, and France 3 Aquitaine did not have the money to carry out such an expensive exercise. The journalists did have an intuitive idea of their audience, however. In France, they essentially took into account their usual viewing public, adding some extra elements such as expatriates and intellectuals in the different countries taking part in the joint venture. The same mental map was also used in the other regions.

The press coverage of *Eurosud* was considerable, probably due to its status as pioneer. Press articles did not indicate how large the audience was and journalists claimed not to have considered the new foreign audience that this joint venture brought them. They were certainly aware that they had a foreign public, but, insofar as the usual regional public was also targeted, they had kept the same production techniques and the same way of handling information. The only time when the diversity of the possible audience was really considered was at the time when the subjects were chosen. After that they acted as usual. It seemed too difficult to take into account the overall public as it was too diverse. No particular effort was made to assess the new audience. The instigator of the project claimed: 'We edited a product of this nature instinctively, not knowing what impact this programme could have.' The partners involved in *Eurosud* were public TV stations, and at that time especially audience size was not as important as a mark of success as it has since become. Generally, the journalists interviewed had a possessive manner when recalling the programme. They seemed to take responsibility for the project and expressed themselves most of the time using the first person. Most had good memories of the production experience, except when talking about the extra work involved.

AN INTERRUPTED IDYLL

The union of transnational regions with a view to creating a common audiovisual production, the principle of a shared editing staff along with the monthly meetings gathering all the partners – all these elements show *Eurosud* to be a programme firmly based on international cooperation. However, looking at how it actually worked in practice, we observe that this so-called equal partnership was not entirely respected. We can perceive a kind of French leadership of the project. The French were in at the origins of the programme, they remained the driving force and the group that changed things, whether through modification of the logo or of the broadcasting methods. When we talk about a leader we think particularly of Jimmy Joncquart. The journalists recognized unanimously the importance of having a leading man in order to carry out a project of this type properly. *Eurosud* was broadcast in three countries for six years, which is a long life-span for this kind of programme. When we interviewed the people concerned about why *Eurosud* ended, the first reasons mentioned were always economic. When the question was put differently, the interviewee suggested other possibilities. But no one talked about problems of understanding, or distance between partners; problems which could have led to failure. The programme did officially stop because of economic difficulties. Spain was the first to admit its inability to carry on with the production, due to the financial crisis of TVE. The Portuguese followed, stating financial problems and a reorientation of their programming teams as the main reasons. The regional station of France 3 Aquitaine also had difficulty in getting financial support for this programme. *Eurosud* did not benefit from any institutional subsidy, and was funded totally by the different editing departments involved.

Once the economic difficulties had been admitted, those interviewed also mentioned human factors, including a general tiredness on the part of the partners involved, who had already invested in the project for six years. They also talked of the problems relating to the presenters. A production in partnership works according to the principle of 'one man – one programme' but it was difficult, during the broadcasting of the programme, to have the same presenters due to frequent political crises in Spanish television. We also mentioned the principle 'one man – one project', and in this case it was Jimmy Joncquart, as father of the project, who supported the programme from the onset; his departure to another regional station could have played a part. And since the programme did not have a production manager, the journalists undertook *Eurosud* production work on top of their usual tasks. All this could have led to weariness.

Other factors were competition between different programmes and especially rivalry between the TV stations of Toulouse and Bordeaux in France. Toulouse co-produced, at the time of *Eurosud*, two other programmes called *Alice* and *Passage*, which they seemed to prefer and which they saw as more important to their own development.

Beyond these reasons, we should consider how difficult it was for geographically and culturally separated people to work together. We might also wonder if the potential impact of such a multi-cultural news programme on the management of TV channels, and on the public, had not changed due to the evolution of the international audiovisual scene. Finally it is possible to speculate about the importance of a contemporary foreign news programme broadcast in France on a regional channel.

Even so, the journalists interviewed seem to be ready to repeat their experience. Thus Bernard Bonnin said: 'If Jimmy Joncquart is willing and gets in touch with us tomorrow we will start again'. Josu Bilbao thinks that the concept should be taken on again because there are no other programmes showing images of people's daily life in different countries. However, the people in charge of programming now seem cautious with regard to the significance that broadcasting such a programme now would have. Among those interviewed we should note the importance they attached to the lack of a production manager for the *Eurosud* programme. It would also be profitable to envisage a certain independence of the programme in relation to different editing staffs, especially from the point of view of the budget. In order to make savings, the monthly meetings could be audio-linked. The current state of intensified competition forces these TV channels to be very successful. Consequently, a partnership could also be considered with private channels.

CONCLUSION

Television is made by men and women, for men and women, and shares in their weaknesses and in their successes. There are stories of mutual irritation and tiredness but also of reciprocal discoveries and friendships. *Eurosud* can be seen as a prime example because a handful of journalists had the idea of doing something that spoke to and about the great shifts which were becoming apparent in a newly emerging Europe, shifts which enabled them to work together. On the other hand, *Eurosud* is not exemplary since no other experience had been or will be identical. The journalists we spoke to had anticipated a triple evolution in the audiovisual area: privatization, a transfer of authority to a supranational level, and decentralization, with increasing autonomy enjoyed by the regions. They sometimes described *Eurosud* as a 'do it yourself' effort. However, this should not be seen as a disparaging comment. If we wish to stress this reality, which is usually carefully hidden, it is to emphasize the ideological nature of the contemporary requirements which want us to be 'professional'.

The coming of *Eurosud* raises pertinent questions about the part television plays in the constitution of a European identity. For EEC authorities, television programmes are clearly identified as being able to develop a common conscience. Dominique Wolton stressed the contradictions in this attitude when he said that EEC television is considered as having an integral political function, which is criticized when it is national and is a factor in the homogenization of different publics. This is the same with mass television (Wolton, 1990: 220; cf. Marchetti, 1997: 106). The international broadcasting of national programmes, or, as in the case of *Eurosud*, of regional programmes, gives us another conception of European identity. As Pascal Marchetti wrote: 'The study of regional television in Europe confirms the homology that exists between programming and identity' (Marchetti, 1997: 110).

The fact that *Eurosud* was a news magazine does not imply, in our mind, that we should put news above entertainment, in terms of intrinsic value or when talking about the construction of a European identity. The theory concerning news, which suggests that a better informed citizen is a better citizen, and that a European citizen aware of European affairs is a better European, is 'a completely idealistic and aggressive vision of a construction of a social order' (Schlesinger, 1997: 108). We chose to discuss a news programme because the intercultural differences are more obvious than in entertainment programmes.

What lesson can we draw from this experience at an intercultural level? The precept in this field is that there is no precept, that we should not trust what has been said before. Interculturality develops of its own accord and does not conform to any kind of formula. On the other hand, 'Interculturality is affected by social representations, such as images and stereotypes and even ideological and political projections. These representations must be recognized from a subjective point of view and objectively due to the progress made in human sciences' (Ladmiral and Lipiansky, 1989: 309). The reactions of those involved in *Eurosud* reveal some of the social misconceptions which structures these representations.

NOTE

1 Our thanks for their help to: Jimmy Joncquart, instigator of the project, manager of France 3 Bretagne; Jean-Claude Sire, in charge of the programming at France 3 Aquitaine; Bernard Bonnin, assistant editorial director at France 3 Aquitaine, and journalist in charge of *Eurosud* for Aquitaine; Josu Bilbao, professor, in charge of *Eurosud* at TVE Bilbao.

ACTIVITIES

1 Analyse themes contained in a transnational programme or a joint venture. Are they 'crossed looks' or mere juxtaposition? Can we find conflictual themes?
2 Three topics of reflection:
'One of the chief dangers potentially involved in the European Union's communications policy would be to allow the process of relinquishing

sovereignty by consent in one direction: that of transnationalization, while attempting to maintain systems of centralized cultural representation in each State. Such a trend would necessarily lead to the reinforcement and dominance of a few national identities, with the consequent impoverishment of the diverse and common European heritage.' (M. de Moragas Spa and C. Garitaonandia (eds) (1995) *Decentralization in the Global Era. Television in the Regions, Nationalities and Small Countries of the European Union*. London: John Libbey)

'And however, we have to face it: European public opinion and European television do not exist, which does not mean that we cannot make Europe but we can at least understand that we have to take into account the different rhythms' (D. Wolton (1990) *Eloge du grand public. Une théorie critique de la télévision* [Apology of the public. A critical theory of television.]. Paris: Flammarion).

'The identity of multicultural man/woman is based, not on 'belongingness' which implies either owning or being owned by culture, but on a style of self-consciousness that is capable of negotiating ever new formations of reality. In this sense multicultural man/woman is a radical departure from the kinds of identities found in both traditional and mass societies. He/she is neither totally apart from his/her culture; he/she lives, instead, on the boundary.' (P.S. Adler (1982) 'Beyond cultural identity: reflections on cultural and multicultural man', in L.A. Samovar and R.E. Porter (eds), *Intercultural Communication: A Reader*. Belmont, CA: Wadsworth, pp. 389–408; quote from p. 391).

SUGGESTIONS FOR FURTHER READING

Blind, S. and Hallenberger, G. (eds) (1996) *European Co-Productions in Television and Film*. Heidelberg: Universitatsverslag C. Winter.

A useful introduction to the politics and aesthetics of television co-production in Europe.

CHAPTER 7

TELEVISION AUDIENCES

Winfried Schulz

It is the audience that makes television a mass medium, and at the same time it is the television programme that creates its mass audience. The interdependence of programmes and their audiences as well as the mass character of television audiences are characteristics which fascinate many observers. A *mass* audience comprises a huge number of people. For instance, 38.8 per cent of the population in Great Britain (around 18 million viewers) followed on TV the funeral ceremony of Princess Diana on 6 September 1997. Other examples of European top programmes of 1997 are listed in Table 7.1. There we see that in Sweden a cross-country skiing report which was aired on 2 March early in the morning reached 21.5 per cent of the population, with an audience share of 87.2 per cent, and in Hungary on 18 February an episode of the American hospital drama series *ER* (*Emergency Room*) reached 52 per cent of the population, with an audience share of 83.8 per cent.

Statistics like those of Table 7.1 are one way of coming to grips with the audience. Programme managers, television producers, writers, performers and advertisers are highly interested in audience statistics, particularly in programme ratings. If a programme has high ratings it is assumed to have met the viewers' needs and interests, which is one criterion of responsiveness and accountability of a television channel (Mitchell and Blumler, 1994). More often, high ratings are regarded as an indication of economic success, particularly from the standpoint of a commercial channel which is catering for a specific segment of the audience market.

Although in both cases the ratings give a quite similar quantitative account of audience size (or programme reach), the statistics have different functions which correlate with two different audience concepts, the audience-as-public and the audience-as-market. It is the mission of a public service channel to be accepted by the audience through serving the interests of a general public or of certain special interest publics. As distinct from this, the objective of a commercial channel is 'audiencemaking' i.e. to attract a

TABLE 7.1 Top rated TV programmes of European countries, 1997

Country	Channel	Title	Genre	Date	Start time	Reach (%)	Share (%)
Austria	ORF1	Villacher Fasching	Entertain.	11/02	20:15	33.0	74.9
Belgium							
Flemish	TV1	Schalkse Ruiters	Entertain.	02/03	20:23	41.9	67.9
French	FTL–TV1	Le 19 Heures	News	09/01	19:00	27.6	64.7
Bulgaria	KANAL 1	Panorama	Magazine	29/02	20:00	57.0	83
Czech Republic	Nova	Miss Desetileti	Entertain.	12/10	21:08	57.6	84
Denmark	DR 1	Handball	Sport	14/12	19:59	52.0	74
Finland	YLE2	Ice Hockey	Sport	03/05	19:45	31	n.a.
France	TF1	TF1 20 heures	News	12/02	20:00	31.7	64.3
Germany	ZDF	Wetten, dass. . .?	Entertain.	13/12	20:16	24.1	50.5
Greece	ET 1	Basketball	Sport	24/04	21:37	19.1	52.6
Hungary	MTV1	ER	Series	18/02	20:16	52	83.8
Ireland	RTE 1	Eurovision Song Contest	Entertain.	03/05	20:00	35	75
Italy	RAI1	Football	Sport	15/11	20:47	38.1	67.7
Netherlands	NED 2	Football	Sport	19/03	20:25	29.7	n.a.
Norway	NRK	Ski Jump	Sport	01/03	13:49	41.1	83.5
Poland	TVP1	Pulkownik kwiatkowski	Movie	11/11	20:10	30.7	70.0
Portugal	SIC	Big Show SIC especial	Entertain.	12/06	21:30	23.2	73.6
Slovakia	STV1	Pocasie	News	26/07	20:01	45	62
Spain	ANTENA 3	Football	Sport	30/01	21:31	32.9	60.2
Sweden	SVT1	Cross-Country Skiing	Sport	02/03	07:40	21.5	87.2
Switzerland							
German	SF 1	Tagesschau	News	05/01	19:30	27.3	64.1
French	TSR	TJ-soir	News	08/12	19:30	27.2	65.4
Italian	TSI	Telegiornale sera	News	17/11	20:00	31.7	66.9
United Kingdom	BBC 1	Funeral of Diana	Other	06/09	11:00	38.8	61

For each country the programme with the highest audience share in 1997 was selected.
Source: Television 98

mass audience and thus create a market which can be offered to advertisers (Ettema and Whitney, 1994).

The audience, the mass, the public and the market are collectivities which can be characterized in statistical terms. Later we will outline some of the methods by which researchers generate audience statistics. In addition to the quantitative approach we will look at qualitative research as the dominant paradigm of audience analysis in the academic world. A characteristic of qualitative approaches is to decompose the collectivity of the audience into its 'members' and to study the viewing behaviour of individuals in their social contexts.

Mapping audience size and composition is one of the objectives of quantitative audience research, particularly if it is oriented to the responsiveness or marketability of television programmes. In addition, practitioners as well as academic scholars are interested in explaining audience behaviour and establishing models of programme choice. Audience research has accompanied the development of the television medium from its very beginning and has resulted in a plethora of empirical findings and theoretical explanations. Later we draw upon this stock of knowledge.

AUDIENCE ANALYSIS

Europe's television audiences are worth about 28 billion Euro per year. This is the amount for which the television industry in the 15 European Union countries sold its audiences to advertisers in 1997. The major part of this advertising budget was allocated on the basis of ratings statistics. No other field of communication studies has as much commercial relevance and far-reaching practical consequences as audience research. In this section we will show how television ratings are generated and reported. In addition to the most common and highly standardized methods we will look at some alternative audience measures, including qualitative research.

Peoplemeter ratings

Ratings are the most frequently used measures of audience size. Audience ratings tell how many viewers were exposed to specific programme content on particular TV channels in certain time slots. The measure of exposure is often assumed to indicate an act of choice in which an individual selects from a range of available programming (Webster and Wagschlag, 1985). Less modestly interpreted, exposure is assumed to imply attention to television, programme preference or acceptance and even an effect on the viewer. Quite often the ratings serve as the prime criterion of TV advertising effect. These aspects make ratings a feedback information which programme managers, producers, writers, performers and advertisers often rely on.

Ratings provide a yardstick for comparing different programmes and channels with respect to audience exposure. To serve these functions the audience measurements have to be standardized and reliable. In most countries this is secured by rules set up by the advertising industry in cooperation with TV organizations and research companies. An initiative of the European Broadcasting Union (EBU) – Joint Industry Group on Audience Research Methodology is directed at harmonizing and making these rules compatible across countries (EBU, 1997).

Peoplemeter is the name of a complex measurement system that has become the *de facto* standard technique of audience measurement across the world. The key element of this system is meter equipment attached to each TV set to record continuously when the set is switched on, to which channel it is tuned, and which household member is watching. A remote handset with push buttons assigned to each household member (with extra buttons for guests) serves to register the individual viewing periods. When a person begins viewing and ends viewing, he or she is supposed to signal this by pressing the button.

The data logistics of the peoplemeter system allows for a very quick inspection of preliminary results as well as elaborate statistical analysis. In most countries results are available within 24 hours, even to the public (for instance displayed on teletext every morning). The peoplemeter system produces a huge data stream. Viewing acts are measured continuously day and night all year round and could, in principle, be reported second by second. In practice the data are processed, simplified and aggregated. One common technique for information reduction is to register only viewing acts which exceed a certain *persistence threshold* (for instance, three minutes consecutively tuned to a channel). The meter systems of different countries vary in this and other parameters, and there are also some differences in the arithmetic procedures used in calculating audience size. Box 7.1 lists some basic terms and calculations which are in use internationally.

The peoplemeter ratings can be generalized to the whole audience only if they are based on a representative sample of television households. The selected households form a *panel*, a term which expresses that they remain members of the sample for a longer time, often for years. Recruiting and maintaining the peoplemeter sample is critical to the method since the selected households have to allow metering equipment to be installed and have to be willing to use a keypad to register their viewing acts.

Since ratings are based on – sometimes relatively small – samples they can only be taken as estimates. Ratings statistics are more or less affected by sampling error, depending on the sample size. A large sample provides more precise results and, more important, allows for detailed reporting about demographic sub-groups. As Table 7.2 shows, sample sizes of meter systems vary over a wide range from below 500 to over 5,000 households

Box 7.1

Basic concepts of ratings research

Television ratings are used by the broadcasting industry to measure the audience for a programme or a commercial break. A rating is the average percentage of a population viewing across a specified period of time (such as a programme duration or quarter-hour). Ratings can relate to individuals as well as to households. By multiplying the ratings with the base number of the population, ratings are converted into numbers of viewers.

Share is the percentage of the population tuned to a particular programme or channel out of all those using television at that time. Share is calculated on the base only of those individuals who are registered as viewing during the specific time period.

Amount of viewing is the amount of time that a person is registered as viewing television on an average day. Amount of viewing is expressed as an average in minutes per head of population (see Figure 7.1, p. 124).

Reach is the percentage of the population who saw a specified amount of a programme, or of a channel's output, over a specified period. In Great Britain, the defined conventional amount of time is three consecutive minutes, but it can be any length of time. The average daily reach for a programme, for example, is the proportion of the population who, each day averaged over the week, watched at least three consecutive minutes of the programme.

Frequency is the number of times that these viewers (included in the reach) have been exposed to the message. Information about frequency of exposure typically relates to a particular advertisement or advertising campaign. It is expressed as an average (e.g. 'the average frequency of exposure to this campaign was 1.6'). More precise information is the full distribution from which the average is derived.

In a few countries audience measurement routinely includes an **Appreciation Index**, a score (e.g. on a scale from 0 to 100) which indicates how much each broadcast is liked by its viewers.

A concept which is used quite commonly in advertising is **gross rating points** (GRP). The GRPs are simply the product of reach and frequency (Reach × Frequency = GRP). GRPs serve as a measure of the overall size or total weight of an ad campaign.

in accordance with the financial capacity of the television industry in different countries. The sample size is the major factor which determines the cost of a meter system.

Due to its commercial relevance, ratings research itself has become a major business. For example, in Germany the TV companies invest about 14 million Euro per year in the peoplemeter system. The whole amount is absorbed by GfK, a major marketing company. Internationally operating companies like Audits of Great Britain (AGB) and the American supplier Nielsen provide peoplemeter services in several countries (see Table 7.2).

TABLE 7.2 Peoplemeter services

Country	Service	Launch	Panel size (households)
Austria	Teletest	1991	1200
Belgium			
North	NV Audimetrie S.A.	1989	750
South	NV Audimetrie S.A.	1985	750
Czech Republic	TN AGB MF	1997	660
Denmark	Gallup A/S	1992	500
Finland	Finnpanel OY	1987	475
France	Mediametrie	1986	2300
Germany	GFK	1985	5200
Greece	AGB	1987	700
Hungary	AGB	1994	620
Ireland	A:C:Nielsen	1996	600
Italy	Auditel/AGB	1986	5076
Netherlands	Intomart BV	1987	1000
Norway	MMI	1992	500
Poland	AGB	1997	1250
Portugal	AGB	1990	620
Spain	Sofres; A.M	1993	2500
Sweden	MMS	1993	650
Switzerland	IHA	1985	1650
Turkey	AGB Anadolu	1989	1300
United Kingdom	Barb	1984	4435
United States	Nielsen TV Index	1987	5000

Source: Television 98

Alternative ratings measures

The peoplemeter system is a relatively recent methodology. It was developed by AGB in Britain and launched in the mid-1980s. AGB exported the system to a number of European countries and tried also, though without success, to challenge Nielsen on the US market (see Table 7.2). The measurement of audiences is originally an American 'invention' which dates back to around 1930 when the advertising industry demanded more precise information about the audiences created by radio as a new mass medium (Beville, 1988). Since then, a number of social science methods have been adopted and accommodated to media analysis and to the needs of programme producers, advertisers and their agencies. Most of these are still in use, although the peoplemeter is considered the most advanced method. Other methods have their specific advantages too and, on the other hand, the peoplemeter has certain disadvantages.

The most obvious problem with the peoplemeter are the high costs of implementing, maintaining and operating the system. Only a highly developed television system and advertising market can afford to invest many millions per year to register viewing behaviour second by second all year round. So the system has hardly been implemented in less developed countries, including Eastern Europe. A second critical point is the obtrusiveness of the system. Panel households have to agree to have technical devices attached to all audiovisual equipment in the home, to cooperate by pushing a button each time they begin and end TV viewing, and thus to be monitored continuously day and night. The obtrusiveness of the method may result in response errors and thus affect the validity and the representativeness of the audience data.

The **household meter** which preceded the peoplemeter was in certain respects a somewhat less problematic technology. A household meter is connected to the TV set and records all tuning activities. It is unobtrusive in so far as it does not require any effort on the part of the viewer. However, it does not give any information about the viewing behaviour of individuals, and this is the main disadvantage which finally led to its substitution by the peoplemeter.

Self-administered **diaries** as an audience measure are widely used all over the world. The diary is a paper booklet which is delivered to a representative sample of viewers. Sample members are asked to record their media use over a one-week period. The booklet provides a grid for every day which divides the day into quarter-hour segments, usually beginning very early in the morning and ending late after midnight. Booklet keepers are supposed to record all viewing acts during the time segments they occur, the channels and titles of programmes they watch, and the family members and guests who are in the audience.

Like the peoplemeter, the diary generates information about individual viewing behaviour. But the method has several weaknesses. It is quite demanding and vulnerable to response errors, particularly in expanding TV markets due to the proliferation of channels and the use of remote control devices.

Measures of the audience's **programme appreciation** with more or less standardized scales, sometimes called 'qualitative ratings', make use of a special version of the diary method. They are supposed to give an account of how involved the audience feels with the programme or, in other words, how much viewers like what they watch. Like the quantitative ratings, the appreciation measures are of interest mainly to practitioners since there is evidence that the more involved audience members feel in a particular programme, the more likely they are to watch that programme all the way through and pay attention to advertisements shown in it (Gunter and Wober, 1992: 3). However, since liking and actual viewing are highly correlated (Barwise and Ehrenberg, 1988: 50 ff.) practitioners in several countries have decided to do without appreciation measures and rely on quantitative ratings only.

Qualitative ratings are in regular use, e.g. in Great Britain, Canada, Australia and the Netherlands. For example, in Britain a representative panel of viewers are expected to complete a booklet every week and rate how interesting and/or enjoyable they found those programmes they happened to watch.

Interviewing is also a widely used method to collect data about television audiences based on a representative sample of the population. A survey questionaire has the potential to generate a wealth of quantitative and qualitative information about the behaviour and the characteristics of viewers. Its main disadvantage is that it cannot record viewing behaviour as it occurs and is, instead, dependent on the respondents' memory. To limit response errors due to memory failure, the detailed recording of media use behaviour is usually confined to 'yesterday' or to the 24 hour time span before the interview.

The **survey**, either as an in-person interview or, more often, as a telephone interview, is a widely used method for obtaining ratings of radio programmes. In television, research interviews play a role as a supplemental method, e.g. for contacting respondents as diary keepers, or for recruiting members of a meter sample. A peoplemeter system requires survey interviewing for establishing and maintaining the panel and for providing information about audience characteristics which can be combined with the viewing data.

Qualitative audience research

All ratings measures give only a rather crude quantitative account of audience exposure. Even appreciation measures, although they go beyond mere programme exposure, still share most of the characteristics – and limitations – of quantitative ratings. Critics of ratings research such as Ang (1991) and Morley (1992) point to the abstract nature of the ratings which treat viewers as numbers and viewing as a context-free and one-dimensional activity, i.e. detached from the viewer's social situation and disregarding concomitant activities of TV viewing.

As distinct from this, qualitative studies aim at describing television viewing as a complex practice in the context of everyday life and examining the ways in which audiences make sense of television. Qualitative studies have a long tradition in media research which goes back to the 1920s, and there are several different research perspectives with backgrounds in, among others, psychology, social phenomenology, ethnography, literary studies and cultural studies (Höijer, 1998; Jensen and Rosengren, 1990). According to Lindlof (1991) five different 'styles' of qualitative audience studies can be discerned:

The **social phenomenological** style builds on ethnomethodology, symbolic interactionism and cultural hermeneutics. A typical research question in this context is how mass-mediated symbolic activities contribute to the social construction of reality, e.g. how children understand and make sense of a television programme (Wolf, 1987).

The **communication rules** style is concerned with the systems of interpersonal norms and how they are performed in social situations, for example the social conduct for viewing television in public places (Lemish,

1982). As a largely American approach it is based on rules theory and conversational analysis.

Cultural studies originated in Great Britain and became influential on audience research worldwide. They are rooted in political economy and the Birmingham School of critical cultural theory. A model of encoding–decoding is at the centre of this research style as well as the idea that 'ideology as *sent* is not the same as ideology as *taken*' (McQuail, 1994: 101). Audience members may resist or subvert dominant ideologies of television by decoding messages according to their social or class position. Morley's widely recognized studies of family television viewing may serve to illustrate the critical studies approach (Morley, 1988, see below, p. 122).

A similar interest in the decoding and interpretation of the television 'text' characterizes **reception analysis.** This approach has been strongly influenced by cognitive psychology in addition to literary criticism, semiotics and cultural studies. Empirical studies sometimes include a content analysis of television messages. A key concept of reception analysis is the audience as an *interpretive community*. Interpretive communities share similar strategies for decoding the television 'texts', for instance certain programme genres. These strategies are contingent on the social positions of the viewers in society, shaped, among others, by gender, social class, or the experience of subcultures (Lindlof, 1988). Liebes and Katz' (1986) examination of cultural differences in TV viewing is a good example. Through focus group discussions the authors compared the readings of an episode of the *Dallas* series by different ethnic communities in Israel and matched groups of second-generation Americans.

Feminist research may be considered a style of its own although it shares many features with other qualitative approaches, particularly with cultural studies. Feminist studies focus on gender as a cultural construct. A central concern is with women's subordinate role in society and their use of television as a means to express their own aspirations and identities. An example is the study by Press (1989) which demonstrates that American women receive television entertainment programming in class-specific ways.

Despite their different roots and backgrounds most qualitative studies subscribe to the following methodological orientations:

- Qualitative inquiry is 'local and particularistic', i.e. the analysis focuses on individual viewers, dyads, families or subcultures rather than on abstract statistical aggregates.
- Television viewing is studied in the context of everyday activities since it is normally enmeshed with other domestic practices and family interactions.
- The viewer is seen as an active interpreter of television rather than as a passive spectator; the focus is on how viewers make sense of television and achieve meaning in social interaction.
- Television content is a polysemic 'text' which lends itself to many different 'readings', i.e. ways of decoding and of sense-making, depending on the social position and outlook of the viewer.

- Researchers emphasize inductive and interpretative methods by applying 'thick' descriptions of situations, focus groups and in-depth interviewing as well as participant observation.
- Results are often based on relatively small numbers of respondents who are not necessarily selected according to random sampling statistics; correspondingly, the results are presented verbally and as descriptive typologies rather than in numerical form and statistical tables.

A widely recognized example of qualitative research is Morley's (1988) study of 18 families living in the area of South London. The author addressed by in-depth interviewing the following topics:

1 power and control over programme choice
2 styles of viewing
3 planned and unplanned viewing
4 television-related talk
5 use of video
6 'solo' viewing and guilty pleasures
7 programme type preferences
8 national versus local news programming

In addition to in-depth interviewing the **focus group** is a frequently used research method in qualitative audience research. Introduced as early as the 1940s by Paul F. Lazarsfeld and Robert K. Merton (Merton, 1987) it originally served to supplement quantitative media effects research. Focus groups can help to pin down those aspects of a complex stimulus from which observed media effects might have originated. After this early episode the academic interest in focus groups disappeared and emerged again only in the 1980s, mainly in market research. It also became used mostly as a stand-alone method, in reception research and as a preferred instrument in critical audience research. Focus groups are also instrumental in programme development and thus serve to incorporate viewers' reactions in the TV production process.

For a focus group study a number of subjects are brought together to discuss an issue in the presence of a moderator. Often the discussion starts from a media presentation, e.g. a television programme. The discussion is usually taped and transcribed (for more details see Lunt and Livingstone, 1996; Morrison, 1998).

Field work with qualitative methods normally generates large amounts of raw material like interviewing protocols, taped recordings and their transcripts, observational notes and written summaries. Whereas standardized, quantitative studies call for high investment prior to the field work in setting up and pre-testing data collection instruments, like questionaires, diaries or meters, qualitative reception studies require considerable efforts to screen and structure the raw materials after they have been collected.

Analysing and constructing meaningful results from qualitative data is highly demanding with respect to the creativity of the researcher. One major problem is how to structure and aggregate the data without either losing the differences between individuals and groups or claiming false generalities on the basis of single cases. Livingstone (1992) suggests, among others, borrowing from methods of cognitive psychology, e.g. multidimensional scaling, for analysing audience interpretations (for further methodological suggestions refer to Höijer, 1998; Jensen and Jankowski, 1991; Lull, 1990: 174 ff.).

AUDIENCE BEHAVIOUR

The perspective of ratings research is limited to programme exposure, whereas reception studies try to get a broader and deeper impression of the television experience and its impact on the viewer. In addition, there is a wealth of research looking at cognitive, behavioural, societal and other consequences of television viewing. Approaches of the latter type are usually categorized as *effects research*, indicating that they hypothesize television as the cause of whatever consequences the inquiry focuses on.

In the first part of this section we will look at audience behaviour defined as exposure and show some salient viewing patterns. In the second part, we will discuss different explanations of audience self-selection and television use. Our outline takes advantage of available results of empirical research. Questions of effects of television viewing are beyond the scope of this chapter.

Viewing patterns and audience structures

Like all media use behaviour, television viewing is dependent on time as a resource. Several time-based statistics give an account of how people watch TV. For instance, there are data about how much time the population of different countries devotes to television viewing on an average day. Figure 7.1 shows that Americans and Hungarians watch TV almost four hours per day, whereas Czechs and German speaking Swiss spend hardly more than half that much time viewing. These results are calculated, like all the other statistics presented in this section, from peoplemeter ratings.

For practical purposes of the television industry it is important to know how audiences allocate their viewing time to different channels. Pie charts are appropriate visualizations of the resulting statistics of audience shares. These charts give an impression of the relative market strength of the different channels and of the overall structure of the television market. Figure 7.2 contrasts, as extremely different examples of market structure,

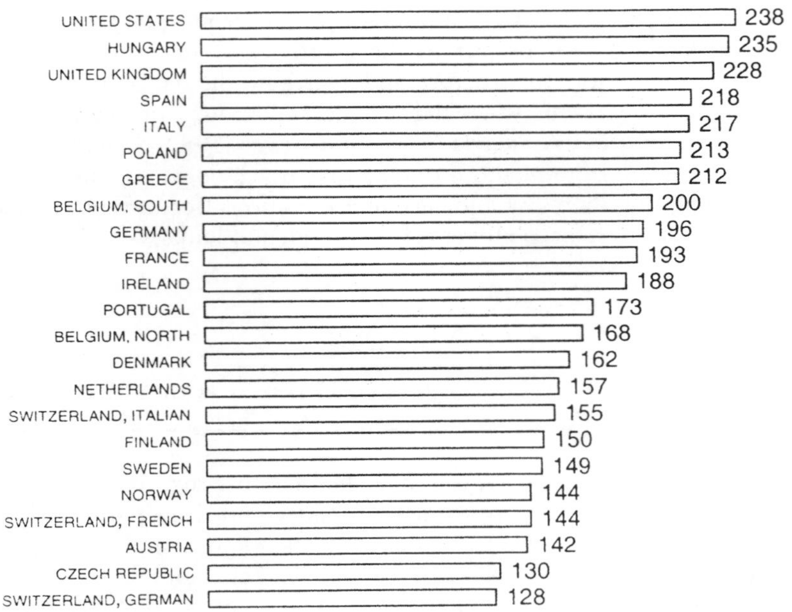

FIGURE 7.1 Average daily viewing time per individual (in minutes) (*Television 98*)

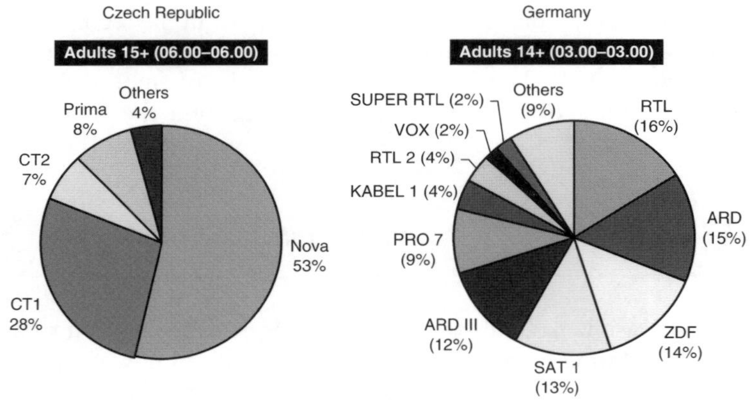

FIGURE 7.2 Audience shares of the main channels (*Television 98*)

the situations in the Czech Republic and in Germany. The Czech audience is highly concentrated on only two channels with a share of more than 80 per cent. Nova alone, a commercial channel, accounts for more than half of the audience market. As distinct from this, the highly competitive market in Germany is divided into a number of small segments. The major channels have a share which ranges from 9 to 16 per cent. In addition to such accounts of the overall market structure, audience statistics and respective pie charts are available on the basis of smaller and more specific

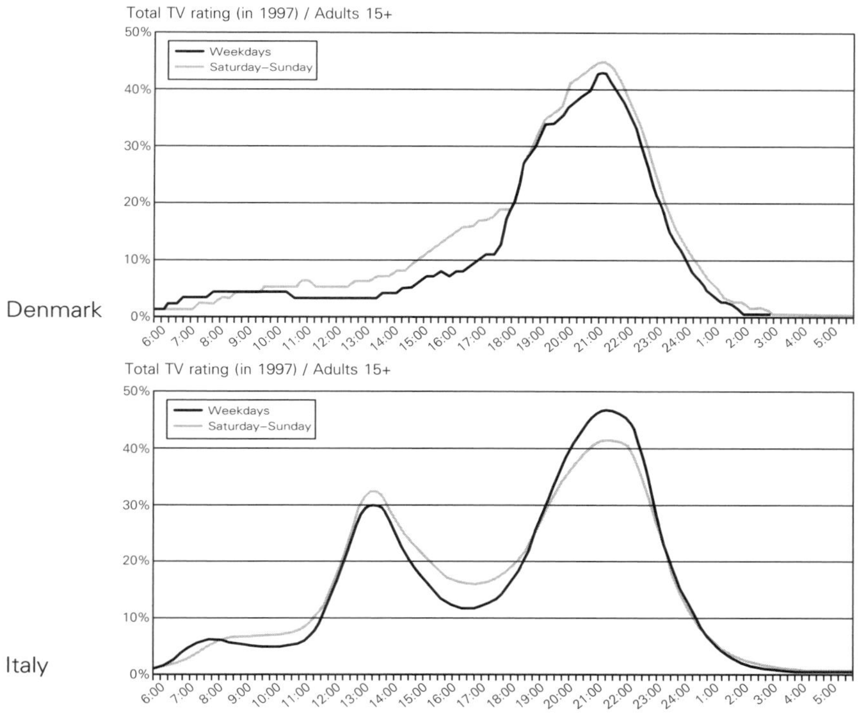

FIGURE 7.3 Daily patterns of the television audience (*Television 98*)

time units, for example, displaying market shares for a certain day or for the prime-time period of that day or for the hour between 7 and 8 p.m. or for any other time slot.

Another perspective on time is to examine how many people watch at a given hour of the day. Figure 7.3 demonstrates this by plotting over the time axis the percentage of the population exposed to television on an average day. The two selected examples illustrate two prevailing patterns of viewing behaviour. The pattern of Denmark with just one peak in the evening, the usual prime time, can be found almost everywhere in Northern and Central Europe. A pattern with a second peak around mid-afternoon which is represented here by the case of Italy is typical of the Mediterranean countries (and is also found in Belgium). Obviously, television viewing for many people of these countries is a way of spending their siesta.

For practical purposes as well as for the scholarly interests in viewing behaviour, it is useful and quite common to look at various population sub-groups, in addition to the whole population. There are two different statistical approaches to this.

1 The first approach resembles the calculation of reach or share for the total population (see Box 7.1 above) with the only difference that we take as the 100 per cent basis for such calculations certain population

TABLE 7.3 Audience composition of the major German television channels (%)[1]

	ARD	ZDF	RTL	SAT1	PRO 7	Total population[2]
Male	47.5	47.7	47.8	49.5	53.0	47.6
Female	52.5	52.3	52.2	50.5	47.0	52.4
Age						
14–49	46.5	44.1	59.2	58.0	69.4	56.3
50 and older	53.5	55.9	40.8	42.0	30.6	43.7
Household income						
lowest	36.5	37.4	35.7	36.1	33.9	34.6
lower middle	24.1	24.0	25.5	25.4	24.9	24.0
upper middle	25.6	25.2	26.5	26.3	28.2	26.9
highest	13.8	13.4	12.3	12.2	13.0	14.5
Total	100	100	100	100	100	100
Viewers[3]	(35.73)	(28.91)	(25.79)	(22.12)	(13.69)	(63.73)

1. ARD and ZDF are public service channels; the other channels are commercially operated.
2. Aged 14 and over.
3. Average daily reach.

Source: Allensbacher Werbetraeger-Analyse 1998

sub-groups. For example, as a service to advertisers the managers of a commercial channel may show their *reach* among different age groups, particularly among the younger generations. Or a public service channel may present such figures for demonstrating its responsiveness to the interests of elderly people. Similar operations are applicable to calculations of audience share.

2 We will gain essentially the same information by taking as the 100 per cent basis the total audience of a particular channel (or of a specified programme) and inspect its *composition* according to categories of gender, age, socio-economic background and other variables (as an illustration see Table 7.3). In addition to demographics some studies also provide information about interests, lifestyle, buying and consumption patterns and many other characteristics of viewers. With regard to their respective interests and expectations, programme makers and advertisers may assess such composition profiles in terms of *audience quality*.

Explaining programme choice

The aggregate patterns of audience behaviour we have looked at in the previous section result from individual programme choices. In order to explain these choices, audience factors as well as media factors, individual traits as well as structural constraints have to be considered (Webster and Wagschlag, 1985; Webster and Phalen, 1997).

Selective exposure is a well established concept of communication research which helps us to understand a person's choice of programming

(Zillmann and Bryant, 1985). It is based on the assumption that people tend to expose themselves to messages that are consistent with their predispositions and avoid material that challenges their existing beliefs and attitudes. In its original version, developed by Lazarsfeld, Berelson and Gaudet (1944) in the context of an election campaign, the concept served to explain the reception of political propaganda and the self-selection of partisan audiences. Other authors soon extended the concept to consumer behaviour (Festinger, 1957). Like the principle of selective exposure, another classic of communication research, the *uses-and-gratifications* approach, explains selection processes by individual traits of audience members. A person's needs and motives in interaction with his or her perceived satisfactions resulting from media use are assumed to direct actual choices (Katz et al., 1974).

A less ambitious way to explain viewer preferences is to refer simply to demographic factors. It can easily be demonstrated by ratings data that age and socio-economic status are useful predictors of television behaviour. This can be seen in Table 7.3, which shows that age and income (as an indicator of socio-economic status) divide the audiences of the major German television channels. Generally, amount of viewing time and frequency of TV exposure increase with age, but are lower among the upper strata of the population. Of course, the demographics indicate that differences in people's circumstances of living and in lifestyles actually determine their different information and entertainment preferences.

In empirical analyses the concepts which focus on individual viewer traits and preferences usually have limited explanatory power (Barwise and Ehrenberg, 1988: 28). This is partly due to the fact that television viewing quite often is a group activity. In some viewing situations a person may not be able to act on his or her preferences because someone else in the family is in command of the remote control device. In other situations the members of a family may negotiate their choices of programming. In addition, individual programme preferences can direct a person's selection process only to the degree that the programmes differ distinctively in character and he or she is aware of such differences as well as the available options. Particularly if there is a broad offer, as is in most cable systems, viewers actually lack full awareness of choices. These and other factors modify the influence of individual preferences on programme exposure.

A person's media environment constraints the selection process in many respects. The range of *available television channels* is one important factor which, in turn, depends on other conditions like the structure of the broadcasting system, the access to cable and/or satellite transmission and the decision of a household to subscribe to cable or to buy a satellite receiver. These factors contribute to the differences in the structure of the audience market illustrated in Figure 7.2 above. In a number of European countries, for example in Greece, Italy and Spain and in most of Eastern Europe, the choice of domestic television programmes (programmes in a language which the majority of the population can understand) is still quite limited, and the majority of the population has access neither to cable nor to direct satellite transmission. But even in media-rich environments many viewers develop a certain *channel repertoire* which comprises only a small subset of the total number of channels available to them (Ferguson and Perse, 1993).

Audience availability is, like channel availability, one of the crucial structural factors that determine exposure to television. The concept of audience availability refers to the number of people who are likely to be using television at any point in time. Figure 7.3 illustrates typical patterns of audience availability which are due to daily routines, to physiological necessities like sleeping or eating and to working commitments. In addition to the time of the day the weekday and the seasons play a role. The viewing behaviour on weekends is different from the weekday pattern, and during winter months people spend more time with television than in the summer.

Differences in the amount of viewing across countries as displayed by Figure 7.1 may indicate that there are also national peculiarities other than the structure of the television industry and the availability of cable and satellite technology. Are Hungarians really TV addicts while the Czechs watch so much less? Do the British use TV so differently from people in Austria?

The viewers viewed

Perhaps the differences across countries are, at least partly, due to weaknesses of the ratings methodology. This is an obvious suspicion if one considers the differences in the peoplemeter methodology which still exist across countries, in spite of the harmonization attempts of the EBU. Differences pertain, among others, to the definition of the universe of television households, the method of sampling, and the definition and measuring of viewing acts. To what degree the results of Figure 7.1 are affected by such factors is an open question.

In addition to the critique of the metering of audiences by academic scholars, which has already been mentioned, there is always a lot of critical discussion in the profession among those who supply or use the ratings (see ARF/ESOMAR, 1992). One central issue is the definition and measurement of the viewing act. The discussion has been stimulated by a number of qualitative studies which look more closely at what viewers do when they are viewing, for instance by observing people in their living room through a video camera (Bechtel et al., 1972; Collett, 1987; see Figure 7.4). 'Eavesdropping' research of this kind as well as other observation studies have demonstrated that viewers are inattentive for a considerable amount of time; they are, as Lull (1990: 30) describes it, 'e.g. singing, ironing, sorting clothes, talking, mimicking the television, dancing, doing exercises, posing, dressing, fighting, eating' and, not so rarely, sleeping (see also Gunter and Svennevig, 1987).

FIGURE 7.4 The viewer viewed (Collett, 1987)

Such findings put the validity of the metering data into question. If a housewife is ironing and talking to her husband while TV is on, does she count as 'watching' television? And what about the other family members in the room? Her husband is reading the newspaper and her daughter is listening to a CD with her headphones on, while both are, from time to time, glancing at the TV screen. Who in this family is part of the television audience?

These questions are not at all problematic for qualitative studies. Instead of counting viewers, qualitative research is interested in studying as comprehensively and in as detailed a way as possible how people behave in front of the screen, how they experience television viewing, how they interpet and make sense of the programme. Morley, for example, writes about the objectives of his in-depth interviewing of selected families in South London that he 'wanted to get insights into the criteria used by viewers in making choices and in responding (positively or negatively) to different types of programming and scheduling' (Morley, 1988: 32). Another example is Lull's ethnographic research 'inside family viewing'. The author observed that television serves as a constant background and as a behavioural regulator for family life. Television facilitates communication and interpersonal contact or avoidance; it is a resource for learning and for family role fulfilment, for instance in the regulation of children's television viewing by a parent. A typology proposed by Lull (1990) gives an account of the social uses of television (see Box 7.2).

Box 7.2

Social uses of television

Structural

Environmental: background noise; companionship; entertainment.

Regulative: punctuation of time and activity; talk patterns.

Relational

Communication facilitation: experience illustration; common ground; conversational entrance, anxiety reduction; agenda for talk; value clarification.

Affiliation/avoidance: physical, verbal contact/neglect; family solidarity; family relaxation; conflict reduction; relationship maintenance.

Social learning: decision making; behaviour modelling; problem solving; value transmission; legitimization; information dissemination; substitute schooling.

Competence/dominance: role enactment; role reinforcement; substitute role portrayal; intellectual validation; authority exercise; gatekeeping; argument facilitation.

(Lull, 1990: 36)

CONSTRUCTING THE AUDIENCE

In spite of almost five decades of systematic inquiry into the television audience the object under study seems to have remained an unknown species. As Ang suspects, the 'television audience' exists only in discursive form: 'it is nothing more than a statistical construct, which does not reflect a pre-existent, real entity, but evokes it' (Ang, 1991: 94). And Dahlgren (1998) asks whether it is 'even meaningful to use the concept of "audience" at all?' Questions challenging the conventional wisdom are becoming increasingly critical as the media landscape changes. In this final section we will discuss ways of coping with different problems arising from what Ang and Dahlgren call 'the elusive audience'.

The television audience is in certain respects fundamentally different from, for example, the audience of a theatre performance or of a rock concert. Audience members at the theatre and at the concert can be specified not only in terms of time and location, i.e. we know exactly where and when they attend the event. They also are real individuals who can be observed in person and identified by name, at least in principle. As distinct from this, the audience of a television programme is dispersed over many locations, sometimes all over the world. Normally the members of this audience are anonymous, and we do not know where those who watch are located, when they start and when they stop viewing and how long they attend. The only information we usually get is some sort of ratings statistics. But this information pertains, like all sample-based statistics, only to the *aggregate* of viewers as a whole and cannot be transformed into information about individuals.

Audience research has developed different strategies for coping with these problems. Qualitative approaches avoid conceiving of the audience as an anonymous aggregate and instead look at *individualized viewers*, such as children, housewives, married couples or, frequently, at families in their natural habitat (Lindlof, 1987). Quantitative approaches, on the other hand, focus on *audience variables* which characterize persons as belonging to a specific gender, age cohort, socio-economic class, marriage status or other social category. The focus is on abstract statistical constructs like reach and share, as well as on audience flow and the calculation of rates of audience duplication and audience inheritance (Cooper, 1996; Webster and Phalen, 1997). This looks like a revival of the audience-as-a-mass concept which was developed in the early days of broadcasting (Blumer, 1939), even though empirical findings show remarkable regularities in audience behaviour if aggregated by statistical methods (as illustrated by Figure 7.3 above).

Despite critical questions like those posed by Ang and Dahlgren, the audience as a construct of a collectivity endures in the minds of scholars and in the terminology they use. Even the adherents of qualitative research when speaking, for example, of 'natural audiences' or of 'interpretive communities' refer to the audience as a collectivity. This may be seen as an attempt at reconciling the micro-perspective with common macro-terminology.

Quantitative and qualitatitive approaches have overlapping interests, particularly an interest in understanding and explaining viewer behaviour by 'disaggregating' the mass (Webster and Phalen, 1997: 121) or 'deconstructing' the audience (Lindlof, 1991). In fact, the quantitative–qualitative divide is to a certain degree arbitrary and often overstated. What seems to be an opposition is partly due to a mutual misunderstanding of each other's goals and methods. The best approach to the television audience is a combination of qualitative and quantitative studies. Good scholarship takes advantage of both types of method.

In addition to the micro–macro antagonism and the quantitative–qualitative divide the discourse of audience research is marked by the active–passive duality. There has been an ongoing discussion for decades whether the audiences should be looked at as a passive mass of spectators or as *active* users who make motivated choices on grounds of individual needs and interests. The central terms of this discourse are charged so that active media use is supposed to be 'better' than passive spectatorship (McQuail, 1997: 22). In addition, the active–passive duality is rhetorically linked to the qualitative–quantitative controversy by claims of the adherents of both methodological approaches that each is subscribing to the 'politically correct' concept of an active audience.

Based on these and other terminological oppositions and differentiations a number of audience constructs have been proposed in the research literature, most of which are expressed by an 'audience-as' formula. We have mentioned already the *audience-as-interpretive-community* and the *audience-as-mass* the second of which is sometimes opposed to the *audience-as-public*. Whereas the former two are, although differently, created by mass communication, a public exists already *before* it is addressed by some kind of communication and thus becomes an audience.

Concepts which relate to the interests of both commercial television and advertisers are the *audience-as-market* and the *audience-as-commodity*. McQuail defines the market concept as an 'aggregate of actual or potential consumers of media services and products, with a known socio-economic profile' (McQuail, 1997: 8). Audience markets, specified for instance in terms of socio-demographic or lifestyle categories, are targeted by the managers of TV programming in order to achieve a maximum of share (see Hujanen, Chapter 4). One of the motives behind this strategy is to sell the share of a certain audience market to advertisers.

Media marketing practitioners quite normally assign economic value to the audience and think of an audience as a commodity. The currencies for trading in audiences are CPM, CPP and CPGRP, which refer to the cost to reach 1,000 members of a target audience, to the cost per ratings point and to the cost per gross rating point, respectively (for more details including factors determining the economic value of audiences refer to Webster and Lichty, 1991: Chapter 8; Webster and Phalen, 1997).

There is a concerned debate based on the criticism that market and commodity models increasingly dominate the perspective on television audiences and that commercial interests may jeopardize the traditional values of European broadcasting (Blumler, 1992). Since commercial broadcasting was introduced in most European countries in the 1980s, television has become big business, and so has ratings research. While commercial companies concentrate on the 'bookkeeping' type of quantitative research, most academics retreat to qualititative studies. These developments contributed to the schisms in the field of audience research.

Concerns are also voiced about the future of the audience in light of ongoing changes in the media landscape. New media technologies, like VCRs, cable and direct satellite transmission, seem to have a substantial impact on the formation and behaviour of television audiences. In this respect, the most relevant features of new media are (Webster and Phalen, 1997, 102 ff.):

- Television content is more diverse due to the proliferation of channels and programming.
- Content is correlated with channels due to the introduction of monothematic channels.
- Channels are differentially available due to technological, economic and regulatory factors.

It is widely hypothesized that an increasing *audience fragmentation* will result from these factors. Germany may serve as an example of a television market with a relatively high degree of audience fragmentation (see Figure 7.2 above). As the number of programming choices and the competition among channels have increased, the audience has dispersed over a number of channels. Fragmentation 'does appear to spell the end of the audience as a social collectivity – a formation with the possibility of a shared experience and sense of common belonging' (McQuail, 1997: 133). However, market shares represent the allocation of viewing time on the aggregate level and say hardly anything about the range of individual choices. Take for example 50 viewers and a supply of 50 channels in a cable system. If all viewers spread out their viewing budget over all 50 channels this may generate the same market shares as we would get if each viewer allocated his or her total viewing time to just one channel, but in each case to a different one. Only the latter situation would resemble what McQuail pictures as 'the end of the audience'. Webster and Phalen (1997: 110 ff.) have introduced the term *audience polarization* for such a situation, namely the tendency of individuals to move to the extremes of either consuming or avoiding some channels or some class of media content.

Empirical evidence so far does not bespeak the end of the television audience as a collectivity. As Table 7.1 shows, there are still occasions when the majority of the nation gathers in front of the screen to witness the same media event. Even in a media-rich society like Germany with a growing segment of viewers who practise a high channel repertoire there are yet no indications of audience polarization. Rather than moving to the extremes and concentrating on some channels, while avoiding others, it is typical of the 'avant-garde' viewers to take advantage of the range of choices offered by an expanding television system (Schulz, 2000). As earlier studies have concluded, audience responses to the new media environment seem to be more evolutionary than revolutionary (Becker and Schoenbach, 1989; Neuman, 1992).

ACTIVITIES

1 Find out sources in your country where you can get the results of television ratings measurement. Set up a list of the ten most widely watched single TV programmes of yesterday (or of last week/month/year). Take the 'reach' figures (if available) as the ranking criterion.

- What may have contributed to the high ratings of the top programmes in the list?
- To what degree do these ratings indicate the appreciation of programmes by their audiences?
- How will the rankings change if you substitute the reach figures by market share figures? Can you give reasons for these changes?

2 Set up a table (like Table 7.3 above) for the audience composition of the leading television channels in your country.

In what respect do the composition figures of these channels differ? Can you give reasons for these differences?

3 Observe friends or members of your family while they watch TV.

How attentive or inattentive are they while watching the programme?
Set up a list of activities each person in front of the screen is engaged in while watching television.
Categorize these activities by using the typology proposed by Lull that is displayed in Box 7.2.

SUGGESTIONS FOR FURTHER READING

McQuail, D. (1997) *Audience Analysis*. Thousand Oaks, CA: Sage.

This is a comprehensive overview of audience research which covers both social scientific and humanistic approaches. The author puts special emphasis on theories and concepts of audience analysis. He discusses research traditions as well as ongoing controversies between different schools of audience research.

Webster, J.G. and Phalen, P.F. (1997) *The Mass Audience. Rediscovering the Dominant Model*. Mahwah, NJ: Lawrence Erlbaum.

Focusing on the television audience, this book demonstrates different techniques for analysing mass audience behaviour. The authors discuss concepts of media economics and the role of research in creating the audience commodity. They also consider developments in the new media environment.

III

TELEVISION GENRES: BORDERS AND FLOWS

INTRODUCTION

Jan Wieten

In Part III several of the main themes that have been discussed in previous chapters reappear in the context of studies of particular television genres. Together with Moran's and Laborde and Perrot's chapters in Part II, a wide array of programme genres is covered, from talk shows and soaps to current affairs, and from high art to the clips of music television. But that is necessary, for television is all these things. By taking a closer look at the various concrete ways in which television manifests itself, we may hope to find evidence of the profound transitions that societies in Europe and television itself are going through. In one way or another all the case studies in this section illuminate the general trends that have been pointed out before.

'Borders and flows', the subtitle of this section, points to one of the effects of increased competition in television: the development of new and hybrid programme forms that transcend conventional boundaries between genres in a quest for audiences. In public service broadcasting, information, culture and entertainment consciously used to be kept separate. New hybrid forms – such as the ones for which the term infotainment is often used – raise questions about the consequences of mixing up news and entertainment for the quality of information. Others, on the other hand, expect the market-driven new genres to make relevant information about the world we live in more accessible and understandable for larger groups of people. The case studies in this part should provide a good impression of both old and new programme formats.

In their study of MTV-Europe Keith Roe and Gust De Meyer do not just give an idea of how this European branch of the international music television channel works; they also offer insight into the complex nature of the relationship between the global and the local. The success of MTV is commonly ascribed to the universality of the language of music, and placed in the wider context of the discourse surrounding the globalization of culture. But the reality is less simple. The ideology of cultural homogenization fails to distinguish, as they point out, between globalization of the economy (which is real) and globalization of culture (which is doubtful).

In Europe MTV had to adapt to musical, cultural and linguistic diversity. Spoken language in particular has proved to be a major obstacle to the success of MTV-Europe (and a boost to its regional competitors). The aim of this research is to find out the extent of use of local languages and artists in the four regional services of MTV-Europe. Roe and De Meyer conclude that MTV has been only moderately successful in this respect, as its programming is still dominated by Anglo-American artists and even more by the use of English in songs, although there is more diversity in the languages in which programmes are hosted.

Like Roe and De Meyer in this chapter, Albert Moran's chapter about European adaptations of *The Restless Years* in Part II and Sari Näsi's case study of European television news in Chapter 13 question the rather too naive ideas we may have about cultural globalization.

In a different way culture is also the central issue in Marit Bakke's discussion of 'Arts Television: Questions of Culture' in Chapter 9. But here the tension is between ideas of one 'national' or 'high' culture and European societies that have become multicultural. Bakke looks at the performance of television as a means for the dissemination of art and culture and she points to ways of finding out about it with the help of publicly available data such as policy documents and EBU statistics and classifications.

Seen from a cultural policy perspective, television is an immensely important instrument for reaching people with art (even if the art world itself has strong reservations). It can reach more people than any other means of distributing cultural objects. But dissemination of culture is not the highly estimated, unproblematic task of broadcasting that it used to be. Culture itself has become a controversial concept. It has to do with the dominant values of a society. In a more and more culturally diversified Europe this makes it difficult to operationalize. It is not the only problem that producers of art programmes on television have to face. Competition with commercial broadcasters for audiences, and lower budgets tend to marginalize culture and arts programmes on television. The uncertainty that prevails manifests itself also in experiments with new forms and new styles, and a tendency to 'hide' culture in other programme categories such as news or talk shows.

Perhaps even more problematical are the consequences of a greater dependency on audiences and advertisers in another traditional stronghold of public service broadcasting: news and information. In an increasingly competitive television environment, it may be profitable to popularize the news and to develop formats in which information is made more entertaining. Jan Wieten and Graham Murdock studied two programme categories in the infotainment genre: breakfast television and talk shows.

In Chapter 10 Jan Wieten presents a study of history and presentational styles of commercial and public breakfast television programmes in a number of European countries. Breakfast television is a typical example of an established American commercial television format that was introduced in Europe when commercial broadcasters started to show an interest in the early morning market. Despite its strongly built-in audience orientation, and its mix of information, service and entertainment, there are few signs that the genre as a whole has commercialized since it made its appearance in Europe in the early 1980s. But there is a tendency for public and commercial television to diverge to two different models of making early morning television. The stylistic differences between breakfast magazines and more traditional news programmes indicate that breakfast TV wants to be 'read' differently than the news. But unlike the news, and also unlike other infotainment-type programmes, breakfast television employs many different modes of address within its general warm and friendly framework.

Talk shows have much more popular appeal and have received considerably more attention than breakfast television. A reason may be that talk shows have sometimes been hailed for their openness to everyday experience and for demolishing traditional hierarchies. Like breakfast TV, talk shows originated in America and their spread in Europe has been caused by the extension of broadcast hours and the increased competition for audiences, which put a premium on cheap programming with proven popular appeal. The main types are political talk shows, celebrity talk shows and participatory talk shows. In his analysis in Chapter 11, Graham Murdock is less optimistic about the genre than its ardent supporters. In American talk shows a tendency has been noticed to move from 'personalizing the political' to 'sensationalizing the personal'. That tendency is still less marked in Europe, but it is already clearly noticeable in Britain. Therefore the claim that the talk show genre addresses some key conditions of contemporary democracy better than public service models is highly questionable.

In 'Television Current Affairs: The Case of Northern Ireland' Greg McLaughlin in Chapter 12 analyses British television series about the conflict in Northern Ireland that were made before and after the beginning of the peace process. His conclusion is that there is less difference than one would expect given the changing public consensus about the conflict and the more tolerant atmosphere since Labour came to power. Broadcasting had to function under the double-bind of economic deregulation, which limits the amount of money for programmes, and political regulation, which restricts editorial independence. Public service means to protect against political interference and commercial power, but tolerance for its independence was limited when the security of the state was at stake. Although that has changed, McLaughlin shows that the new situation is hardly better. Economic deregulation has led to a more consumerist orientation, even in public broadcasting. It has shunted television journalism out of controversial political and investigative reporting. Therefore the more recent programmes do not challenge prejudice more than did the ones that were produced before the peace process started. Instead they follow a path that is safe and uncontroversial.

In the last chapter, Sari Näsi analyses national and international news about a truckers' strike in France. This topic gives her a chance to confront theories about the ways in which media report about labour disputes with theories about the globalization and domestication of international news. International news must be anchored in narrative frameworks that can be recognized by local audiences in order to be understood. She finds different patterns of news reporting, but a rather prevalent one in which a purely national bias evaporates the issues involved in the dispute and in which all conflicting parties melt into an amorphous 'them', the French 'bad guys', as opposed to us, 'good guys'.

Together these empirical studies, by their range of topics and the variety of methodological approaches, illustrate, and sometimes even challenge, the more theoretical and general analyses of developments and trends in the first parts of the book. Studies like these are also indispensable building blocks for theories and reflections about the forces at work in television and the media in general. It is our hope that they will stimulate the reader to further probe the contemporary links between television and society.

CHAPTER 8

MUSIC TELEVISION: MTV-EUROPE

Keith Roe and Gust De Meyer

MTV (Music Television) can be viewed wherever in the world satellite-TV reception is possible. However, it is not just because of its global character (which it shares for example with CNN) that MTV is important. MTV is also special because it claims to be different from other channels, to be based on a completely new concept of television and the viewer. In this chapter we shall examine this unique form of television, first by tracing its origins and development, secondly by examining the marketing concept upon which it is based, thirdly by focusing on some of the specific problems faced by MTV-Europe, and finally, on the basis of an empirical study of MTV-Europe's programming, by addressing the question: how European is MTV-Europe?

THE DEVELOPMENT OF MTV

MTV made its début on 1 August 1981 on 225 cable systems reaching 2.1 million households in the United States. Its first ever video clip, 'Video Killed the Radio Star' by Buggles, was clearly intended to be prophetic. By the end of 1983 the channel was available to 18 million American households. As the number of viewers rose, so did advertising revenue, with the result that, after heavy loses in the first two years, MTV became profitable in 1984 and, by 1985, was earning $31 million from revenues of $96 million (Montavelli, 1986; Denisoff, 1988; Banks, 1996).

In 1987, MTV moved across the Atlantic, although it was not the first music video channel to appear on European cable systems, this distinction being held by the short-lived Music Box. Moves into Eastern Europe, Latin America, Asia, Japan and Australasia soon followed, so that by

MTV IN THE UK & IRELAND
SCHEDULE & HIGHLIGHTS • FEBRUARY 8th - 14th '99

Times: 06.00, 08.00, 09.00, 10.00, 11.00, 12.00, 13.00, 14.00, 15.00, 16.00, 17.00, 18.00, 19.00, 20.00, 21.00, 22.00, 23.00, 24.00, 01.00, 02.00, 03.00, 04.00, 05.00

MONDAY 8th	TUESDAY 9th	WEDNESDAY 10th	THURSDAY 11th	FRIDAY 12th	SATURDAY 13th	SUNDAY 14th
MAD 4 HITS	MAD 4 HITS	MAD 4 HITS	MAD 4 HITS	MAD 4 HITS	MAD 4 HITS	MAD 4 HITS
MTV BYTESIZE	MTV BYTESIZE	MTV BYTESIZE	MTV BYTESIZE	MTV BYTESIZE	MTV BYTESIZE	MTV BYTESIZE
HYPE 1.3.99	HYPE 1.3.99	HYPE 1.3.99	HYPE 1.3.99	HYPE 1.3.99	EUROPEAN TOP 20	HIT LIST UK
MAD 4 HITS	MAD 4 HITS	MAD 4 HITS	MAD 4 HITS	MAD 4 HITS	MTV NEWS	MTV NEWS
US TOP 20	HIT LIST UK	EUROPEAN TOP 20	50 '90S	DANCEFLOOR CHART SHOW	GREATEST LOVE SONGS OF THE '90S WEEKEND	GREATEST LOVE SONGS OF THE '90S WEEKEND
MTV BYTESIZE	MTV BYTESIZE	MTV BYTESIZE	MTV BYTESIZE	MTV BYTESIZE	SELECT MTV	UK SINGLED OUT VALENTINE'S EDITION
SELECT MTV	SELECT MTV	SELECT MTV	SELECT MTV	SELECT MTV	MTV NEWS	SELECT MTV
MTV BYTESIZE	MTV BYTESIZE	MTV BYTESIZE	MTV BYTESIZE	MTV NEWS	GREATEST LOVE SONGS OF THE '90S WEEKEND	MTV NEWS
HYPE 1.3.99	HYPE 1.3.99	HYPE 1.3.99	HYPE 1.3.99	UK SINGLED OUT	DANCEFLOOR CHART SHOW	GREATEST LOVE SONGS OF THE '90S WEEKEND
HIT LIST UK	US TOP 20	THE LICK R&B CHART SHOW	EUROPEAN TOP 20	HYPE 1.3.99	MAD 4 HITS	MTV NEWS
MAD 4 HITS	MAD 4 HITS	MAD 4 HITS	MAD 4 HITS	DANCEFLOOR CHART SHOW	MTV NEWS	50 '90's
SAY WHAT?	MTV MEGAMIX	ARTIST CUT	SAY WHAT?	MTV MEGAMIX	BEAVIS & BUTTHEAD DOUBLE BILL	MTV LIVE
MOVIE SPECIAL	SUPER ADVENTURE TEAM	MTV LIVE	THE LATE LICK	MTV NEWS	THE GRIND DOUBLE BILL	HYPE 1.3.99
UK SINGLED OUT	SIFL & OLLY	BIORHYTHM: MIKE TYSON	NON STOP HITS	UK SINGLED OUT	HYPE 1.3.99	THE LATE LICK
NON STOP HITS	NON STOP HITS	NON STOP HITS	MTV UNPLUGGED WITH BRYAN ADAMS	THE GRIND DOUBLE BILL	SATURDAY NIGHT MUSIC MIX	50 '90's
SUPEROCK	ALTERNATIVE NATION	YO!	NIGHT VIDEOS	PARTYZONE	CHILL OUT ZONE	MTV LIVE
MOVIE SPECIAL	SUPER ADVENTURE TEAM	MTV LIVE		MTV NEWS	NIGHT VIDEOS	NIGHT VIDEOS
UK SINGLED OUT	SIFL & OLLY	BIORHYTHM: MIKE TYSON		UK SINGLED OUT		
NIGHT VIDEOS	NIGHT VIDEOS	NIGHT VIDEOS		CLUB MIX		
				MTV MEGAMIX		
				PARTYZONE		
				NIGHT VIDEOS		

GREATEST LOVE SONGS OF THE '90S WEEKEND

HIGHLIGHTS

HIGHLIGHT

GREATEST LOVE SONGS OF THE 90's WEEKEND
13th & 14th February

If your heart's been through the blender or you're floating on butterflies, you won't want to miss this an entire weekend of love songs on MTV. We embrace SAINT VALENTINE, by drip-feeding you with the sweetest, sexiest and most seductive music of all time. So snuggle up with your significant other or grab a pal for a music marathon that you will fall in love with.
of Madonna, Celine Dion, Mariah Carey, Boyzone and many more 'legends of lurve'.
Valentines Day also marks the start of the second series 'Singled Out UK'. Sexy Sarah Cawood and raunchy Richard Blackwood bring people together with an atomic bang.

infonet

SUBJECT TO CHANGE

1995 MTV could claim to reach 320 million households in 90 countries on 5 continents, 24 hours a day (Burnett, 1996), thus fulfilling its early marketing slogan of 'One Planet One Music'.

Box 8.1

MTV's global march

1981	USA	1992	Nigeria
1987	Western Europe	1993	Former Soviet Union
1989	Eastern Europe	1993	Latin America
1990	Brazil	1995	Asia
1990	Israel	1996	India
1992	Japan	1997	Australia + New Zealand

Source: Bekaert, 1998a

In the early 1990s MTV was the fastest growing cable and satellite channel in Europe, with distribution growing from 2.2 million households in 1987, through 20 million in 1990, to 56 million in 1996 (Bekaert, 1998a). Initially, the general format of MTV-Europe copied that of the parent American station. Later, however, this was perceived to be a mistake (see Roe and Wallis, 1989; Burnett, 1990) and efforts were made to adapt its content and style to the European context.

Box 8.2

The growth of MTV-Europe

Year	Number of subscriber households (millions)
1987	2.2
1988	6.8
1989	11.9
1990	20.0
1991	32.5
1992	43.0
1993	58.0
1994	60.0
1995	51.6
1996	56.0

Source: Bekaert, 1998a

THE CONCEPT OF MUSIC TELEVISION

According to one of its creators, Robert W. Pittman (1990), MTV was specifically conceived and designed for the generation of *TV babies* because, having grown up with television, they communicate, process information, and form ideas in ways different from those of their parents. Pittman argued that, while the latter are 'the one thing at a time' generation, the TV babies by contrast, 'really can do their homework, watch television, talk on the phone and listen to the radio all at the same time'; simultaneously processing information from each source into a different cluster of thoughts. Moreover, he observed, they seem to perceive visual messages better and they can *read* a picture and understand body language at a glance. The task for television makers, he concluded, was to learn to speak the language of this television generation.

After extensive market research the grammar of this 'new language' was seen as the integration of television and rock music in the now well established music-video clip format. As Hartman (1987: 19) pointed out, this potent mix had long been used in TV commercials (and, more recently, in longer music videos), 'but not in as dynamic a fashion and not with such spectacular results as MTV achieved in penetrating the youth and young-adult market'. Moreover, such an integration promised solutions to perceived problems in both the television and the music industry. At that time, contemporary music radio was losing its audience (Straw, 1988), the recording industry was in a recession (Burnett, 1990), and TV producers had always been comparatively unsuccessful in reaching the notoriously elusive 12–34 age group. The basic original format of MTV was based on that of Top 40 radio programming (indeed another of MTV's founders, John Lacke, called MTV 'visual radio'), with planned song rotation (Roe and Wallis, 1989). However, after some audience decline in the mid-1980s, MTV reduced its dependence on the standard music video clip in favour of more general lifestyle programming.

The main purpose of MTV is to deliver a particular audience segment to advertisers (for more on this kind of strategy see Chapters 1 and 4 of this volume). According to one of MTV-Europe's earliest publicity brochures,

> Audience research surveys prove that MTV-Europe delivers the audiences advertisers want to reach . . . Nobody reaches the elusive affluent 16–34 audience like MTV . . . MTV re-writes the rules of European advertising . . . Now advertisers can hit the 16–34 age group with MTV's laser-sharp targeting . . . MTV reaches its viewers all over Europe with consistent clarity. It's about the cars they drive, the clothes they wear, the foods they fuel themselves with, MTV is their choice. (Roe and Wallis, 1989: 37)

In order to fulfil this promise to deliver a particular youth market to particular advertisers, everything on MTV – from the looks and presentation style of the VJs (video jockeys) to the music, and the videos themselves –

must fit into the narrow-casting description of what is perceived to appeal to this audience group, namely a non-stop, on tap, creation of moods, feelings and emotions within a youth culture lifestyle that viewers can buy into (Savage, 1987; Burnett, 1990). In other words, MTV programme content and advertising become to a large extent indistinguishable.

As a result of its success MTV also had a profound effect on the whole recording music industry. Suddenly artists and labels felt themselves required to produce sophisticated, expensive music videos in order to promote their products. Consequently, according to some observers, music video has not necessarily been an unqualified blessing for the recording industry, especially since there is little firm evidence that music videos actually lead to increased sales of recordings; or that they make any economic sense at all. Moreover, some artists are concerned that music television has resulted in the domination of visual images of 'pretty people' at the expense of musical talent (Burnett, 1996); a domination which, according to some critics, has also led to the reinforcement of racial and sexual stereotypes (Brown and Campbell, 1986; Kaplan, 1987; Seidman, 1992).

THE MTV AUDIENCE

Although there have been many studies of MTV, the great majority have dealt with the content and style of the channel (usually in terms of its alleged racist, sexist and postmodern character) rather than with its audience (see, for example, Baxter et al. 1985; Caplan, 1985; Aufderheide, 1986; Elg and Roe, 1986; Sherman and Dominick, 1986; Hansen and Hansen, 1990; Hansen and Krygowski, 1994; Tapper et al., 1994; McKee and Pardun, 1999).

In an early study of the American audience Sun and Lull (1986) identified the importance of the visual aspect of music videos (combined with a generalized attraction to the musical content of MTV) as central to their appeal. They also found the main motives for viewing to be entertainment, information, social interaction (talking about videos with friends), and the fact that videos assisted in the interpretation of lyrics. Meanwhile, Brown, Campbell and Fischer reported that, by that time, 'music videos already have become an important part of the American adolescent's pattern of media use' (1986: 28). In their study, the primary motivations for viewing were entertainment, diversion and filling time, social interaction, and to receive instruction on how to dance and what to wear to be fashionable. However, the fact that significant racial and gender differences were found suggested that different adolescent sub-groups use videos for different reasons, a conclusion which was supported by Brown and Schulze's (1990) finding that audience interpretations of music videos vary according to race, gender and *fandom*.

Box 8.3

Reasons for watching MTV

Entertainment	Relaxation
Social interaction	Relieving boredom
Information	Passing time
Interpreting lyrics	Mood control

Correlates of MTV-use
Age
Gender
Ethnicity
Socio-economic status
School achievement

In Europe, the Swedish audience for the music videos on Music Box and Sky Channel was studied by Roe and Lövgren (1988). They found that music video TV was already being used on a daily basis by the majority of adolescents in cabled areas. On weekdays, the average time per day spent watching music videos was just under an hour, rising to about 1.25 hours at weekends, although there were some gender differences in this respect. The main motivations for use were found to be passing the time, listening to lyrics, facilitating social activity, and mood control. They also found that school achievement and commitment to school were related to music video use, with low achieving adolescents with a negative attitude to school watching significantly more (cf. Roe, 1985, 1992, 1993, 1994).

In a study of Flemish adolescents (aged 12-18 years) Roe and Cammaer (1993) found high levels of familiarity with MTV contents. Less than 2 per cent of respondents stated that they knew nothing about MTV, while 73 per cent were able to name at least five MTV programmes. 26 per cent watched the channel on a daily basis, with a further 16 per cent watching at least every other day, and only 10 per cent reporting never watching MTV (and of these, one-third were unable to receive the channel). There was a tendency for frequency of viewing to increase with age, mainly as a result of falling levels of non-viewing. However, most MTV use was found to be unplanned and erratic with viewers zapping in and out of the channel on a regular basis. Further evidence that MTV was regarded as an 'on tap' resource for unplanned viewing was supported by the fact that few ever bothered to use a VCR to record specific MTV programmes. As in other studies, significant gender (and here socio-economic status) differences were found with respect to most aspects of MTV use.

In this Flemish study, the strongest motive for watching MTV was 'to hear the music'. Next came 'relaxation', 'to relieve boredom', 'for information', and 'to be able to talk to others about it', in that order. Attitudes to MTV were generally positive. When asked to rate MTV in terms of seven pairs of positive and negative adjectives, on every dimension the mean fell on the positive side of the scale. MTV was rated most positively in terms of being cool, novel, exciting, and amusing. However, there was less consensus with regard to the musical balance of MTV. Only in one case was there a clear majority opinion: namely, that there was too much rap on MTV. For other music types opinion was more divided and it was concluded that, given the diversity of musical tastes, MTV could do no more than please most of the people some of the time (Roe and Cammaer, 1993).

MTV-EUROPE CONFRONTED BY LINGUISTIC AND CULTURAL DIVERSITY

Although its growth in terms of household connection figures has been spectacular, MTV-Europe did not enjoy the same immediate financial success as the American parent company and has always suffered from the problem of adapting the channel to the musical, cultural, and linguistic diversity of the continent.

Initially, MTV tackled the problem of satisfying the heterogeneity of music tastes among its audience by putting together varied play lists and strict application of the '5 minute rule', which works on the principle that if the viewer doesn't like what's on at any particular moment, s/he knows that in five minutes time something else will come along. The main problem for MTV-Europe was that, in the vast majority of cases, even this 'something else' tended to be American, leading to accusations that MTV was trying to steamroller Europe with American music and that, in reality, globalization merely meant Americanization. From the beginning MTV-Europe has denied this charge, claiming that it wanted to pay more attention to the European music scene, but that the real problem was the insufficient number of quality European music videos being produced (Roe and Wallis, 1989).

Since MTV-Europe is dependent on the international music industry for its programme content (for example, music-video clips), it has always been forced to operate within the structural and economic parameters set by that industry, in particular its Anglo-American dominance. Thus, even when MTV-Europe attempted to reduce its dependence on American music, non-American tended in practice to mean British, with the result that in the early years of MTV-Europe, Anglo-American music accounted for 83 per cent of the videos in the total playlist (Burnett, 1990).

Given the world-wide popularity of Anglo-American music, this in itself does not pose too much of a problem for MTV-Europe. However, it does tend to exacerbate the second cultural problem with which any trans-national channel in Europe is inevitably confronted, namely, the continents' linguistic diversity.

Initially, MTV-Europe decided to concentrate on English as its main language because it was perceived to be the most widely spoken, especially among young people. Early experiments with programmes in other

languages (for instance, Dutch) had merely led to complaints from viewers in other areas. Moreover, language was regarded as of secondary importance compared to the universal language of (Anglo-American) popular music. There is evidence that MTV-Europe's early (American) programmers overestimated the level of comprehension of English among young people on the continent (Roe and Wallis, 1989). However, since the programme format consisted almost entirely of music videos interspersed by minimal '5 minute rule' links from VJs, language continued to be perceived as unproblematic.

For a time research tended to support this view. For example, even in language-conscious Flanders, the majority of Roe and Cammaer's (1993) 12–18-year-old respondents did not perceive language to be a problem on MTV-Europe, with 20 per cent claiming to understand all, and 52 per cent most of the English spoken on the channel and only 24 per cent stating that they would watch more MTV if there were more programmes in Dutch (the language of Flanders).

But subsequent developments have undermined these assumptions. Firstly, after suffering problems of audience fatigue similar to those earlier experienced by the parent American station, MTV-Europe followed the latter's policy of reducing the predominance of the video-clip rotation format in favour of other, more talk-based types of programming. However, this resulted not only in greater demands being made on viewers' language comprehension, but to a growing perception that MTV was becoming just another entertainment channel and in danger of losing its special music identity, leading to the cancellation of some non-music programming (*Music and Copyright*, 1997: 123).

Second and far more seriously, the launch of the German language music television station VIVA in one of MTV-Europe's most important markets brought direct competition for advertising revenue. VIVA was set up by four international record companies (PolyGram, EMI, Sony and Warner) in October 1993 and began transmission two months later. By 1997, VIVA was reaching 22 million homes in Germany, Austria and Switzerland, could be received in 96 per cent of German cabled households, and had become more popular than MTV-Europe in its home territories (*Music and Copyright*, 1997: 117). A year later VIVA had further increased its audience in Germany by 26 per cent and was being watched by an estimated 3.9 million viewers a day (6.9 per cent of the German population aged 14-plus), compared to 2.7 million for MTV (*Music and Copyright*, 1998: 142). In the wake of its success a sister channel (VIVA2) was launched early in 1995 to cater for an older age group (as a competitor to MTV's adult music channel VH-1). It too was successful, reaching 63 per cent of all German cabled homes within two years.

VIVA's formula was not only based on having its VJs speak German rather than English. The management policy of having a quota of German music of 40 per cent for VIVA and 30 per cent for VIVA2 appears to have struck a positive chord with the audience, as well as having stimulated domestic production of records and video clips (*Music and Copyright*, 1997: 117).

It was not long before the success of VIVA called forth imitators in other countries. In the Netherlands, for example, TMF (The Music Factory) was launched in May 1995 and, like VIVA in Germany, it soon displaced MTV-Europe as the most popular music television station in its domestic market (*Het Nieuwsblad*, 12 September 1998). The policy of TMF is to feature Dutch VJs who put a lot of emphasis on Dutch musical products and, like VIVA, it works with a 40 per cent quota of domestic video clips. As a result the number of Dutch hits in the national hit parade has risen steadily in the past three years (http://www.tmf.be).

In October 1998, urged on by its success in the Netherlands, TMF established a separate Flemish service (TMF-Vlaanderen) based on the same formula of trying to reflect national tastes and promote local artists and, once again, the formula proved to be successful (Sobemap, 1998). MTV-Europe has admitted that the success of these national imitators (and of VIVA, in particular), forced it to rethink its structure and programming strategy. Its response, in March 1996, was to create three zones of regionalized programming: central, northern and southern, followed in July 1997 by a separate UK/Ireland service.

This regional expansion strategy involved variations in both musical and linguistic content. MTV-UK has a very British character and is dominated by Anglo-American music. MTV-Central is aimed primarily at German speaking Europe (although it can also be seen in Eastern Europe), with a large number of programmes being presented in that language and 20–25 per cent of the video clips featuring local artists. MTV-Southern targeted Italy, where MTV-Europe had always been weak. After its relaunch in September 1997, it contained a substantial number of programmes in Italian and 30–35 per cent of the video clips reportedly feature local artists

(Bekaert, 1998b). Within a few months it had become available to 75 per cent of the Italian population. In France and Spain, however, expansion has proved far more difficult. Levels of cable and satellite penetration remain low in both countries and France has laws specifying language content quotas for television. Consequently, MTV has been more interested in creating more local programming for the Netherlands and Scandinavia than increasing its reach in France (*Music and Copyright*, 1997: 123). For example, recently the daily show *Nordic Top 5*, consisting of nothing but music produced in Sweden, Denmark, Norway and Finland, was created. According to MTV, 'the really exciting thing with this show is that for the first time we can give room for artists singing in their native language' (http://www.mtve.com).

MTV-Northern was designed to cover the areas not served by the other three and can be received in 25 European and three non-European (Egypt, Israel and South Africa) countries. As a result of this diversity (and notwithstanding developments such as *Nordic Top 5*), it lacks any real profile and remains English language based and Anglo-American dominated (Bekaert, 1998b).

MTV AND GLOBALIZATION

The experience of MTV-Europe can be placed in the context of the contemporary discourse surrounding the globalization of culture. Globalization refers to 'the idea that the world is becoming one place as opposed to a myriad of relatively independent, different and faraway places' (Riley and Monge, 1998: 355). Proponents of this theory claim that technologies such as communications satellites cut across local and national cultures, thereby stimulating the creation of a global community sharing common values and lifestyles. Conversely, critics claim that the theory of globalization underestimates the resilience of local identity and cultural differences. (Waisbord, 1998).

In part these differences of perception result from a failure to differentiate the undoubted commodification of the global *economy* from the empirically far more dubious homogenization of global *culture*. The fact that transnational corporations seek to promote an *ideology* of cultural homogenization should not, as Wheeler (1998) argued, deceive us into believing that this desire automatically and uniformly results in shared feelings of cultural community or conformity to a single shared global identity transcending differences rooted in local and national cultures. In other words, it is necessary to avoid flattening out the concept of global culture, of reducing it merely to common patterns of commodity consumption. As Wheeler asked sarcastically, 'Does global culture mean the whole world loves McDonald's cheeseburgers and Mickey Mouse? Do the foundations of global community involve everyone in the world watching CNN . . . and in English?' (1998: 361).

And, we may add, watching MTV – and in English?

In fact, the case of MTV demonstrates that the concept of the globalization of culture is multidimensional, involving complex, sometimes contradictory, forms of cultural hybridity (cf. Tomlinson, 1999). On one level it is a spectacular example of the validity of the globalization thesis in that it uses contemporary technology to deliver essentially the same product (predominantly British–American music video clips) and the same commodity advertisements (cola, sports shoes, jeans, etc.) to the same demographic group all over the world – and it has (until now at least) been financially successful in this enterprise. On another level, however, the experience of MTV has been an excellent illustration of the limitations of the globalization idea. Confronted by European cultural and linguistic diversity, MTV has been forced to retreat from its original 'One Planet One Music' (and 'one language') concept. Moreover, espousing as it does the ideology of globalization, MTV did not compromise willingly with such diversity – it was not until competition from local music television stations began hitting viewing figures (and thereby advertising revenue and profits) that anything but lip-service was paid to the idea of regionalizing European services to cater for local variations.

However, as we have seen, while regionalization has been successful in areas (such as Italy) where the service was previously weak, in areas such as Germany and the Low Countries, where local competition has been effective, MTV-Europe still lags behind in popularity. If the universal language of music has been unable fully to deliver global homogenization, then it is difficult to see how other types of services can hope to succeed except in a very limited superficial sense. Significantly, in September 1997, CNN also adopted a regionalized structure designed to deliver specific services to different parts of the world.

HOW EUROPEAN IS MTV-EUROPE?

The question we may be permitted to ask, then, is: does MTV-Europe's regional policy represent a genuine attempt to cater for the local tastes and cultural and linguistic diversity of the continent, or is it merely a cosmetic attempt to cover the standard Anglo-American 'global' product with a local gloss? In order to address this question the results of a content analysis of the programming of MTV-Europe's four regional services will be presented. Specifically, we shall examine the extent to which the four main regional services of MTV-Europe feature local languages and artists. It was hypothesized that, although there would be significant differences between them in these respects, all would remain dominated by Anglo-American music.

Between November 1998 and February 1999 one week was randomly chosen for each service during which, on each day, a different 3–4 hour block was recorded between 12.00 and 24.00 hours. The design involved coding the music, non-music, and advertising content of each of the services in terms of musical genre, language employed, and the geographical origin of the artists featured. In cases where the latter was unknown, secondary sources such as the Internet were used.

RESULTS

Programmes (excluding advertising spots) were first coded as consisting mostly of non-stop video clips, non-music, or mixed. The results (see Table 8.1) indicate that, while MTV-UK and MTV-Southern are remarkably similar in their make-up, there appears to be wide variation between MTV-Northern and MTV-Central, with non-music programming most common on the former and non-stop video clips featuring most on the latter.

Music genres were coded and then grouped into more general categories. Once again some variation between the four services appears (see Table 8.2). Mainstream pop is the largest category on UK and Northern, dominates on Southern, and comes a very poor second on Central. Black music, on the other hand, dominates Central, comes second on UK and Northern, and is comparatively infrequent on Southern. Dance music appears most often on Northern and Southern, while rock can be seen most on UK. Finally, it is worth noting that, added together, pop and rock top 50 per cent on all the services except Central.

Given the concern traditionally expressed over the dominance of British–American music on MTV, the geographical origin of the artists was coded. The results (see Table 8.3) clearly indicate that this imbalance continues, with artists from the British Isles and North America together topping 90 per cent on UK and reaching 85 per cent on Northern, 80 per cent on Central and 73 per cent on Southern. Central is the most American dominated and Southern the least while, not surprisingly, British artists can be found most on UK (where, however, they still underscore Americans). In line with the regionalization policy, Italian and German artists feature to some extent on their respective services. Beyond this, only Swedish and to a lesser extent French and Australian artists manifest any consistent presence across the four services.

Examining the language in which the songs were sung we find an even greater domination of English, with 100 per cent of artists on UK and Northern singing in that language, compared to 93 per cent and 87 per cent respectively on Central and Southern. Clearly, given the results in Table 8.3, a number of artists from these countries (and all of those from Sweden) sing in English rather than in their native tongue.

TABLE 8.1 Music and non-music programmes on MTV-Europe (%)

Programme type	**Service**			
	UK	**Northern**	**Central**	**Southern**
Non-stop video clips	48	22	66	46
Mixed	26	28	21	27
Non-music	26	50	13	27

TABLE 8.2 Different types of music on MTV-Europe (%)

Music type	**Service**			
	UK	**Northern**	**Central**	**Southern**
Mainstream pop	33.5	38.6	14.7	45.7
Rock	23.8	12.7	9.9	17.3
Black music (rap, hip-hop, etc.)	33.0	29.4	63.7	11.7
Dance	8.1	18.3	11.4	18.8
Other	1.6	1.0	0.4	6.6

TABLE 8.3 Geographical origin of the artists featured on MTV (%)

Origin artists	**Service**			
	UK	**Northern**	**Central**	**Southern**
North America	49.7	49.7	65.1	36.1
British Isles	41.5	35.9	15.5	36.6
France	1.6	3.6	3.6	1.0
Germany	0.5	1.0	11.1	3.1
Spain	–	0.5	0.4	–
Italy	–	1.0	–	16.5
Netherlands	–	1.0	–	–
Belgium	–	0.5	–	–
Sweden	3.3	5.1	2.8	2.1
Denmark	–	0.5	–	0.5
Iceland	–	–	0.4	–
Australia	1.6	1.0	0.8	3.1
Other	1.6	–	–	1.0

In line with the regional strategy, however, the language in which programmes were hosted, as well as in advertisements, manifested greater linguistic variation (see Table 8.4). Thus, although English continues to dominate UK and Northern, German dominates Central, and Italian (to a lesser extent) is the main language of Southern. Otherwise, only occasional advertisements in French and Dutch were found.

Finally, given the discussion surrounding the globalization of commodities referred to above, the advertisements appearing on the four MTV-Europe services were coded with reference to the products featured. The

TABLE 8.4 Language of programmes and advertisements on MTV (%)

Language	Service			
	UK	Northern	Central	Southern
English	100	83	17	27
German	–	–	83	–
Italian	–	–	–	67
French	–	7	–	6
Dutch	–	10	–	–

TABLE 8.5 Types of product advertised on MTV-Europe (%)

	Service			
	UK	Northern	Central	Southern
CDs	19.4	5.4	24.3	12.0
Cosmetics	24.2	6.9	14.5	19.5
Films	18.5	15.8	13.8	12.7
PC/Internet	–	13.6	8.0	5.9
Leisure/sportswear	–	23.4	1.6	9.9
Soft drinks/junk food	9.7	2.1	11.3	7.6
Beer/alcohol	6.8	0.7	0.4	5.5
Electrical	10.6	2.2	2.3	7.9
Motor vehicles	–	8.2	1.2	2.2
Banks	2.9	–	2.0	–
Telephone	2.0	–	5.7	6.9
Jewellery/watches	–	7.2	1.6	7.7
Local events	–	11.1	–	2.4
Furniture	–	–	6.9	–
Food (general)	5.8	3.2	1.2	–
Magazines	–	–	4.8	–

results (see Table 8.5), while showing some variation across the regions, do indicate that certain types of commodities tend to dominate MTV-Europe's advertising with, in each case, one category accounting for 20–25 per cent of advertising spots. Moreover, the top three products on UK, Central and Southern are the same (CDs, cosmetics and films). Overall, five types of product – CDs, cosmetics, films, leisure/sportswear, and PC/Internet – account for about 62 per cent of MTV-Europe's advertising spots. Finally, it is worth noting that MTV-UK featured the narrowest range of products, and had the least amount of advertising.

These results can be summarized as follows: 82 per cent of the video clips analysed featured British–American artists and 95 per cent of the lyrics were in English. The advertisements seen on MTV-Europe, too, show a remarkable degree of homogeneity, with four types of product (CDs, cosmetics, films, and leisure/sportswear) dominating. Only the dominant spoken language showed substantial variation: English on UK and Northern, German on Central, and Italian on Southern.

CONCLUSION

The purpose of this chapter was to examine the development and current status of music television in Europe. We noted that MTV is based on an original concept of television and the viewer, a concept based on the assumption that a certain type of content appeals universally to young people everywhere. However, in Europe, MTV's global aspirations have been confronted and constrained by the cultural and linguistic diversity of the continent. At first, MTV-Europe resisted any compromise with this diversity, but subsequently the emergence of local competition in a number of important markets forced MTV-Europe to split its programming into four main regional units designed better to represent local languages and music cultures.

The question then addressed was whether this policy of regionalization represents a genuine attempt to accommodate European linguistic and cultural diversity, or whether it is merely a strategy designed to camouflage the continuing globalization and homogenization of music and commodity consumption. To examine this issue a comparative content analysis of MTV-Europe's four regional services was conducted.

The results indicate that, while MTV-Central and MTV-Southern have indeed abandoned English as their dominant spoken language, in the origins of the artists and the language of the songs purveyed by MTV-Europe, nothing appears to have changed: 10 years ago 83 per cent of the video clips on MTV-Europe featured British or American artists; today that figure is 82 per cent. Even on MTV-Central and MTV-Southern, German and Italian artists account for only 11 per cent and 17 per cent, respectively, of video clips. Moreover, the fact that 95 per cent of the artists in our study sang in English indicates that some choose that language in preference to their own, presumably in order to increase their chances of receiving international playtime. In terms of its advertising, too, MTV-Europe manifests a very narrow range of products, with five types accounting for over 60 per cent of all advertising spots.

Given these results, we can conclude that it is spoken language (rather than musical tastes) which has proved to be the main obstacle to the success of MTV-Europe. Moreover, despite its regional strategy, own-language rivals continue to out-compete MTV-Europe in a number of important markets, enabling them to target audiences for advertising more effectively. Given all of these developments, it is expected that MTV-Europe will be forced to continue its policy of regional differentiation. In particular, it is likely that the polyglot MTV-Northern service, currently lacking any real profile (and containing the most non-music content), will be carved up into separate segments, with the Nordic area and Dutch speaking Europe the leading candidates for further autonomy. Whether this will result in more Nordic and Dutch/Flemish artists singing in their native languages rather than in English, however, remains to be seen.

ACKNOWLEDGEMENT

The authors would like to express their thanks to Michele Bekaert for her assistance in the preparation of this chapter.

ACTIVITIES

1 Analyse the content of the music programmes on general public and commercial television stations.

- Compare these music programmes with the content of your MTV service.
- Where they exist, analyse the content of the specialist music TV stations that compete directly with MTV. Compare their content to that of your MTV service.
- Compare the hit parade of your country with the video-clip play lists on MTV and on other competing music TV stations.

2 Discuss the relationship between linguistic and cultural diversity on the one hand and universal content appeals on the other.

SUGGESTIONS FOR FURTHER READING

Banks, J. (1996) *Monopoly Television: MTV's Quest to Control the Music*. Boulder, CO: Westview Press.

Banks, J. (1997) 'MTV and the globalization of popular culture', *Gazette*, 59 (1): 43–60.

The central theme of both is that of MTV as a globalising force intended to take control of the music.

Burnett, R. (1996) *The Global Jukebox*. London: Routledge.

General overview concerning musical globalization, especially documented with facts and viewpoints about MTV.

Denisoff, S.R. (1988) *Inside MTV*. New Brunswick, NJ: Transaction Books.

A critical examination of the history, programming policy, advertising and general ideology of MTV.

Morley, D. and Robins, K. (1995) *Spaces of Identity: Global Media Electronic Landscapes, and Cultural Boundaries*. London: Routledge.

Globalization and local cultural identity and the impact of the electronic media in general.

Tomlinson, J. (1999) *Globalization and Culture*. Cambridge: Polity Press.

Most recently published comprehensive overview of the theory of cultural globalization, which is regarded as involving complex and sometimes contradictory forms of hybridity.

CHAPTER 9

ARTS TELEVISION: QUESTIONS OF CULTURE

Marit Bakke

> There really is a mission for cultural and arts programmes. Television is the active, border-crossing 'Encyclopedia' or 'New Museum' of the day which in many ways, and not the least through broadcasting programmes on the art and culture, can help to orient the cultural context for the next decades in a direction that could suit us a bit more. (Hermans, 1988)

> our culture is sliding into a culture of spectacle. Media and spectacle-orientated performances and events with reference to art create a negative energy, turning art into an 'art event', a spectacle to be consumed for and by everyone. The attention for art roused by spectacle is bad since it is not founded on content, but on the effect of its media existence. I contest the idea that all these media operations 'serve' art, resulting in an increase of real interest for art for more and more people. (Vercruysse, 1992)

> Culture and the media are inextricably bound together: the media reflect images of ourselves and our acts. We are bombarded by images and words every day, and we possess a myriad of tools which allow us to communicate. In much of the world television has become the primary vehicle for culture. All cultural policies must accordingly take into account the impact and importance of the media. How can we ensure that in every country, the media provide diversified programmes which not only promote a shared national identity but also give pluralistic expression to the variety of social, political and cultural values? (UNESCO, 1998)

The traditional cultural institutions of Europe have been theatres, concert halls, museums, art galleries, book stores and libraries – places to visit. The expansion of printed and later of electronic mass media has made it possible for the art objects and cultural events in these locations to be distributed in other, more extensive public arenas, helping to create what André Malraux called, in a memorable phrase, 'a museum without walls'. They translated geographical places into symbolic spaces. Public service broadcasting (PSB) in particular has often been characterized as a universal arena for the dissemination of culture in addition to news, information and entertainment. However, presenting arts and culture on TV is not a

PLATE 9.1 **Michael Sandle, *A Mighty Blow for Freedom/Fuck the Media*, 1988.**

Bronze, 300 × 130 × 220 cm. Photo by M. Sandle, reproduced courtesy of the artist.

Sandle (b. 1936) is a British sculptor who has lived and worked in Germany since 1973. He is noted for his dramatic but ominous bronze sculptures and public monuments which use allegorical figures and symbolism in order to explore such serious themes as war, dealth, violence and capitalist decay. Sandle's contempt for the modern electronic media – which he equates with manipulation, propaganda and mediocrity – is clear in this bronze: a surreal, over life-size female figure with 'a tremendous torque in the torso' smashes a TV set with great ferocity. (It seems the artist once destroyed his own TV set in a fit of anger prompted by poor picture reception and the triviality of the programmes.) In Sandle's view, the art of sculpture should 'not let itself be misused as an adjunct to the entertainment industry'.

Sandle's gesture of protest does not alter the fact that the fine arts still have to function within a culture dominated by the mass media, nor does it alter the fact that artists are embroiled in the mass media whether they like it or not (artists are profiled in magazines and TV arts programmes; documentary films are made about them and they are interviewed in the press and on radio; their works are recorded in photographs; and their exhibitions are advertised). As those who kick in their TV screens soon discover, the loss of a few sets has virtually no impact on the institution of television.

straightforward matter. The quotes at the beginning of this chapter express a range of views on the relationship between mass media and the field of culture and the arts. Plate 9.1 (from Walker, 1994: 16) represents one artist's view of the artistic potential that television has to offer.

Of course, there are other, perhaps more urgent, questions which could be asked as European nation states become more and more multiethnic, and consequently multicultural, on the one hand, and at the same time develop increasingly supranational forms of cooperation. Questions such as: whose art and which culture are we talking about? In previous chapters Brants and De Bens and Dahlgren have sketched the changing frameworks within which television and culture meet and interact. In the context of this chapter we focus on a rather more specific issue: how television operates as a means for the dissemination of art and the products of cultural work. Also we look at how to find out about television's performance in this field with the help of publicly available data taken from official policy documents and the programme classifications and statistics of the European Broadcasting Union (EBU). We are focusing here on the possibilities and limitations of EBU data in relation to art and culture in television, but the general principles would apply to the use of such data in other areas as well.

Although the written and visual quotes at the beginning of the chapter cannot be taken as proof of a general tendency, it may nevertheless be significant that broadcasters are more likely to see the mass media as a valid and valued means of cultural dissemination than people in the arts world. These conflicting evaluations can be partly explained by the different conceptions in each field of what culture is and by differences of opinion about the suitability of television as a medium for promoting culture. The changing character of broadcasting, from primarily being regarded as a cultural institution to a more and more market-driven institution during the 1980s, may be another explanatory factor for the more negative attitude in the world of the arts. Syvertsen (1991: 344) relates the changes in broadcasting to 'a more general social trend whereby "culture" is gradually losing out to "business"' (see also Dahlgren, Chapter 2 in this volume). Both the arts and the mass media are established social institutions within modern societies. Although their relationship is sometimes infused with mistrust, and may even be characterized by a sense of superiority of one sector over the other, more often they cooperate in order to distribute art works or to create media products with a particular artistic touch.

This chapter thus addresses two basic questions: (1) To what extent can television be seen as a cultural institution and as a means for the dissemination of culture? (2) How is television dealing with the task of being a cultural institution? The answers to these questions will vary with different goals for culture policy as well as for media policy, with different definitions of culture and with varying opinions in the arts and media field about potentials and problems in the arts/culture and mass media relationship.

CULTURE AND BROADCASTING

As pointed out by Peter Dahlgren in Chapter 2, mass media, and public service broadcasting in particular, are in a stage of transition. The overall diversity of television is being challenged by ideological forces, by commercialization, and by transnationalization. Less popular cultural forms and informational programming are being marginalized. The public service idea in broadcasting has been discussed traditionally from a cultural policy perspective. It has been seen as a means to secure so-called external benefits, that is, to take care of certain collective needs in a democratic society. From this viewpoint broadcasting appears as a key arena for the production and distribution of cultural goods in the shape of programmes about drama, music, handicraft, literature and architecture. Contributing to preserving the cultural heritage, enhancing cultural identity, and encouraging the creation of new cultural objects is seen as part of broadcasting's obligation to treat its audience as citizens.

The external benefits of culture goods may then be listed as follows (Heilbrun and Gray, 1993: 205–209):

1 *Availability*: Certain culture goods should be available regardless of whether or not individuals are using them all the time or not, e.g. public libraries;
2 *Legacy* for future generations (cultural heritage);
3 *National identity and prestige* – local and national identity as well as national prestige abroad;
4 Contribution to *liberal education* and arts participation;
5 Encouragement for *artistic innovation* which, in turn, can add to the cultural heritage.

In most European countries these external benefits have been seen as important goals for culture and media policy.

Electronic and print media's production and distribution systems definitely offer possibilities for making cultural goods plentiful, cheap and widely available. However, these features are exactly that those parts of the arts community regard as detrimental to the quality and status of the arts. Mass production, they argue, imposes a special format on cultural goods, and mass distribution takes away the genuine aesthetic experiences that an immediate listening, watching or reading of cultural objects offers. Thus, it is argued, the mass media turn the cultural world into an instrument of the cultural industry.

The challenge for the cultural and art world is to consider the potential which modern electronic media offer. Should they be met with scepticism in Vercruysse's terms or with enthusiasm in Herman's terms? Let us take music as an example. Music is presented in a variety of public arenas: concert halls and festivals for live performances by symphony orchestras, chamber music ensembles, groups and soloists; radio and TV broadcasting which can reach a large audience; music videos, CDs and records which can be rented or bought. Among these arenas, national broadcasting is the only one that provides universal distribution, making it the most accessible 'concert hall'. The record industry's advantage is that it offers a wide selection of music, but access depends on the location of record stores and on how expensive the records are. A concert hall, represents the least accessible arena for listening to music.

Seen from an audience's perspective of easy access to cultural goods, public broadcasting appears to be the best-suited arena. First, technically, both radio and television can reach nationwide audiences. Secondly, more people with medium to low education than with high education watch television. Thus television has a potential for reaching people who are not regularly attending traditional cultural arenas like theatre performances, concerts and art galleries.

However, television as an art arena becomes problematic if we look at it from the perspective of the arts and cultural world. Television and art, the latter with connotations of creativity, complexity and individuality, would seem to be two completely different worlds. The specific characteristics of electronic mass media are prone to put certain restrictions on content. At a general level as Gaye Tuchman (1983: 336) has argued, mass media are *distribution* systems for popular culture rather than *production* systems for 'high culture'. A consequence may be the one indicated by Vercruysse, that mass media are spectacle oriented, leaving out what some have called 'genuine' art.

Seen from a cultural policy perspective, the current situation within the cultural field as well as within the world of television offers two challenges. The first one implies a choice between 'policies designed to reinvigorate public communications systems, which are relatively independent of both the state and the market, and policies which aim to marginalize or eradicate them' (Murdock, 1992: 18). The aim should be to broaden the cultural communication system. That is, to make artistic and cultural objects available to other audience groups than the ones that use the traditional cultural institutions. Thus electronic media, and particularly television, should be seen as a means for the democratization of culture: not just to facilitate a wider distribution, but even to overcome some of the class differences which so far have been observed in cultural consumption. Instead of adopting the Frankfurt School's negative view of media as devastating for the project of enlightenment, one could view them – as means for revitalizing it.

Another challenge for television is how to function as an instrument of cultural identity and national integration in a multicultural environment. Dealing with increasing diversity in cultural expression is, at least in part, a question of access. Thus the task would be to establish and preserve conditions under which many alternative voices, 'regardless of intrinsic merit or truth, find a hearing, provided that they emerge from those whom society is supposed to benefit – its individual members and constituent groups' (McQuail and van Cuilenburg, 1983: 146).

These two issues are connected with the concept of *control*: control of broadcasting *networks*, and control of broadcasting *content* (Bakke, 1986). Both types of control regulate the degree to which various cultural interests and representations obtain *access* to broadcasting networks, and, in turn, can be disseminated to a wider audience. If 'alternative voices' do not have direct access, it is left to those who do control them or to the market to secure their access to broadcasting channels.

The common thread in these reflections is that mass media, including television, are institutions that are supposed to serve the *public* interest, represented by individual citizens and by society as a whole. The current changes within media systems could put at stake a number of vulnerable values cherished by public service broadcasting (Blumler, 1992) because they may affect programme quality; regional, linguistic, political and cultural diversity; and cultural identity (cf. Dahlgren, Chapter 2 in this volume).

THE CONCEPT OF CULTURE

Until now we have used terms such as 'art', and 'culture' and 'cultural' in several different ways. That is not unusual. Culture is a very elusive concept. Not surprisingly there is abundant literature offering the reader an equally abundant variety of interpretations and definitions of the term. Kroeber and Kluckhohn (1963) collected a total of 164 (!) definitions of culture (cf. Williams, 1967). It can mean anything that is not 'nature', it may be used as another word for 'civilization', or it may describe the values, beliefs, norms and customs of a society or groups within it, together with all the various forms through which shared meanings are expressed. This last sense encourages us to look at 'culture' in complex societies not as a single, unitary system, but as a shifting array of 'subcultures', produced by groups (such as young people, black people or women) with sets of values that are different from the 'dominant' culture, or to focus on 'countercultures', whose values are in conflict with the dominant culture (Yinger, 1960).

In this discussion so far, we have used the term culture also in a much more restricted sense, in which it comes close to being a synonym for the 'art' and 'cultural objects' promoted by the central institutions of society. This is the culture taught in schools and universities or displayed in public museums. It is a highly selective definition that excludes many forms of artistic expression that have a vigorous life at the grassroots. Which brings us to the question of power: whose definitions of what counts as 'culture' prevail in the major spaces of public culture?

It is essential to be aware of the different meanings and uses to which the term 'culture' may be put. Terms and concepts are never neutral. The use of words like subculture or counter-culture, for instance, implies a hierarchy in which one form of culture is perceived as superior or more important and presented as a universal standard against which other forms are judged and found to be inferior. These words say something about who and what is included in and excluded from the central arenas of public life.

In common use in European societies for example, *culture* stands for a whole set of shared values and ideas that may be experienced as 'natural', but which are products of a history in which capitalism, Judaeo-Christian beliefs, ideals of enlightenment, of nationality and of individuality have been major influences.

An awareness of such implications of key words is needed even more now that globalization, represented by migration, tourism and the exchange of popular culture, has blurred the distinction between a dominant culture and subcultures, be they based on ethnic, linguistic, age or other characteristics. It also has challenged the notion of culture being attached to particular nation states, and broadened our conception of 'art' beyond a European context. In a multicultural environment established definitions of culture need to be questioned continually.

Though meanings and uses should be differentiated, they are hard to separate. Our concepts of culture are interrelated. We may narrow down our use of the term in this chapter to aesthetic expressions, that is, to the arts, yet this definition is still strongly related to the values expressed by the 'culture', or rather the 'dominant' culture, of our society. The dissemination and democratization of art through the media is also important from a cultural policy perspective because it is a way of preserving and renewing the values, norms and other shared meanings of our societies. In the conventional way of thinking the idea of art is firmly attached to our dominant notions of national and more generally of European cultural heritages, and identified with so-called fine or high art. With globalization and the diversification of European societies however, this perspective has been challenged. We should keep this firmly in mind as we go about finding answers to the two questions that we raised at the beginning:

1 To what extent can television be seen as a cultural institution and as a means for the dissemination of culture?
2 How is television dealing with the task of being a cultural institution?

HOW DO WE ANALYSE THE CULTURAL ASPECTS OF BROADCASTING?

There is a long tradition for analysing programme content in terms of cultural imperialism and Americanization. The theoretical basis for this has been the assumption that programmes reflect the values and images of a specific culture and produce meanings that cement particular social identities. Accordingly, the research has focused on the meanings mobilized by various formats and genres – e.g. soap operas – as well as on the ratio between home production and imported programmes (De Bens et al., 1992). While the latter approach primarily invites a discussion of the relevant factors forming social and cultural identities in general, the former looks more at media content as texts which contain meanings and pleasures which, in turn, are circulated among different audience groups.

Our task is a simpler one. Although fully aware of the limitations, we have chosen to focus here on the objects and events promoted by the major established institutions of culture. What we have to find out then is how television performs its cultural task of broadcasting theatre performances, of creating its own drama productions, of transmitting concerts, of presenting and commenting upon original visual arts and literature. One dilemma facing the people in charge of making such programmes would, of course, be to make a choice between the myriad artistic manifestations that exist, either as part of our cultural heritage or as creations of living artists and cultural workers. One might expect that such choices between cultural objects, events and activities would be made on the basis of some kind of 'high-quality' standards. But quality is as elusive a concept as culture, and quality in culture even more so. There are no objective and value-free standards to measure quality in the arts. That also makes it difficult to apply a criterion such as 'quality' in our research.

How, then, do we measure media, performance and television's performance in particular? Such an analysis can usefully begin by looking at two elements: (1) the idea of the 'arts' as defined by broadcasting corporations, and (2) the 'arts' as presented in broadcasting content.

POLICY STATEMENTS BY BROADCASTING CORPORATIONS

To what extent do public broadcasting systems in Europe see the dissemination of art as their task? And not as expressed in policy statements, but in actual programme practices? An overview of important media policy issues which was made over ten years ago (Bakke, 1986: 139) showed that high quality was stressed as an important aspect of media content. This goal was also expressed in terms of securing high culture and keeping the public from consuming mediocre mass culture. In France, Italy, The Netherlands, Finland, Norway and Denmark politicians and broadcasting companies regarded national identity as a key cultural issue within media policy (Bakke, 1986: 135). A concern for cultural identity and pluralism was later observed by Hoffmann-Riem (1992: 185), who describes how public broadcasting systems in Spain, the United Kingdom, Belgium and Germany have created particular services for regional audiences and for different language groups. These are manifested in Catalan and Basque in Spain, in Welsh in the United Kingdom, in French and Flemish in Belgium, and for the different *Länder* in Germany.

The two examples below represent views expressed by the Norwegian Broadcasting Corporation, a public service company. The first quote is from a letter that the Corporation sent to the Ministry of Culture in 1987, asking to become a semi-private institution (NRK, 1987: 9):

> A strong national broadcasting is necessary in order to give Norwegian culture, in the broad sense, a strong foothold and a chance for growth. However, NRK is more than a distributor of culture. Radio and television must play a role as creators of culture. With its ability to reach and unite great parts of the population, NRK might altogether be the most important single cultural institution.
>
> The goal for our cultural programmes is to offer current information about art and culture, science and music as well as creating an interest for cultural fulfilment and experience. (NRK, 1994: 12; author's translation)

ANALYSING CULTURAL CONTENT IN TV PROGRAMMES

A research project usually develops when we are faced with unsolved problems – e.g. the causes of cancer – or when we want to explore certain themes. Formulating in advance a number of puzzling or intriguing questions enables us to focus our research, both in terms of establishing a fruitful theoretical basis as well as choosing the relevant methods. One extra advantage of doing this work is that we may reduce the time spent on data collection. The same goes for content analysis.

Terms like *diversity*, *national identity*, *group values*, and *art forms* have been mentioned in previous sections. These can be spelled out in four research topics for analysing culture content in television:

1. diversity with respect to culture and art forms, i.e. movies, theatre, music, literature, visual arts, crafts, architecture;
2. diversity with respect to groups with specific values. This can also be called cultural pluralism in terms of regional, ethnic, age, language, and other differences;
3. national identity in terms of national cultural content;
4. diversity with respect to forms of presentation:

   - live transmission from concerts, theatres, etc., or indirect dissemination (e.g. records);
   - presentation as news or as background information and commentaries in particular magazines.

These research topics can be analysed empirically using either existing data or data which we collect ourselves. The first procedure saves us from the very time-consuming task of doing a content analysis. However, in comparative research it is important that the same categories are applied in each country, and this is not always the case. Another drawback is that the categories may not be completely relevant for our research questions. The solution, then, can be to choose the second procedure and do our own registration. We shall look at some of the benefits as well as problems involved when applying each of these methods.

Since 1981 the European Broadcasting Union has had a common system for gathering statistics about programming output from public service radio and television channels in Europe. The registration procedure uses a set of categories that the member broadcasting corporations have agreed upon within the EBU Statistics Group. This classification system is the basis for the empirical illustrations in this chapter. Since 1999 the programme registration has applied seven main genres and six selected genres, Fiction/Drama and Entertainment belong among the main genres, while Cinema Movies and Art/Culture are among the selected genres.

The most recent data available are from 1997. Boxes 9.1 and 9.2 illustrate how such data can be used in an empirical analysis of the theoretical themes mentioned earlier. From the nine main categories used between 1981 and 1988 we have selected the following to explore the issue of culture content in television programmes: Fiction, Light Entertainment, Music, Sports, Arts/Humanities/Sciences, and Religion.

Looking at these selected programme categories, Fiction has the highest percentage of total programme time in both the four Nordic countries and the five other European countries. In two of the Nordic television channels (TV2 in Finland and NRK1 in Norway), and in two of the European channels (ORF1 in Austria and ARD in Germany), Sports programmes have the second highest percentage programme time. Sports programmes also come in second place together with Arts/Humanities/Sciences in SVT1 in Sweden as well as in MTV2 in Hungary and in the Italian television channel RAI 3.

Table 9.1 shows the channels in which Arts/Humanities/Sciences programmes comprised the highest percentages in 1997.

EBU statistics for each year between 1991 and 1995 indicate that these 1997 percentages give a fairly representative picture of the general share of each country's total television programme time that is spent on the Arts/Humanities/Sciences category. The exception is the German channel ZDF, where the percentage increased from 4–5 per cent during the early 1990s to 16 per cent in 1997. A closer study of the television systems during these years could tell us more about the scheduling of arts and culture programmes; whether they are included in the overall programming in traditional public service channels, or presented in more specialized culture and arts channels, like ARTE.

The definitions in Box 9.2 show that Fiction includes cinema movies, and because of their length, they naturally account for much of the output in terms of time. Another option could be to see whether the different types of programmes have been 'on the air' at all. If we want to discuss the extent to which television channels fulfil their tasks as mediators of culture, this procedure is a tricky one. A low percentage of Arts/Humanities/Sciences programmes, for instance, could indeed be interpreted as just a token contribution to the principle of diversity in culture content. Sports programmes are intentionally included in the figures in order to focus on

Box 9.1

The EBU Statistics Group classification systems for registering television programme output

A. Classification system applied between 1981 and 1998
(The definitions of all categories appear in Box 9.2)

FICTION

Series
Serials
Sitcoms
Single plays
Movies
Telefilms
Animation

LIGHT ENTERTAINMENT

Games
Quizzes/Contests
Talk/chat shows
Shows/Variety/Humour/Satire

SPORTS

Sports events
Sports magazines

MUSIC

Opera
Musicals/Operetta
Folk music and dance
Serious music
Light/Pop/Rock
Pop video
Ballet and contemporary dance

NEWS

Newscasts/flashes
News magazines
Weather forecast

INFORMATION

Current affairs
Parliamentary broadcasting

EDUCATION

ARTS/HUMANITIES/SCIENCES

RELIGION

Categories added in 1997:

INFOTAINMENT

HUMAN INTEREST

B. Classification system that was proposed in 1999

Main genres:
News
Other factual/information
Fiction/Drama
Entertainment
Sport
Religious services

Selected genres:
Children's
Animation
Documentaries
Art/Culture
Music

Box 9.2

Definitions of programme categories

FICTION
Series: drama productions consisting of separate stories sharing title and characters.
Serials: drama productions consisting of a continuing story in episodes.
Sitcom: dramatized series in a humorous style and performed by a more or less fixed cast.
Movies: full-length films originally produced for the cinema.
Telefilms: full-length feature films produced for TV.

LIGHT ENTERTAINMENT
Programmes intended primarily to entertain, excluding programmes in which the musical element is predominant.
Games: competitions of pure entertainment (normally contests) of low production value.
Quizzes/Contests: game shows calling into play the competitors' special knowledge and intelligence and/or which involve considerable production work and form part of a broadcaster's mission in the field of cultural formation and education.
Talk and chat shows: consisting mainly of entertaining talks, interviews, etc.

MUSIC
Programmes in which music plays a predominant role.

SPORTS
Sports events: the transmission live or deferred of the whole or very large extracts of sports events as presented by the event organizer.
Sports magazines: regular programmes with varied sports content.

INFORMATION
Programmes intended primarily to inform about facts, events, theories or forecasts, or to provide explanatory background information (excluding educational programmes, sports and news).

RELIGION
Programmes based on different forms of religion, or similarly inspirational programmes intended to edify the audience. Informational programmes about religion should be included under Arts/Humanities/Sciences.

ARTS/HUMANITIES/SCIENCES
Programmes concerned with the enrichment of knowledge in a non-didactic way regarding various spheres and phenomena in the arts, literature, linguistics, philosophy, sciences.

INFOTAINMENT
Programmes intended primarily to inform but with substantial entertaining elements.

HUMAN INTEREST
Real-life stories with background narrative.

TABLE 9.1 The share of Arts/Humanities/Sciences television programmes in Nordic countries and some European countries, 1997 (%)*

Nordic countries		Other European countries	
DR2 (Denmark)	18	ZDF (Germany)	16
NRK2 (Norway)	17	TVP1 (Poland)	14
SVT1 (Sweden)	15	RAI3 (Italy)	13
SVT2 (Sweden)	14	MTV2 (Hungary)	12
		ORF2 (Austria)	10

* Channels are ranked in order from high to low percentages of total programme time.

TABLE 9.2 Share of own production of total Arts/Humanities/Sciences television programme time, and own production of total programme time in television channels in Nordic countries and in other European countries, 1997 (%)

Nordic countries			Other European countries		
Channel	Arts	Total own production*	Channel	Arts	Total own production*
NRK1 (Norway)	33	42	TVP1 (Poland)	66	48
DR2 (Denmark)	32	28	RAI2 (Italy)	58	44
YLE TV2 (Finland)	26	31	RAI3 (Italy)	52	54
SVT2 (Sweden)	24	48	MTV1 (Hungary)	49	32
DR1 (Denmark)	23	39	ZDF (Germany)	40	37
NRK2 (Norway)	19	29	MTV2 (Hungary)	38	47
YLE TV1 (Finland)	18	39	TVP2 (Poland)	33	42
MTV3 (Finland)	4	31	RAI1 (Italy)	33	55
			ORF2 (Austria)	22	25

* Excluding presentation, advertising, text news.

the various conceptions of culture that were discussed earlier. Neither Sports nor Light entertainment belongs within a narrow definition of culture as arts. However, they may very well be included in a broad definition of culture that would comprise leisure time activities. This concept can even be observed in public administration, as is the case in Norway, where the Norwegian Ministry of Culture has a separate division for sports affairs.

So far we have not dealt explicitly with any of the themes described earlier on. The EBU statistics also include origin of programmes. Home production is usually regarded as reflecting one's own country's social, political and cultural values, thus contributing to a sense of national identity among the audience. Table 9.2 illustrates this aspect.

The great variety in the definitions and operationalizations of the concept of culture is a major problem for comparative research. This is also the case with EBU statistics, and they should be applied with caution. In its instructions to participating broadcasting organizations, it emphasizes that:

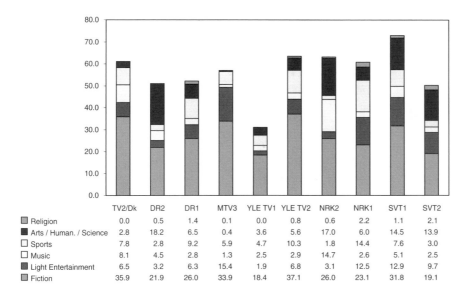

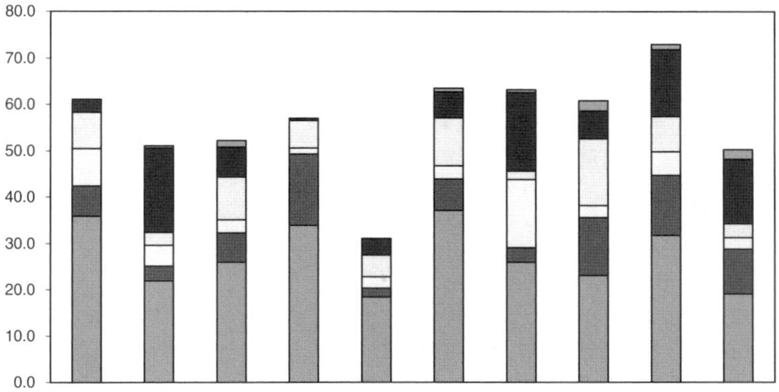

	TV2/Dk	DR2	DR1	MTV3	YLE TV1	YLE TV2	NRK2	NRK1	SVT1	SVT2
Religion	0.0	0.5	1.4	0.1	0.0	0.8	0.6	2.2	1.1	2.1
Arts / Human. / Science	2.8	18.2	6.5	0.4	3.6	5.6	17.0	6.0	14.5	13.9
Sports	7.8	2.8	9.2	5.9	4.7	10.3	1.8	14.4	7.6	3.0
Music	8.1	4.5	2.8	1.3	2.5	2.9	14.7	2.6	5.1	2.5
Light Entertainment	6.5	3.2	6.3	15.4	1.9	6.8	3.1	12.5	12.9	9.7
Fiction	35.9	21.9	26.0	33.9	18.4	37.1	26.0	23.1	31.8	19.1

FIGURE 9.1 Culture programmes in TV channels in Denmark, Finland, Norway and Sweden (% of total programme time, 1997)

'The attribution of specific types of programming to the seven main genres listed here should be according to your own organization's interpretation.' Thus the output statistics may reflect each broadcasting company's specific definitions of, for example, culture content. Furthermore, this is usually connected with each country's values and conceptions of culture.

In an attempt to compensate for such methodological faults, EBU has recommended its member broadcasting companies to apply the ESCORT classification system. This comprises four dimensions: Intention, Format, Content and Target Group. Television programmes can be classified on all four, giving a multidimensional description. ESCORT includes several categories which are useful for analysing the themes concerning the coverage of different types of culture and of cultural pluralism (ethnic groups, etc.). The Content dimension includes: Non-Fiction, Drama, Entertainment and Music. Furthermore, among the Non-fiction categories (which cover documentary and current affairs programmes) we find Plastic Arts, Theatre/Cinema, Literature, and Languages as well as Sports and Leisure, while Drama comprises Popular drama, Serious drama, Docu-drama and Poems/Stories.

Thus the ESCORT classification system facilitates a more nuanced analysis of culture content in television programmes. This means, for instance, that we can focus on traditional art forms – the so called fine arts – or apply any of the other conceptions of culture. Firstly, we may have access to data that can be applied in relation to the first topic, diversity with respect to culture and art forms. This multifaceted approach is also facilitated by the fourth classification dimension: Target Group. In addition to General

Audience, the target groups are defined according to Age, Regional/Local, Minorities, Occupations, and other Special Interests (motorists, tourists, women – indeed!). This is the type of data we need in order to delve into another of our theoretical themes, the question of cultural pluralism that has been emphasized by McQuail and van Cuilenburg (1983) and has been an important issue in several countries.

Finally, the Format classification dimension enables us to analyse how the programmes were presented, for instance as magazines, commentaries, documentaries or hosted shows.

Despite the fact that the EBU Statistics Group Classification System and the ESCORT system combined offer a very extensive set of tools for analysing television content, they are limited with respect to more detailed studies of qualitative aspects of programme presentation. One analytic approach is to look at changes over time. The creation of public service broadcasting in the 1920s was founded with certain aims: to educate, inform, and enlighten the audience as citizens (cf. Brants and De Bens, Chapter 1 in this volume). The programmes should offer the very best, often in the form of lectures by professionals within literature, social and natural sciences, etc. Live transmissions of concerts were also common. The same educational framework was transferred to public service TV during the 1940s, and prevailed until the early 1980s. Then, public service broadcasting was challenged by the commercial channels' music video programme format, in particular represented by MTV (cf. Roe and De Meyer, Chapter 8 in this volume). This had consequences also for cultural coverage in television. Many public service stations were afraid of losing young audiences to commercial channels (Schulz, Chapter 7 in this volume); on the other hand, television journalists and producers became interested in experimenting with new formats.

A feeling developed that it was necessary to find a compromise between television programmes as an art form in themselves and their use as means for cultural dissemination. Public service television also had to balance addressing the audience as consumers and addressing them as citizens. The consumer mode implied a programme format with frequent camera changes, unproblematic content, and a certain amount of humour. The citizen mode implied a slower tempo, focusing on specific cultural events and art works in studio talks, and on theatre and concert transmissions.

Towards the end of the 20th century, journalists and producers in the cultural divisions of European broadcasting corporations experienced a worsening of the conditions for making programmes about art and culture. There was less money available, and culture programmes were increasingly scheduled after prime time, when the audiences are small. The strategies chosen by PSB to cope with this difficult situation vary between the European countries. For instance, Scandinavian public television stations have tried to present art and culture in different programme formats. One format is the talk show host briefly interviewing an artist (primarily an entertainment programme), another format is a 45-minute conversation between a journalist and an artist or a writer, or the format can be an almost lecture type presentation of a special issue. Documentaries and taped or live transmissions are other optional formats. Thus art and culture can be covered by several departments: news, factual/documentary, entertainment, as well as culture. Many stations have almost stopped covering art and culture, leaving the task to niche channels, like ARTE.

The general situation of cultural institutions in a country may also affect a television station's decisions. The more accessible traditional cultural arenas are to the public, the less important are television channels to enable the audience to gain access to art and culture. The opposite is the case in countries with a scattered population and where distance from theatres, concert halls and art galleries are long. The debates that are going on in many countries, as well as the continuous experimenting with new forms and new styles, are not just symptoms of the ongoing struggle between the world of art and the world of television. They also betray the uncertainty that prevails among media producers as European societies change and old established concepts of culture are increasingly difficult to apply.

ACKNOWLEDGEMENT

I want to thank Jan Ivar Hansen, Head of Division for Personnel and Economy in the Norwegian Broadcasting Corporation, for generous assistance with figures and other information.

ACTIVITIES

1 Which concept of culture is expressed in each of the three quotes and in the visual representation in the introductory section?

2 Collect policy documents from television companies or stations in your own country, and describe the goals they have formulated for the coverage of culture.

   - How has culture been defined?
   - Have the television stations stated any obligations regarding their coverage of culture?
   - Is there any mention of cultures other than the 'main' one?

3 Select from television channels in your own country one programme about traditional art and one popular music video. Compare the two programmes with respect to their forms of presentation: differential use of visual elements and sound, just presenting (art) objects, transmitting live performance, or culture within another framework; and their pace

(length of programme, items, etc.), or other aspects that strike you. Also compare the scheduling of such programmes during the week and during the day (e.g. weekends, afternoon, prime time, late hours).

4 Compare a commercial television channel with a public service channel in your own country with respect to the programme formats that are used for presenting art and culture. Discuss the differences that you find.

SUGGESTIONS FOR FURTHER READING

Griswold, W. (1994) *Cultures and Societies in a Changing World*. Thousand Oaks, CA, London and New Delhi: Pine Forge Press.

This book gives a broad perspective on arts and cultural analysis. It offers a specific theoretical framework for studying the relationship between cultural objects (symbols, beliefs, values and practices), cultural creators (e.g. artists and organizations), cultural receivers (e.g. arts audiences), and the social world (the context in which culture is created and experienced). The book has a comparative approach and presents examples from Nigeria, China and the United States.

Hayward, Ph. (1988) *Picture This: Media Representation of Visual Art and Artists*. London: John Libbey.

This describes positive and negative aspects of mediating visual arts through mass media. The artist's role is discussed.

Williams, R. (1975) *Television. Technology and Cultural Form*. New York: Schocken Books.

In this, by now classic book, Raymond Williams explores issues related to technological determinants and restrictions on the production of television content

CHAPTER 10

BREAKFAST TELEVISION: INFOTAINERS AT DAYBREAK

Jan Wieten

Early morning television has something to do with time. And it does not make a secret of it. It is already in the name. Most early morning programmes have something like 'Good Morning', 'Breakfast', or simply 'Morning' in their titles. Even if we happened to miss the title of the programme, we would notice the link with time at first glance by the almost inevitable clock that is imposed on the screen all of the time, that is to say, except during commercial breaks. Breakfast television 'thematizes' itself, according to Paddy Scannell (1996: 149), 'in all its ways of attending to the present moment and producing it as the moment it is: breakfast time, time-to-get-up, to wash, shave, dress, clean teeth, snatch a bite to eat and off to school, factory, shop, office or wherever.' It is, as it were, 'obsessed with its own liveness', as Jane Feuer (1983: 17) argues in her famous essay about ABC's early morning show *Good Morning America.*

Time is a different matter here than in other television programmes. When we watch a movie or a soap on TV we are expected to forget time, but in morning television we are constantly reminded of it. The presenters tell us that we should keep watching, they promise that there are many interesting things yet to come, and they inform us of the exact time when these will turn up. But at the same time, more than at any other moment during the day, the television screen concedes by its clock that there may be more urgent matters that we have to deal with than watching TV.

Like the evening news, but in a different way, breakfast television is situated at one of the transitional points in our daily life cycle. The evening news marks our daily transformation from a public into a private function, whereas early morning TV accompanies us on the way from private to public (Morse, 1986; Corner, 1995; Allan, 1998). Breakfast news bridges the gap between a period of leisure in the home and the demands of the working day that lies ahead. The news in the morning must inform us not only about what has happened during the night, but also about events that are likely to occur during the day, and thus prepare us for the things we may have to face. Most of us have little time between getting up and leaving home. During this short period there are many other things to do that can come in the way of watching TV, or that keep us from watching with undivided attention. A difficult situation, especially for television, because it demands attention from both eyes and ears. It leads to a different use of television than that of evening audiences. Morning viewers may be expected to turn the TV set on, as they would have turned on the radio earlier on, and use it in much the same way as their radio (Alasuutari, 1997). Sound may therefore be more important in breakfast television than in other comparable TV genres (Altman, 1986). The need to solicit and grasp attention segment by segment by self-promotion, direct address and centrality given to sound (Ellis, 1982) is even more urgent in breakfast TV than in television generally.

Makers of early morning programmes have to deal with a shifting audience. It is constantly changing in composition, under the force of the schedules of activities outside the home. However, apart from these hurried viewers, the available audience also consists of people with different morning rituals – housewives, unemployed, older people – whose share grows as the morning proceeds. They are important as well. For it is difficult to find special market niches at this time of day that can be exploited successfully. So the target often is the total available audience, and a format has to be found that implicates, in Scannell's words (1996: 149), 'adults, children, women and men' and attends to each 'in some way in particular services'. Compatibility (see Hujanen, Chapter 4 in this volume) is seen as a necessity in breakfast TV, but as difficult to achieve. A fast, rolling format may serve the interests of the hasty shifting part of the audience, but other viewers may find little gratification in a programme that constantly repeats itself.

Most producers of breakfast television programmes also believe that a different style of television is needed, because of the different psychological make-up of morning and of evening audiences. Many of them seem to think that what we need most in the morning is a friendly and reassuring companion to help us make our daily transfer from the warmth of the home to the cold world outside. Breakfast TV is offered to us as such good company. It is, according to Daniel Hallin (1994: 92), all about friendly and interesting people who 'have conversations with other friendly and interesting people, and the viewer is invited to join them'. Some would say that it has to be that way. For, as Tauno Aijälä, a founding father of breakfast TV in Finland, argues, there is only one or at best a few ways of doing early morning television right, and only a few rules to obey, given the time of day and the characteristics of the morning audience.[1]

Given these conditions, it is not hard to understand that many broadcasters have made quite an effort to find out about the early morning audience (Feuer, 1983; Barwise and Ehrenberg, 1988; Madge, 1989). The problem they face is not dissimilar to the one faced by television in general, as it has to deal with audiences with an ever-widening choice of channels, and equipped with the means to move smoothly and swiftly from one to the other. Only breakfast television had to cope with these facts of life from the beginning, and it chose its format accordingly.

COMPARATIVE ANALYSIS OF BREAKFAST TELEVISION

Not all programmes which are broadcast between 5.30 and 9.30 on weekday mornings (or corresponding later hours during weekends) are referred to as early morning television, or breakfast television. Many European television stations feature reruns of soaps, sitcoms of the previous day, educational programmes or programmes for children at this time of day, but most of these are not especially made for the early morning. We shall employ names like breakfast television, in accordance with common use, for the programmes that were designed with this particular time slot in mind, and which generally have the format of a magazine, and a basic structure of regularly repeated or updated news broadcasts. As principal feature of a magazine we take diversity of content within an identifiable unit.

Although breakfast magazines will be discussed here as programmes, which may be identified in the normal ways as units (e.g. by name, hosting, style, a beginning and an end), there may be reason to treat them not as single programmes but as combinations of programmes, because of their extreme length, some content characteristics and their shifting audience.

Before daytime television arrived most news bulletins were scheduled in evening time slots. The main television newscasts of the public channels in Europe have had the same length and occupied the same place in the programme schedules for decades. Watching the evening news has become a ritual in almost every European household since the 1950s. But the highest density of news bulletins can now be found between 6 and 9 in the morning, the broadcast hours of most of the breakfast television programmes. These news bulletins, usually every half-hour, are an important structuring element of early morning magazines.

In between the news bulletins may come teasers and headlines, sometimes as continuously moving zips at the bottom of the screen. A separate weather report almost always accompanies the news. Traffic news is also a common feature. At regular intervals sports, economics or other sections may be added to the bulletins. Some countries also have regular regional news inserts.

The other items of the magazine are as it were wrapped around the newscasts. The opening of the magazine by the presenters precedes the first news bulletin, and the programme is normally closed in the same way after the last newscast. All breakfast magazines contain interviews with experts/commentators and people in the news, predominantly done live in the studio (but also by phone or satellite), as well as some pre-recorded items from correspondents or reporters. Reports and other items may be

TABLE 10.1 Content of commercial and public breakfast television in Finland (May 1998)

	Huomenta Suomi 1998 %	Aamu-TV 1998 %
News	17	33
News in Swedish		6
Economic news	5	
Sports	5	16
Weather	6	4
News	**33**	**59**
Chat/newspapers	6	2
Studio interview	12	17
Report + interview	15	14
Report	3	5
Talk	**36**	**38**
For children	4	3
Performance + interview	4	
Exercises	6	
Cooking	6	
Viewer interactive		
Other	**20**	**3**
Commercials	**11**	

repeated during the course of the programme. The range of subjects is wider than is normal in news and current affairs programmes, and would include topics from such areas as science, culture, education, environment and nature, show business, movies, literature, and popular music. Many programmes have a cartoon or other small item for children, almost all programmes have a newspaper roundup. Mainly the commercial programmes contain a range of service sections: from lifestyle, home, cooking, aerobics and health or beauty advice, to automobile and wine tests. Phone-ins, games, and live performances by musicians and other artists are also more common in the breakfast magazines of the commercial broadcasters than in the others. The on-screen clock with programme logo and the constant reminders of things to come are services provided by all breakfast programmes.

The public breakfast TV programmes are generally a bit more structured and news oriented than the commercial ones, but the term 'magazine' applies to them too (Table 10.1). Practically all programmes show some internal development during the two or more hours of the show. Usually the first hours contain more hard news items and economic news, whereas the last hour is more lifestyle oriented, targeted at a predominantly female and older audience. This structuring has the additional advantage of creating friendly environments for certain kinds of advertising.

In Europe breakfast magazines are a recent phenomenon. They made their appearance in the 1980s and the early 1990s, and it should therefore come as no surprise that the advent of breakfast TV is often logically connected to the major upheaval that took place in television during these years. Many authors mention the appearance of breakfast television magazines, almost in passing, as one of the symptoms of a process of popularization, commercialization and Americanization of European television and television journalism (Corner, 1995; Franklin, 1997). Dahlgren (1995: 53–55), discussing this 'dominant trend', ranges breakfast television, with tabloid-style news broadcasts, vox pop talk shows, and transnational satellite TV news, as among the results of intense experimentation with new formats that betrays uncertainty about what is good journalism (see also Munson, 1993). Hallin (1994: 91) classifies early morning TV as first of all 'entertainment', when compared to the evening news broadcasts of the American networks, which in his view are still primarily 'journalism', even though they are set within an entertainment medium. According to Corner (1995: 75) magazine formats in general have become the focus of much recent development in the competition for 'watchability' and the search for successful blends of journalism, features and 'chat'.

Television journalism in general has been criticized for trivializing important issues by juxtaposing them with frivolous items, producing only an illusion of informedness among its viewers (Dahlgren, 1995: 46). Wilson (1984: 8) contends that breakfast television programmes try to create 'a sense of family normality out of the least amenable material: world news and current affairs'. Even in more traditional news and current affairs programmes such popularizing tendencies have been observed as an increased emphasis on human interest, sensationalism, personalized presentation and happy talk. But the position of the new hybrid genres is different and is often considered even more problematic, because of their conscious mixing of two 'irreconcilable' elements: information and entertainment (see also Dahlgren, Chapter 2 in this volume). The European Broadcasting Union (EBU) recently had to devise a new programme category, as Bakke explained (in Chapter 9), to cope with *infotainment* programmes. It demonstrates not only that the phenomenon is seen as new, but also that it is widespread and expected to stay. EBU defines infotainment as 'Programmes intended primarily to inform but with substantial entertaining elements'.

A study of early morning television may add to our understanding of infotainment and other trends in television journalism and the news, and perhaps even help us to get a clearer picture of the future. In this case study we will focus on two aspects: the development of breakfast television and the style of early morning programmes. It is mainly based on analysis of eight breakfast television programmes in four European countries (Table 10.2). Four of these are produced by commercial broadcasters and four by public broadcasting organizations.[2]

A closer look at the history of breakfast television may help to find out if its spread adds support to the thesis of a general popularization and commercialization of television news. In that case we should also find evidence of such popularizing tendencies in the development of early morning television itself. A comparison of programmes produced by public and by

TABLE 10.2 Eight breakfast television programmes

Station	Country/type	Programme	Broadcast time	Main presenters (May 1998)
MTV3	Finland/commercial	Huomenta Suomi	weekdays 6–9 also on Saturday and Sunday	Lauri Karhuvaara/Mari Sarolahti Lauri Karhuvaara/Pirkko Arstila Liisa Riekki/Heikki Huttunen Liisa Riekki/Sakari Kilpelä
YLE	Finland/public	Aamu-TV	weekdays 6–9.10	Leena Pakkanen/Arto Nyberg Leo Riski/Satu-Lotta Peltola
KRO	Netherlands/public	Ontbijt TV	weekdays 7.30–9	Rocky Tuhuteru Dieuwertje Blok
SVT	Sweden/public	Rapport Morgon	weekdays 6.30–9.30	Marianne Rundström Staffan Dopping
TV4	Sweden/commercial	Nyhetsmorgon	weekdays 6–9.20	Malou von Sivers/Bengt Magnusson
BBC	UK/public	Breakfast News	weekdays 6–9 6–7 Business Breakfast on Sunday: Breakfast with Frost	Justin Webb/Sophie Raworth Andrew Harvey/Liz MacKean
Channel 4 Planet 24	UK/commercial	The Big Breakfast	weekdays 7–9	Johnny Vaughan/Denise van Outen
GMTV (ITV channel 3)	UK/commercial	GMTV	weekdays 6–9.25 6–7 The News Hour 8.50–9.25 Lorraine Live Similar on Sunday	Eamonn Holmes/Fiona Phillips (6–7 Penny Smith/John Stapleton)

commercial broadcasters could shed light on the thesis that one of the ways in which this trend manifests itself is by an increasing convergence of private and public broadcasting (see Dahlgren, and Brants and De Bens, Chapters 2 and 1 in this volume).

About the character of breakfast television as infotainment and its relationship to older television journalism formats such as traditional news broadcasts we may find out by a comparative analysis of the styles, the presentational forms, of breakfast television and the news. In our case comparing the styles of the two is made easy in a sense because we find them both in early morning magazines. The particular ways in which the news is incorporated in the programmes may, we hope, also shed some light on the character of both.

A comparative analysis could also make clear if the suggestion that there is a (one) particular breakfast television style is perhaps premature. There may be at least two (a commercial and a public broadcasting one, for instance, as the literature about broadcast strategies and convergence suggests), or perhaps several, if we assume that national culture also has an impact on the styles employed in broadcasting and the news (e.g. Levo-Henriksson, 1994). This would make it interesting to look at stylistic similarities and differences between the programmes produced by public and commercial broadcasting organizations and in different countries as well.

HISTORY OF BREAKFAST TELEVISION

The word *new* is often used in connection with early morning television. Breakfast TV is indeed a new television format, but only as far as Europe is concerned. In this part of the world it came into existence as a product of the extension of broadcasting time to the early hours of the day which followed the arrival of cable and satellite channels and the collapse of most of the public broadcasting monopolies in the 1980s and early 1990s. In almost all cases – e.g. in Belgium, Britain, Germany, Finland, The Netherlands, Sweden – the initiative seems to have been with the commercial broadcasters.[3]

It is also seen as new in the sense of being one of a number of recent types of programmes that defy existing categorizations of television genres, for which the rather imprecise term 'infotainment' is employed. Yet another reason to call it new lies in the ways in which it has adapted to the modern – or rather postmodern – viewers, described above, people with little time and attention for whom television has become a side-show, not unlike radio, next to more urgent matters to be dealt with.

Breakfast television is far from new, however, if we look beyond Europe and beyond public broadcasting. Actually early morning magazines belong to the oldest formats in television. *Today*, the popular breakfast show of the American network NBC, is one of the two longest running programmes on American television. Since 1952 (!) when it started, its general format has remained remarkably unchanged. *Today*, and America's other major breakfast show, ABC's *Good Morning America* (1975), are the most profitable news programmes of these American networks. Not that this kind of programme was completely unknown in Europe, even in European public broadcasting. Radio used similar early morning programme formats long before television entered this field. *Tonight*, an investigative television magazine, started by the BBC in response to the challenge of commercial television in 1957, could be regarded as another predecessor as far as the general formula is concerned. And of course print media have offered diverse matters within one format for ages!

Still, the American example seems to have been influential when it came to filling up the first hours of the day in European television. It is not too difficult to see that the breakfast magazines in Europe share features with shows like *Today* or *Good Morning America*. Added to the fact that commercial broadcasters in Europe were the first to adopt the format, there may be reason to suspect that we may indeed have here an example of the Americanization of television and television journalism.

The United Kingdom was the first country in Europe to begin with breakfast television. When the Independent Broadcasting Authority (IBA) announced in 1980 that it would issue a licence for (commercial) breakfast time television, public broadcaster BBC decided within a week that it would start its own breakfast TV programme. The two programmes began within two weeks of each other in early 1983, first the BBC and then on the ITV channel, TV-am, led by some of the most famous journalists in Britain, people like David Frost, Angela Rippon, Anna Ford and Michael Parkinson. Channel 4 launched its first breakfast service in 1989. As in the United Kingdom, public and commercial breakfast television in Sweden began within a short time of each other, but in Finland, Germany and the Netherlands it took public broadcasters several years to decide that they too should produce an early morning programme.

Perhaps the prime reason why public broadcasters felt that they could not let the challenge of the new stations go unanswered lies in the nature of the programmes that the commercial operators scheduled for this time of day, i.e. *news* magazines. The provision of information is a core business of any public broadcasting service, and to leave this to private contenders would, in the long run, have touched upon the very legitimacy of public service broadcasting. The immediate cause, which made broadcasters realize that a regular provision with television news at the break of day would be a good thing, sometimes lay in a major news event such as the Gulf War.

At first BBC's *Breakfast Time* was a relaxed, light news magazine, TV-am's *Good Morning Britain*, with its self-proclaimed 'mission to explain' (Day-Lewis, 1989: 10), by far the more serious, perhaps over-intellectual, one. TV-am at first stayed far behind BBC *Breakfast Time* in the ratings, until it popularized and introduced Roland Rat, a puppet, as co-host! Consciously or not TV-am thus applied the same strategy that NBC had employed successfully in the early 1950s when J. Fred Muggs, a live chimpanzee, was launched as co-host to boost the ratings of *Today*. Despite all these efforts TV-am (Mrs Thatcher's favourite morning programme) lost its licence, when it was to be renewed in the early 1990s. It was given to GMTV, which offered a more middle-of-the-road breakfast magazine. Around the same time BBC's *Breakfast Time* became the more focused and serious *Breakfast News*. Channel 4 found out that its news-oriented breakfast programme *Channel 4 Daily* could not compete with the other two. It was replaced in 1992 by the immediately successful, hilarious *Big Breakfast. The Big Breakfast* is targeted at a much younger age group than either *GMTV* or *Breakfast News*, and only in its basic structure is it similar to other breakfast news. As part of recent plans to restructure its total news output the BBC (1998) has decided to change the formula of *Breakfast News* again and make it more accessible.

Established in 1989, MTV3's *Huomenta Suomi* ([Good] Morning Finland) became the first breakfast TV programme in Northern Europe. The response from Finnish public broadcaster YLE came more than seven years later, and only after extensive research had been done, to test the feasibility of another early morning service next to the successful commercial one. YLE's morning programme *Aamu-TV* (Morning TV) was a bit like *Huomenta Suomi* at first, but soon adopted a more serious and more news-focused formula.

The two Swedish breakfast TV programmes *Nyhetsmorgon* (September 1992) and *Rapport Morgon* (January 1993) set out with roughly similar light formulas. SVT's *Rapport Morgon* soon found out that it could not compete with commercial TV4 along these lines. *Rapport Morgon* became a serious news magazine but is slightly modifying that policy now.

RTL4 (at that time called RTL-Veronique), the first commercial broadcaster in the Netherlands, began with breakfast TV in 1989, the first year of its existence, but gave up after one year because of low ratings for the programme. In 1994 three Dutch public broadcasters, KRO, NCRV and IKON,[4] joined forces to produce *Ontbijt TV* (Breakfast TV), at first a light TV copy of a popular radio programme called the Breakfast Club. After the first year KRO continued on its own. Since that time the programme has gradually become more serious and journalistic.

STYLE OF BREAKFAST TELEVISION

The style of a programme has to do with more or less permanent outward appearances, with modes of address and with all kinds of visual characteristics. Style, as opposed to content, has to do with *how* things are communicated. Not that the two are separate, for style reflects the motives of the makers, it says something about the kind of organization that produces the programme, and even about the society that we live in, its power structure and its values. Style also positions us as viewers, it gives us the clues that we need to make sense of what we hear and see, preferably in the way it was intended (cf. Morley, 1980; Fiske, 1987). Although there is an element of fashion in style – styles change and in breakfast TV more quickly than in the news – it is still a relatively stable element. We may expect that the style of tomorrow's breakfast news will be the same as today's.

In trying to find out about the style of breakfast magazines,[5] as compared to the news, we concentrated on visual aspects of the programmes. We looked at the opening sequences of breakfast television and the news bulletins in breakfast programmes, at the sets they use, at the presenters and their style of presentation, and at how the news is integrated in the programme. This way we expect to learn about some important, directly visible consequences of juxtaposing or mixing news, information, entertainment and consumer service and advice in one programme format, as in breakfast television or in infotainment generally.

Television news is a thoroughly researched genre and its conventions are well documented.[6] Over the years it has acquired a form which makes it almost immediately recognizable. A television newscast in Japan looks pretty much the same as one in Russia or Indonesia or the United States. Its outward appearances are functional to what news and journalism stand for in our societies. They all work together to convey the impression that both messengers and messages are credible, authoritative, serious, factual, unbiased and independent and that what they tell us is new and worth knowing.

The opening sequences

The news bulletins in breakfast television programmes do not all have a distinct title sequence. But if they do, it is normally identical or at least similar to news broadcasts on the same channel during the rest of the day. The signature tunes used to introduce news programmes often sound rather ominous, and suggest a sense of urgency by the use of gongs and similar devices. Almost all the opening graphics of the news broadcasts show maps, or turning globes or display a typical newsroom or video screens in a television control room. Blue is a dominant colour. There is little difference in this respect between different countries or between commercial and public broadcasters.

Breakfast television introductions tell a different story.[7] The music is unpretentious and light-hearted in almost all cases. What most opening sequences first of all display is an impression of undefined topical diversity. References to the time of day, symbolized by suns, skies at the break of dawn, lighthouses, alarm and other clocks, are common. So are symbols of breakfast like coffeepots, mugs, rolls and cereal. Other early morning activities such as taking a shower may also be referred to. When it comes to titles, *Good morning*, with its suggestion of warmth and friendliness is popular, especially with commercial broadcasters.[8]

Most of the symbols that are used have to do with home, with the private sphere, but not all point that way. Sometimes camera views as well as graphics tell about television and the way it is made. Only a few programmes (of some public broadcasters) exclusively use symbols that refer to the public world such as globes, maps and news scenes, although many employ these in combination with symbols of timeliness and home.

The set

Newsdesk and *sofa*, the characteristic pieces of furniture of the news and of breakfast television, can be seen as symbolic of two completely different styles. The décor in which the news is presented is almost always easily distinguishable from the set of the magazine, even in the few cases when the news does not have an opening of its own. News stage props represent the world of journalism or point to the world outside, to things that have to do with the public sphere. The newsreader (in breakfast TV news it is usually one person) is seated behind the same sort of desk as is used in other news broadcasts. The scene portrayed behind the presenter is most often a newsroom with computers, video screens and busy journalists moving around. It is businesslike. The designs of the sets of the magazines are more diverse. Even though the more or less archetypal picture of people seated on a sofa or in easy chairs around a low table with coffee mugs in the décor of a living room is not unrealistic, normally the contrast between *newsdesk* and *sofa* is less marked. Quite a few programmes do not have sofas; others do not hide that they are broadcast from a studio, not a home.

A more characteristic feature is that almost all magazines move from one setting to another during the programme, some designed in a more newsy fashion, others in the relaxed living-room style (Plates 10.1 a–g). Typically the opening announcements and welcome are done by the presenters from behind a desk or a high table, whereas guests are received on the sofas. The tendency is strongest in the magazines of the commercial channels with their wider range of topics. The type of the set is linked to the type of the subject. MTV3's *Huomenta Suomi* used to apply this method most consistently, sticking closely to the conventions of existing genres.[9] It ('it' includes the presenters) moved from magazine studio to news studio and back, placing every topic in a context which gave it its intended proper meanings: a chat with a movie actor was done on the magazine set, an interview with a minister in the newsroom (but only if the subject was considered hard news). *Go'morgen Danmark*, of Danish semi-commercial broadcaster TV2, does the same but in an overall more homely setting. Magazine items are positioned in different rooms of a house that is, or is made to appear, the location of the programme.

PLATE 10.1 Presenter roles in breakfast television: Liisa Riekki (with Heikki Huttunen) in *Huomenta Suomi*, 8 May 1998.

10.1a. 6.00 a.m. Opening chat.
10.1b. 6.28 a.m. Newspaper roundup.
10.1c. 6.50 a.m. Double studio interview.
10.1d. 7.39 a.m. One-to-one interview in news studio.
10.1e. 8.27 a.m. Inspection of recipe. *'What a coincidence. This pie looks really French to me and later on we will have some French music coming up.'*
10.1f. 8.50 a.m. Interview with Debussy performers (pianist Pascal Devoyon and cellist Martti Rousi).
10.1g. 8.58 a.m. Closing chat.

On the whole the stage props of a breakfast magazine make a different impression than the sets of news programmes. Coffee mugs are indeed a common feature, and a casual display of morning newspapers also belongs to the paraphernalia of early morning television. The furniture is of a more easy type than in the news. In the place of the stern newsdesk with the presenter behind it are tables that invite people to sit themselves in a relaxed way. As a backdrop behind (or rather around) this scene there may be plants and a bookcase and views through virtual or real windows. Through the windows people walking, or traffic moving by, may be seen, or the townscape of a rather nondescript city. It is an outside world closer to home than is signified by the globes and the maps behind the readers of the news. The colours we see most prominently displayed are warm: yellow, red and orange. The presenters tend to be dressed less formally than is common in the news, although the 'brightly knitted sweaters' that were a trademark of BBC's *Breakfast Time* in the 1980s are now very much a thing of the past (Fry, 1983: 14).

Camerawork is also less static and more relaxed in breakfast magazines than in the news. Top shots, long shots, and extreme close-ups, seldom used in news broadcasts, are common in morning magazines. Moreover the visualization of the actual making of live television, by showing cameramen and other technical staff at work, has become a matter of routine in many shows, with *Big Breakfast*'s habit of dragging the technical crew into the show an interesting but extreme example of this tendency. The making of television is demystified in a way that is normally not seen in the news genre.

Presentation and presenters

Although news conventions have shifted to less formal styles, the presentation of the news is still predominantly in the public address mode (Corner, 1995). It is mostly static: the anchor remains in place. He or she addresses the viewer by speaking from behind the desk, straight into the camera (in practice straight into the teleprompter). From time to time the papers on the desk may be consulted. The tone is solemn. A faint smile is permitted at the beginning and the end of the news.

The conventions of breakfast TV presentation are different. The presenters are mobile and flexible. They move from one situation to another and adopt the style and mode of address that is required by the circumstances. On the whole these are less formal and more colloquial than in typical newscasts. Informal modes of address, like first names, are more commonly used than in the news broadcasts. Studio interviews are live and are aired unedited. The style of interviewing is relatively relaxed, more inquisitive than interrogating. In breakfast television programmes autocue is used only during newscasts and for service announcements. Even when making these kinds of announcement many magazine presenters use the teleprompter also as cue for improvisation. Humour, spontaneity, and a talent for improvisation are highly valued in breakfast TV presenters, especially in commercial stations. They are supposed to make use of these talents, but newsreaders are not permitted to indulge in such frivolous chatting. This contrast is most obvious at the points of transition between the magazine and the news.

The presenters of the television news act as functionaries. They are not expected to speak for themselves as persons. In fact controversy surrounded their appearance on TV screens in the 1950s, which was expected to personalize the news. News presenters have quite consciously been kept relatively anonymous for a long time, at least in much of Europe, and in some places they still are (Morse, 1986; Levo-Henriksson, 1994; Bardoel, 1998). However, anchors of breakfast television programmes are not nameless people, nor are they expected to be. Famous names in television journalism have been involved in breakfast TV, people like Barbara Walters and Sir David Frost. Many of the presenters of early morning television receive high salaries, especially in Britain and the US, even compared to colleagues in other news and current affairs programmes. Presenters in Sweden, Finland and The Netherlands often work in shifts, usually on two or three consecutive days. But in the US and in Britain anchors of breakfast television shows may host their programme five days a week. This is obviously a pattern that is much preferred by the broadcasting organizations themselves (but not always by the presenters), because it helps to establish a clear identity for the programme. Although breakfast magazines are not (yet) named after their hosts, as is more and more the case with talk shows (see Murdock in Chapter 11), their identity is more closely connected to the personality and style of the presenters than the news. A celebrity status may be the result of their prominent roles, but in some cases celebrity may have been the reason to hire someone as anchor of a breakfast television show, in order to attract larger audiences (like champion swimmer Sharron Davies in the case of *The Big Breakfast*).

In most programmes presenters are announced by name, in captions on screen at the beginning of the show. Later on their names are only mentioned when they address each other or are addressed by newsreaders, and other people on the programme, or by guests and experts. In the United States and the United Kingdom announcement by voice-over ('this is . . . with . . .'), or self-announcement ('I am . . .) is more common. Off-screen publicity for presenters varies, but on the whole would seem to be on the increase. Many breakfast television presenters nowadays have their own web pages with their CVs on web-sites of the broadcasting organization or the programme

Phelan (1991: 78) calls news presenters the electronic equivalent of a magazine cover or a newspaper masthead. It is perhaps more appropriate to say, with regard to the anchors of early morning programmes, that they are not only the cover but also the staples in the back that keep the parts together. Even this falls short of what I mean to say. Because viewers cannot browse through a television programme, a magazine format is infinitely more difficult in television than in print. The presenters have to keep a fragmented audience interested, even if the specific item on the screen does not. They create a form of identity and unity in a programme that is not only heterogeneous and segmented, but also repetitive. In breakfast television more is needed to achieve flow (see Hujanen, Chapter 4 in this volume; Williams, 1974; Feuer, 1983) than intelligent programming of the different items alone. It is established primarily by the presenters, who create an identifiable, pleasant and inviting atmosphere, but who also adapt to the specific roles that are required at different points in the programme. A sort of co-existence of information and entertainment is realized by both overcoming and respecting differences between the two.

There are practically always two presenters, one male and the other female. There is an obvious practical reason for this. Presenting a two- to three-hour-long programme is an almost impossible task for one person. Hosting a breakfast show is not just linking topics, but it includes doing all or nearly all of the interviews with guests and experts. Double presentation makes it possible to divide some tasks. This is increasingly the case, even though most producers of breakfast television programmes find the double-interview style more characteristic of breakfast magazines than the turn-taking of one plus one news interviews. Double presentation suggests accessibility. It is thought to produce a friendly atmosphere. It is also considered less exclusive: double interviews in easy chairs or sofas invite the viewer to take part in the discussion.

The combination of the two presenters may be as important as the personal talent and attraction of one of them. According to some authors, it is the combination that works to remove the distance between actors and spectators, by creating the warmth, intimacy and inviting atmosphere of a virtual family to which the viewers may belong (Feuer, 1983; Wilson, 1984; Morse 1986). Jane Feuer (1983: 17) pictures *Good Morning America*'s David Hartman as 'the ultimate father figure' and Wilson portrays BBC's Frank Bough and Selina Scott as a father and his daughter who kept the wheels of the motherless *Breakfast Time* family running (see also Morse, 1986). Pedersen (1999: 96) – in a study of news presenters and gender – argues that the female presenter in such a combination is often trivialized by being positioned as the 'other half' of the couple or as an assistant (cf. van Zoonen, 1991).

We found no such general pattern of typecasting, although presenters like Eamonn Holmes in *GMTV*, John Nicolson of *Breakfast News*, Lasse Bengtsson in *Nyhetsmorgon* and *Huomenta Suomi*'s Lauri Karhuvaara would fit the description of the friendly, relaxed, and fatherly types that Wilson and Feuer may have had in mind. A typical female presenter is harder to find in the European breakfast television programmes that we analysed, although a slight preference among broadcasters may be detected for a contrasting combination of an eager, witty, mildly intellectual type of female anchor, with a fatherly or more populist male presenter. Phelan (1991) contends that hiring charismatic talent is still much of a mystical operation, but broadcasters, even public broadcasters like YLE in Finland, have tried to minimize the risks of getting the wrong person or the wrong combination and the wrong format by extensive pre-testing of presenters and styles of presentation (cf. Feuer, 1983).

Segmentation and flow at the boundaries between news and magazine

Breakfast television broadcasters want to take their audiences along from one segment to another. This means that they must overcome the innate tension between flow and a wide diversity of topics which are governed by different genre conventions. How they do this may be illustrated by looking at the devices that are used to keep news and magazine both separate and together. This does not mean that integration or separation of the newscasts and the rest of the programme is always a matter of principle. For instance, distinction between the two may be caused by the policy of the station to have uniformity in style between all the newscasts on its channel, and integration by such simple practical facts as the size of a studio or the available budget. On the other hand, more and more attention is paid nowadays to the design and the functionality of the set. The result is usually an increased emphasis on one particular house style and an attendant softening of disturbing non-functional stylistic contrasts between parts of the programme.

Normally there is considerable overlap between the content of the magazine and the news. Some distance may be thought useful, however, to keep the cold of some of the harsh events in the news out of the warmth of the magazine. But the normal pattern is one of cross-fertilization. The agenda of breakfast magazines, even of the commercial ones, is set to a large extent by the news. Most of the studio talk is with newsmakers or about people and events in the news. In addition programmes like *Aamu-TV*, *Huomenta Suomi* and *GMTV* use footage of interviews with illustrious guests on the magazine in their newscasts. This kind of symbiosis is harder to achieve where the news organization is completely separate from the magazine, as in Dutch breakfast TV. Although the conventions of news presentation are generally applied, there are also efforts to reconcile the styles of presentation, even where news and magazine are kept separate. This may go two ways. News presentation in *The Big Breakfast* is flashy, almost rap-like, an adaptation to the style of the rest of the programme. *Huomenta Suomi*, on the other hand, adopted strict news conventions to frame some of its studio interviews.

Usually the news is presented by other persons than the magazine. But in BBC *Breakfast News* the presenters of the news are at the same time presenters of the other parts of the programme, either from behind the newsdesk or on easy chairs in a different part of the set.[10] The reverse, but with the same result, is true in TV4 in Sweden: every half-hour one of the presenters of the breakfast show walks away from the sofa, when it is her or his turn to present the news from behind the newsdesk in the news set.

If presenters are different, some unity is re-established by creating, or suggesting, interactivity among the presenters of news and weather and the presenters of the magazine. Oral means (chatting) may be employed, sometimes in combination with visual means (for example, a camera shot in which both can be seen). *GMTV*'s way of handling this is similar to the main American breakfast shows *Today* and *Good Morning America*, with interaction between the anchors of the magazine and the news and a camera view of both (see Box 10.1 and Plate 10.2). French public broadcasting's *Télématin* achieves a similar effect by using split screen with the news and magazine presenters talking to each other. *The Big Breakfast* does it by having its two presenters chat with the presenter of the ITN-produced news who can be watched on a TV set on the floor of the living room which is part of the décor of the programme.

The most commonly employed traditional method for establishing a link is by having the presenters greet each other, or by a simple: 'and now to . . .'. But sometimes achieving flow is made difficult by commercial breaks between news and magazine, or by other interrupting programme slots (cartoons for children, for instance) which make it impossible for presenters to meet, even virtually. And of course, the news itself is an interruption in the continuity of the magazine, which has to be bridged. In these cases audience flow is stimulated by announcements of upcoming topics. This can be done by the presenters, by captions on screen, or by combinations of the two. This way links may even be established between seemingly unrelated items (cf. Plate 1e, where the presenter associates the 'Frenchness' of a pie with French music later in the programme).

DISCUSSION

Infotainment is not a magic formula that guarantees certain and immediate success. In the first place there is no such thing as easy success early in the morning, and secondly, even in countries like Finland and the United Kingdom, where breakfast television has been successful on the whole in attracting a substantial audience,[11] the genre has proved to be very demanding. One reason may be that as a rule information and entertainment are not simply merged in breakfast television, but that they co-exist, one next to the other. The rolling format poses another problem. All this requires a lot of ingenuity on the part of presenters, producers and designers. This might be one of the reasons (next to increased competition) for an observed tendency towards more straightforward entertainment or information types of breakfast television. Increased internal structuring and audience targeting, such as by special lifestyle sections, as in *GMTV* and since early 2000 also in *Huomenta Suomi*, would be a less radical means of reducing the complexity of the format, for both makers and viewers.

Box 10.1 Transitions between breakfast magazine and the news

MTV3 *Huomenta Suomi* (12 May 1998, 6 a.m.)

presenters Lauri Karhuvaara and Pirkko Arstila standing behind high table in studio

Lauri Karhuvaara: What would Finland be without the tango?
Pirkko Arstila: And what would Finland be without Finnish news?
Lauri Karhuvaara: That is right. Let us look at the first news of the morning.

[News jingle, news graphics; caption Uutiset (news); camera shows newsreader behind newsdesk in newsroom; caption: Sari Soininen]

Newsreader Sari Soininen: India's nuclear test yesterday . . .

GMTV (14 May 1998, 7 a.m.)

presenters Eamonn Holmes and Fiona Phillips seated on sofa

Eamonn Holmes: . . . And Deidre Saunders later in the programme to take your calls for whatever kind of eh . . . problem that you've got. Wonder why that made me laugh. Problems are not funny.
Fiona Phillips: They are not. But a problem shared is a problem halved.
Eamonn Holmes: I'll tell you about my problems.
Fiona Phillips: I know your problems.
Eamonn Holmes: You are my problem, Fiona. Well, 09 900 – [*suddenly jumps and points his finger*] camera two, there is a problem, sort that out – 945 945. There you go. And here's the news with Penny Smith. Good morning Penny.

[Camerashot from behind newsreader Penny Smith, seated behind newsdesk, towards Eamonn Holmes and Fiona Phillips on sofa]

Newsreader Penny Smith: Good morning, thank you very much.

[Medium close-up of newsreader at newsdesk, in front of backdrop with globe at top left]

Penny Smith: Good morning, the Ministry of Defence . . .

PLATE 10.2 Camera shot of news presenter Penny Smith and magazine presenters Eamonn Holmes and Fiona Phillips (GMTV)

If we take all European breakfast television together, we do not find a single overall tendency. As a whole it does not seem to have become more popularized than it has been from the start, although some programmes have. The trend among the programmes produced by public broadcasters (BBC, KRO, SVT2 and YLE) has been from light to more serious, an effect which has often been achieved by removing the more purely entertaining items such as the live performances. The development on the side of the commercial broadcasters is contradictory. But *GMTV* and the Swedish and Finnish commercial programmes have basically stuck to their successful mixed formulas. A closer look at the oldest one, *Huomenta Suomi*, shows that its three-tiered structure of equal proportions of news, studio talk and reports, and service and performances has hardly changed over a period of almost ten years.[12] Therefore the history of breakfast television as a whole lends little support to the thesis of increasing tabloidization.[13] And such crude methods of the early days as live chimpanzees and puppet rats to boost the ratings are no longer in use anywhere.

Most of the historical evidence points to a slowly growing divergence between commercial and public types of early morning television. Although national differences may help to explain variations in the degree of informality of style and the structure of the programmes, the influence of audience orientations that go with being a commercial or a public broadcaster seems relatively (and increasingly so) more important.

The divergence of public and commercial breakfast TV is primarily an effect of competition. One interesting distinguishing feature of the competition for the early morning viewer is that in most cases public television entered this field some time after commercial broadcasters had set a standard. Public broadcasters like SVT and YLE first found out that they could not beat the commercial broadcasters with a similar popular format, before they settled for a place closer to the traditional news and current affairs genre. The BBC may become an (important) exception, because it has rejected the restrictions of this option in its plan for the future (BBC News, 1998).

With their more focused, news-oriented magazines public broadcasters serve a comparatively smaller but higher-income, higher-educated, male audience. Although this is perhaps partly a new audience for breakfast TV, this development may be expected to have an impact on the commercial broadcasters. As a consequence they seem to be moving slowly to more focused and structured formats closer to the entertainment side of the infotainment spectrum. The convergence of an earlier phase of breakfast time competition may turn to divergence. What we have now in Europe already resembles a dual form of breakfast television.

One of the most characteristic features of breakfast television is that information, consumer service and entertainment are brought together within one programme. Infotainment is an adequate label for this type of programme format. Does this mean that the criticism of television journalism in general, and of infotainment in particular – that it deflects critical reflection on political questions by trivializing important issues (Dahlgren,

1995) – is applicable to infotainment as practised in breakfast television?

For this the term infotainment is much too unspecific. The infotainment of most European breakfast television programmes is of a type in which information and entertainment are not so much merged (as in other new formats) as held together by a number of aural and visual means, and most of all by a warm and inviting atmosphere, which is created by a certain presentational style and by the framework in which they are presented. In the format of a magazine news and entertainment items co-exist as what they are, with a certain amount of respect for the conventions of each. The typical informal and warm style of early morning television is most pervasive in the programmes of the commercial broadcasters, but there are important differences. In *GMTV* style tends to dominate over content, but in *Huomenta Suomi* content is still the main determinant of style. At the moment these are not really opposites, there is only a relative distance between them. The degree to which style interferes with content may be a more important criterion, though, in deciding whether the above-mentioned criticism applies, than the fact that the serious and the frivolous are put together within one format.

The difference between breakfast TV and other day and night-time infotainment programmes looks much greater than between individual breakfast TV programmes. In early morning television in Europe – this goes for *GMTV* too – a minister of foreign affairs is still more likely to be interviewed about an international conflict than about the conflicts in the relationship with his or her partner (although that subject may be raised too!).

This introduces a final point, which cannot be dealt with on the basis of our research. What kind of judgement should be passed on the genre in terms of the quality, relevance and accessibility of information? Set against established professional standards of good television journalism, as embodied in the traditional news format, the verdict is likely to be negative. Dahlgren (1995) is careful in his assessment of new formats like breakfast television. Hallin, who qualifies the American breakfast news shows as 'entertainment first and journalism second' (1994: 92), found, nevertheless, 'much more substantial coverage than would normally be found on the evening news' (1994: 94). Cottle (1993; cf. 1995) reaches the same conclusion in his study of environment news. There may also be reason to assume that early morning television may be relatively effective in informing people, because it takes the diversity of their backgrounds into account (Hamm, 1990; Perse, 1998).

I have argued that the format of breakfast television is determined to a considerable extent by the conditions of the time of day and the difficult early morning market. Although this is not particularly reassuring in itself, it may help to preserve some features, like being non-confrontational, airing interviews live and unedited, an emphasis on sound and less on pictures, and a slow pace, which run against trends in television journalism in general. There is obviously much more to be found out about this than can be covered in this chapter. What is more, we may have found out something about *how* things are being told in breakfast TV, but we have still hardly touched on *what* is being communicated.

ACTIVITIES

1 A standard rule in comparative research is that the cases should be similar in some fundamental characteristics, but also dissimilar enough to make a comparison worthwhile. The analysis in this chapter is mainly based on a sample of breakfast television programmes in north-western Europe.

- Do you think that the results would have been different if countries in other parts of Europe (or of the world) had been included?
- Why, and in which respects? Try to substantiate your answer by an analysis of history or aspects of style of one or more programmes that were not in the sample.

2 The chapter suggests that the ways in which breakfast television had to adapt to an audience with little time and attention may contain lessons for the television of the future.

- Do you agree with the suggestion in the chapter?
- What kind of lessons could that be?
- Some European countries have 24-hour news television; other countries may follow. What kind of impact might this have on breakfast television?

3 Standard double presentation by a man and a woman in breakfast television implies balance in a quantitative sense.

- Try to find out if their roles are equal.
- Why is this kind of double presentation so popular?
- Do you also find balance when you look at reporters, experts and guests on breakfast TV programmes? How do you explain this?

4 Compare the ways in which interviews are conducted on a breakfast television programme, a news or current affairs programme and a talk show or daytime magazine.

- What kind of people are interviewed (politician, manager, celebrity, artist, 'ordinary' people)? Take one particular kind, e.g. politicians.
- What does the set represent?
- What kinds of topics are discussed and about what do you learn most: political issues, personal backgrounds/problems, emotions, trivialities? What kinds of solutions are proposed and discussed?

- What is the general tone of the interview and the interviewer(s)? How formal, friendly, questioning, pushing, submissive?
- What is the role of the interviewing anchor(s) of the programme? Expert, equal, superior, representing the people?
- What do you think was the best interview? Why? Also try to pass a judgement in terms of 'contribution to democracy' (cf. Dahlgren in Chapter 2).

NOTES

1 Interview with the author, Helsinki, 15 September 1998.

2 It is part of (yet unfinished) comparative research of the development of early morning television in Europe. The project focuses on eight breakfast TV programmes in four European countries (*Aamu-TV* and *Huomenta Suomi* in Finland, *Ontbijt TV* in the Netherlands, *Nyhetsmorgon* and *Rapport Morgon* in Sweden and *The Big Breakfast*, *Breakfast News* and *GMTV* in the United Kingdom). Data are gathered by way of interviews with programmers, programme-makers and presenters (participant), observation (at *Aamu-TV*, *Huomenta Suomi*, *Ontbijt TV*, *Nyhetsmorgon*, *Rapport Morgon* and *Breakfast News*), and analysis of samples of programme output. The paragraph about the history of breakfast television is partly based on interviews at the eight broadcasting organizations, the paragraph about the style of breakfast television on analysis of programmes from the second week of May 1998. Many people at all the broadcasting organizations involved have been giving their (essential) help, for which I am most grateful.

3 The United Kingdom and Finland have had dual broadcasting systems since the 1950s. All commercial broadcasters in the sample have some sort of public service obligation.

4 Public broadcasting in the Netherlands is composed of several more or less independent non-profit broadcasting organizations.

5 In this paragraph we shall use the word programme for the whole breakfast TV programme including the news, and the word magazine for the programme without the typical newscasts.

6 See for instance Corner, 1995; Fairclough, 1995; Hartley, 1982; Heinderyckx, 1993; Fiske, 1987; Kepplinger, 1991; or manuals for journalists like Boyd, 1998.

7 The opening sequence of the news is repeated at every new newscast, but the magazine is treated more as one programme. Viewers are welcomed more explicitly at the opening or just after the first news bulletin than later on during the show.

8 E.g. *Good Morning America* (ABC), *Good Morning Britain* (TV-am), *GMTV* (that is Good Morning TV), *Huomenta Suomi* (MTV3), *Go'morgen Danmark* (TV2), *Goeiemorgen Vlaanderen* (VTM).

9 Since the summer of 1999 all talk is done from the same (restyled) studio, much as in *Go'morgen Danmark*.

10 The BBC has announced that Moira Stuart will present the news on BBC *Breakfast News* when the programme is relaunched in the summer of 2000 (http://www.bbc.co.uk/info/news/news160htm; 12 March 1999).

11 Ratings are notoriously difficult to compare (e.g. Schulz, Chapter 7 in this volume); still it is clear that the breakfast television audience is considerably larger in these countries than for instance in Germany and the Netherlands.

12 Based on analysis of five programmes in the MTV3 archive, which were broadcast between 4 December 1990 and 21 May 1991, and the weekday programmes in the first and second weeks of May 1998. Between 1990–91 and 1998 *Huomenta Suomi* was extended from 130 to 180 minutes.

13 Outside Europe tendencies are not so clear either. A few years ago many observers were surprised by the announcement that *Good Morning America*, which had been produced for decades by the entertainment division of ABC, would be taken over by its news division (Lawrie Mifflin in the *New York Times*, 21 September 1998).

SUGGESTIONS FOR FURTHER READING

Dahlgren, P. (1995) *Television and the Public Sphere. Citizenship, Democracy and the Media*. London: Sage.

Peter Dahlgren discusses current trends in genres of television journalism within the wider framework of theories of civil society and the public sphere and critically analyses the practice of television.

Feuer, J. (1983) 'The concept of live television: ontology as ideology', in E.A. Kaplan (ed.), *Regarding Television: Critical Approaches – an Anthology*, pp. 12–22. Los Angeles: University Publications of America.

Thought-provoking article about liveness as the essence of television, and *Good Morning America* as the programme that epitomizes the concept of an ideology of liveness overcoming fragmentation.

Hartley, J. (1982) *Understanding News*. London: Methuen (later London: Routledge).

An often reprinted critical study of the news and its construction.

Kepplinger, H.M. (1991) 'The impact of presentation techniques: theoretical aspects and empirical findings', in F. Biocca (ed.), *Television and Political Advertising*, Vol. 1: *Psychological Processes*, pp. 173–194. Hillsdale, NJ: Lawrence Erlbaum.

Introduction and overview of what is known about the effects of presentation.

CHAPTER 11

TALK SHOWS: DEMOCRATIC DEBATES AND TABLOID TALES

Graham Murdock

TALKING PICTURES

Television is a machine for assembling images and organizing speech. It invites us to listen as well as to look. Programmes are filled with voices – recounting, arguing, proposing, explaining, joking. Soap opera episodes shift easily between gossip, anecdote and revelation. Major news items move from the anchor's measured summaries of what is happening, to on-the-spot observations from reporters, to interviews with key actors and experts, to eyewitness accounts from those in the thick of the action.

The diversity of talk on television is central to its appeal (Corner, 1999: 45). It offers us the pleasure of eavesdropping on people thinking aloud, telling stories, voicing opinions and struggling to answer awkward questions. But viewers are not simply listening in to conversations conducted elsewhere. Programme presenters talk *to* us, as well as *for* us, frequently turning to the camera to make eye contact and address us directly. The triangular relations between presenters, participants and viewers take on an added dimension when a show is recorded in front of an audience. They become our go-betweens, bridging the public space of the studio and the private space of the home. Audience participation plays an important role in many of television's most popular genres – quiz shows, game shows, video clip shows and situation comedies – but only in 'talk shows' is it tied so securely to the orchestration of talk.

In the professional folklore of programme production, 'talking heads' are often dismissed as a waste of television's visuality, guaranteed to bore the viewers into changing channels. Shows recorded in front of a studio audience avoid these strictures by accentuating movement. The camera follows the ebb and flow of incident, argument and conversation, cutting between the main speakers, holding their faces in close-up at moments of heightened emotion, then pulling back to search the studio audience for resonant responses. Programmes showing someone addressing the camera in an empty studio risk appearing too static and formal. By focusing on people talking 'head to head' in full public view, talk shows promise viewers the excitement of the unrehearsed, the spontaneous and the authentic. In an age where the performances of public figures, from show-business celebrities to politicians and business leaders, are ever more carefully scripted by public relations experts and spin doctors, this is a seductive promise. As one British television producer noted, defending recent talk shows against their critics, 'audience shows can have an emotional honesty that puts a lot of political posturing to shame' (*Guardian Saturday Review*, 1999: 2).

VARIETIES OF TALK

Talk shows draw on a range of different kinds of talk and combine them in a variety of ways to produce both distinctive sub-genres and a series of hybid or mixed forms. Seven sorts of talk are central to the analysis I want to develop here.

Conversation

Commercial television is unashamedly populist. Its drive for ratings puts a premium on elements that cut across divisions within the audience. It continually reassures viewers 'of their wisdom, confirming what they knew to be true all along . . . that the world is a wobbly and treacherous place to live in' (Bauman, 1999: 8). It builds imagined communities around the bedrock experiences of everyday life – love, betrayal, hope, disillusion – and the core elements of commonsense thinking – luck, distrust of authority, and the comforts of money. Its pivotal figures are the soap opera characters, talk show hosts, game show presenters and entertainment show comperes, who link the worlds behind and in front of the screen, reducing distances to almost zero. They offer themselves as 'media friends', people we can imagine 'hanging out together at home, riding in the car, sharing an adventure' (Meyrowitz, 1994: 64). They address us in familiar, conversational tones, sharing jokes, gossip, good-humoured banter, homely advice and offering catch-phrases for everyday use.

Confession

Many admissions of wrongdoing are made to priests or doctors in confidence. But there are also well established forms of public confession.

'True confession' magazines have been a staple of tabloid publishing since the early years of the twentieth century, while programmes like *Truth or Consequences*, 'in which audience members answered questions mailed in by listeners, often accompanied by public humiliation of one sort or another' (Gamson, 1998: 42) were early fixtures in the history of American commercial radio. Television talk shows have adopted both these sources whilst also drawing on styles developed in public forums where confession is witnessed by others. Self-help groups, such as Alcoholics Anonymous, demand complete honesty and openness as a condition of support. Similarly, in evangelical religious meetings converts and backsliders are urged to testify to their sins and repent before the congregation. American talk shows make extensive use of this model so that the verbal interactions between the person confessing, the host and studio audience often resemble the call/response structure of religious 'witnessing' or gospel music. (Landman, 1996: 9). The voicing of often painful experiences is central to the chat show's promise of intimacy and authenticity. Occasionally the host will share their own secrets, as Oprah Winfrey did when she admitted to her constant problems with weight, and talked about her rape at the age of 9, the death of the premature baby she had at 14, and losing her brother to AIDS. These revelations of anxiety and suffering helped to confirm her position as America's most popular talk show compere. This sense of talk shows as a confessional without walls is made explicit in *Confess* on Britain's Channel 4, hosted by a young Catholic priest who invites participants to 'share your sins' and 'relieve your soul'.

Therapy

In contrast to treatments requiring medical intervention such as drugs or electric shocks, the therapeutic style developed by Sigmund Freud which encouraged patients to speak about their repressed experiences quickly became known as the 'talking cure'. However, the time and expense involved put it beyond the reach of most average income earners, leaving a gap that was rapidly filled by the 'agony aunt' columns in popular newspapers, and more recently by the proliferating range of counselling services for moments of personal crisis, from marital breakdown and bereavement to worries about being overweight. American talk shows have taken these new talking cures, combined them with the tabloidization of the 'true confession' magazine, and moved them in front of the camera (Gamson, 1998: 54).

As a number of commentators have pointed out, the populist sensibility that underpins many talk shows, particularly in the United States, consistently denigrates the contributions of academics and professionals. However, 'what is expressed in these shows is not a refusal of knowledge, but of the status of expertise'. They reject 'the arrogance of a discourse that defines itself on the basis of its difference from common-sense' (Carpignano et al.,

1990: 52). As a result, lay knowledge tends to be 'valued as authentic, relevant, coherent, grounded in experience and practical' whereas 'expertise is constructed as alienated, irrelevant, fragmented, superficial, and useless' (Livingstone and Lunt, 1994b: 210). Therapists, on the other hand, often escape this general censure. Their knowledge is presented as easily understood and immediately useful, an impression frequently underlined by shots of the studio audience listening attentively, suggesting that here is one source of authority that people are prepared to accept (Fairclough, 1995: 141).

Storytelling

Talk shows' celebration of grounded experience means that most of the stories recounted are told either by the ordinary people invited on as guests or by members of the studio audience. They offer raw slices of lived experience. Many speak from the margins, giving voice to the hope, disappointment and anger of people who have been ignored, denigrated or demonized by mainstream opinion. As the journalist Barbara Ehrenreich observed (speaking particularly of the new wave of American talk shows), when you watch these programmes you see 'people who have never before been listened to, and certainly never been taken seriously if they were' (in Richardson and Meinhof, 1999: 128).

Interviews

Not all talk shows relate the tribulations and small triumphs of everyday life. A number feature interviews with public figures. Faced with politicians and decision makers, the presenter usually takes the role of the viewer-as-citizen, putting questions that the 'the public' is assumed to want answers to. Distrust of authority figures, and suspicions that 'they' are trying to do 'us' down, are a central theme in populist thinking. Talk shows tap into this. In contrast, when talking to celebrities and stars, presenters speak for the viewer-as-fan, pressing interviewees for ever more intimate details of their professional work, private lives and personal tastes. In response, interviewees will frequently seize the opportunity to promote something.

Sales pitches

Many participants in talk shows are selling something: a new film, record or book, a new policy initiative, or a course of self-help. This is true not only of the celebrities, therapists and politicians whose careers depend on successful 'sales' to the public, but also of some seemingly ordinary participants, like Carol, a guest on *Donahue* (one of America's longest running talk shows) who used her altered face and body to publicize her husband's plastic surgery practice. As she told a researcher, 'you merchandize yourself, and you become known . . . I've always done that, and so I make a good team-mate . . . I've been a very good asset for him in business' (Joyner Priest, 1995: 52). Sometimes the host him/herself may have something to sell. Oprah Winfrey, for example, chairs a book club credited with transforming American reading habits, owns a successful television production company, Harpo, and has published best-selling books based on her fitness and diet programmes. Commercial persuasion on television has long since escaped from the confines of spot advertising and sponsors' announcements. By offering hospitality to a range of sales pitches talk shows contribute to an enveloping culture of promotion which addresses audiences as consumers making choices in the marketplace rather than as citizens pressing for social change.

Argument and debate

Talk shows may also provide important cultural resources for citizenship through the debates they stage on political and social issues. Dispassionate argument, in which speakers submit their propositions to the disciplines of evidence and the risk of refutation by sceptics and opponents, has long been thought of as the cornerstone of democratic culture. Cultivating the habit of rational deliberation in listeners was a major aim of early public service broadcasting, perfectly captured in the title of the BBC programme *The Brains Trust*, an unapologetically paternalistic project. Enlightening the ignorant was intellectuals' sacred duty. In return, listeners were expected to take their expertise 'on trust' and accept that they knew best. From the outset, however, this monopoly was challenged by groups claiming the right to speak for themselves, in their own voice. These demands for extended representation steadily gathered momentum, and were met by new programme forms, including talk shows, offering more pluralistic spaces for public expression and debate. The balance between storytelling and expert testimony is always precarious, however, and generates continual tensions 'between the concrete and the abstract, the disempowered and the powerful, lived-in experience and expertise', testimony and analysis (Livingstone and Lunt, 1994a: 180).

These collisions have prompted two very different critical reactions. Some commentators see talk shows' hospitality to previously neglected issues and voices as a welcome extension of democratic debate. Others accuse them of following the tabloid press in trivializing social issues, replacing rational deliberation with emotive expression, and elevating sensation over the search for feasible solutions. Before we explore this argument further, we need to define the main forms of talk show more carefully.

TALK AS SHOW

The talk shows we are interested in here are made up of three basic elements.

- a presenter, moderator, or chairperson who orchestrates the proceedings;
- various 'guests' who are invited in advance to appear and contribute. They are usually identified by a caption on the screen. Their accounts, opinions and reactions provide the basic raw materials around which the show develops;
- most importantly, there is a studio audience who actively participate in the proceedings either minimally by clapping or booing, or more fully, by contributing their own stories, questions or advice. By turning talk into a public performance, a show, their presence gives the programmes a theatrical quality that marks them off from discussions or interviews recorded without an audience.

These three core features define the basic boundaries of the talk show genre, but within this general frame programme makers can utilize the available resources in several different ways. These variations have produced three basic sub-genres – political talk shows, celebrity talk shows, and participatory talk shows – together with a number of programmes that combine elements from more than one.

Political talk shows are based around interviews with politicians and other key decision makers and/or debates on topics in the news which raise questions about public policies or institutional arrangements. In 1930 the radical German poet and playwright, Bertolt Brecht, called for radio programmes that would transform 'the reports of our rulers into answers to the questions of the ruled' (Brecht, 1979–80: 25–26). A number of political talk shows now do this. The long running weekly BBC programme, *Question Time*, for example, features a panel made up of politicians and other notables who respond to questions previously submitted by members of the studio audience.

Celebrity talk shows are built around interviews with figures from the worlds of fashion, sport, the media and show business and draw freely on the promotional language of public relations and the vernacular tones of fan magazines and gossip columns. The stars appear as both exceptional and ordinary, enjoying a lavish lifestyle but at the same time down to earth, sharing ordinary pleasures and setbacks. Because of their emphasis on establishing intimacy and approachability and their tendency to trade in 'insider' gossip, these programmes are often called 'chat' shows. They are also intended as entertainment, so celebrity guests are often asked to sing or otherwise perform.

Participatory talk shows mobilize the studio audience as active contributors to discussions on social isues or personal dilemmas. They are not simply spectators and listeners but potential speakers and participants. Here the public is 'no longer in the dark of an orchestra. In a sort of democracy of lighting everybody is brought on stage and given their share of illumination' (Carpignano et al., 1990: 47). This type of talk show has expanded rapidly in recent years. In the Netherlands in 1991 for example, an average week's television featured 4.5 such shows. By 1995 this figure had jumped to 25.5. In contrast, the number of political talk shows broadcast remained unchanged at two a week (Leurdijk, 1997: 150).

This basic pattern is repeated in other European countries. It is not difficult to see why. The rapid extension of broadcasting hours, with the addition of breakfast and late-night television, has left more and more space to fill and has stretched production resources. The multiplication of channels, with the launch of new terrestrial commercial stations and the growth of cable and satellite services, has intensified competition for audiences and placed a premium on cheap programming with proven popular appeal. Participatory talk shows meet these criteria perfectly.

They were originally developed for daytime slots in American commercial television but variants of the basic forms are now common across Europe. Enthusiasts welcome their demolition of traditional hierarchies and their openness to everyday experience. Critics see them as further evidence of the Americanization of European broadcasting and the eclipse of public service ideals. Here, as elsewhere, however, this simple opposition of Europe and America conceals more than it reveals. Debates within the United States are marked by the same anxieties over the shifting balance between entertainment and enlightenment, sensation and social responsibility.

MADE IN THE USA: TALK SHOWS AND AMERICAN CULTURE

The issue-oriented participatory talk show was pioneered by Phil Donahue, whose eponymous programme was launched in Dayton, Ohio in 1967. From its first week it included lifestyle topics, such as what kinds of women bachelors found attractive, alongside inquiries into political issues and social institutions, such as the funeral industry. *Donahue* 'took up "public" issues that had heretofore been private and, drawing on a long tradition in women's popular genres . . . spoke . . . the language of subjective, first hand, "authentic" knowledge' (Gamson, 1998: 46). During the 1970s, however, this highly saleable mix came under increasing pressure from social constituencies pressing to have more of their lives and concerns included on the public agenda. *Donahue* responded and by 1979 was achieving higher ratings than the more mainstream political agenda offered by America's long-running current affairs, *The Tonight Show*, prompting the magazine, *Newsweek*, to complain that 'One sometimes suspects that Donahue's idea of a perfect guest is an interracial lesbian couple who have a child by artificial insemination. Sure enough, that couple appeared last March' (quoted in Tavener, 2000: 63). Five years later, in 1984, previously excluded groups found a major forum, when a young, black, former newsreader, Oprah Winfrey, took over an ailing talk show in Chicago. Within a month it had eclipsed *Dohahue* in the ratings and, renamed *The Oprah Winfrey Show*, rapidly gained nationwide distribution. As a black woman Winfrey represented two major constituencies who felt they had been silenced or misrepresented in mainstream programming. Her show played a crucial role in opening up new spaces for women's voices and concerns. She made no secret of this. As she told a female guest on one of her shows in 1989, 'we do program these shows to empower women' (in Squire, 1997: 98). By 1994, when Bradley Greenberg and his colleagues surveyed the 11 highest rating American daytime talk shows, there were two female guests for every male (Greenberg et al., 1997: 416). But the problem of representation was never simply a matter of ratios.

As a number of social theorists have pointed out, established social identities and self-definitions are giving way to blurred boundaries and multiple choices. In this fluid and uncertain situation more and more people are asking 'how we should talk – and argue – about ourselves and others' when we can no longer agree on a shared moral foundation for our discussion (Illouz, 1999: 121). The multiple stories told on participatory talk shows allow both participants and audiences to question established roles, 'try out' new positions and, possibly, to reinvent themselves (Landman, 1996: 2). This can be a painful process.

In a recent interview, Oprah Winfrey expressed mixed feelings about her original shows. On the one hand, she remains proud that she 'highlighted important subjects that were hitherto taboo – child and sexual abuse, divorce, alcoholism'. On the other, she now voices reservations about a production philosophy that 'always considered [it] a great TV moment if you got someone to open up and cry. As I matured I felt bad seeing others expose themselves in a way I knew they'd later regret' (Duncan, 1999: 16). Her solution has been to focus on how women can remake themselves, from a simple change of make-up or clothes to various styles of therapy. It is Samuel Smiles's Victorian handbook on self-help rewritten for the age of niche marketing and dramatized in her own well publicized progress from rural poverty to international success. Her distinctive programming mix is central to the thinking behind Oxygen, the first American cable network aimed exclusively at women, which she launched early in 2000 in partnership with two other successful female entertainment industry executives. As one of her partners, Geraldine Laybourne (architect of the successful Nickelodeon children's channel) explained, 'Oxygen can be today's equivalent of the 1950s back fence, where women can learn, relax, meet, talk, plan, have fun and manage their increasingly complicated lives' (in Tran, 1999: 6). This is a classic instance of brand extension.

Despite her background in news, Winfrey was always strongly linked to the worlds of show business and sales. Her talk show's early success owed much to the Oscar nomination she received for her role in Steven Spielberg's film *The Color Purple*, which, like the show, expertly packaged social commentary as entertainment. As she understood very well, entertainment was always the bottom line for the advertisers who funded the spaces she offered marginalized voices. As she recently told a journalist:

> I work in a profession that pays you based on the numbers watching. If I can draw millions to the TV set to buy products that are advertised I have no guilt . . . although my attitude was, 'Let's get something out of this . . .' Entertainment was the real goal. (Duncan, 1999: 16)

Looking at the programmes introduced in the 1990s, many commentators see this desire to do 'something' socially beneficial with the talk show genre being comprehensively elbowed out by the search for entertainment. One of the casualties of this shift was Phil Donahue, whose pioneering show was cancelled in 1996. He was too 'middle-aged' for the new emphasis on the youth market, too establishment for the new streetwise audience. As a supervising producer on one of the new shows explained: 'Everyone on the show is young, and everybody in the audience is young, and the topics are young . . . Where Donahue might do "Put in jail for a crime they didn't commit", we would do "I get stopped by cops for no reason at all"' (Gamson, 1998: 59).

The drive for the youth market was accompanied by a shift in the backgrounds of the hosts. Whereas both Donahue and Oprah had come from newsdesks, a number of the new entrants came from the heartlands of show business. Ricki Lake, for example, was already well known for her roles in hit box office films such as *Hairspray* and *Serial Mom* before she launched her talk show in 1993. Similarly, Roseanne Barr had become a household name for her role as the matriarch of the dysfunctional working class family in the high rating situation comedy *Roseanne*, before moving on to hosting.

Arguably, popular entertainment genres have also come to play a more central role in organizing talk show formats and styles. The emphasis on discussion and shared solutions has given way to drama, action and confrontation. The shows' themes are often cast in the form of an ultimatum, such as 'Listen, Family, I'm Gay . . . It's not a Phase . . . Get over It!'; 'Your Flirting Has Gone Too Far' or 'Yeah Mom. I'm 13 . . . But I Am Going to Make a Baby' (from recent *Ricki Lake Shows*). These challenges are pursued as three-act dramas, complete with cliffhangers to persuade the audience to return after the advertising break. In the first act, the aggrieved party is invited to tell their story to the audience. The accused is often shown waiting in another part of studio, unable to hear what is being said. In the second act, they are brought out to confront their accuser. Often these mini dramas borrow elements from popular crime shows. A partner accused of infidelity may be asked to take a lie detector test, or as in a recent *Ricki Lake Show* entitled 'The Forensic Test Proved You Cheated!', have their underclothes secretly submitted for DNA testing. In the final act, some resolution is sought. This may take the form of advice from a therapist or expert on human relations, but again, quite often it will borrow from popular courtroom drama. In a recent episode of her show Roseanne Barr put on full judge's regalia and sat po-faced on a dais in front of the American flag, to adjudicate on whether or not a father had the right to forbid his three teenage daughters to have their hair cut in a fashionable bob. After hearing submissions by lawyers for both parties, she found in favour of the daughters, declaring that 'Everyone has the right to feel cute.'

This sentence sums up the central shift in the social focus of daytime American talk shows. Questions of rights are no longer about the distribution of life chances. They are about entitlements to lifestyles. Citizenship has been thoroughly consumerized. Critics see this as further proof of a movement away from personalizing the political by linking individual circumstances to structures of injustice to sensationalizing the personal by focusing relentlessly on broken relationships (Shattuc, 1998). In the process, they argue, 'The studio audience moved from the role of citizens making common-sense judgements to spectators hungering for confrontation' (Shattuc, 1998: 213). They see the new talk shows as a 'recurring nightmare' for the ideal of a democratic public sphere, since instead of constructing a popular site for collective conversation around issues of shared concern, they present the nation to itself 'through the prism . . . of everyday concerns constructed as a spectacle of personal confusion and melodramatic confrontations, of private pain and interpersonal anguish' (Tavener, 2000: 83).

For many observers, the terminal point in this process is represented by the *Jerry Springer Show*, which became notorious soon after its launch in 1991, for allowing its guests to settle their differences with fist fights (which were then quickly broken up by waiting security personnel). As the feminist critic, Camille Paglia, has pointed out, these 'colourful confrontationalism and quick, bruising skirmishes' draw heavily on the youth-oriented styles developed by video games and televised wrestling (Richardson and Meinhof, 1999: 128). And as the French cultural analyst, Roland Barthes, famously observed, 'The virtue of all-in wrestling is that it is the spectacle of excess' (Barthes, 1973: 15). Springer is well aware of this comparison. As he told a journalist: 'There is a lot of wrestling and rolling around that goes on the show. I'll admit that . . . The guy loses the girl. The audience boos the person who can't act correctly' just as the crowd at a wrestling match boos the villain (Marshall, 1999: 24). But it is precisely the quality of excess and the denigration of rational debate that has most angered Springer's critics.

Interestingly, Springer came to television after a successful career as a populist politician. Although he was forced to resign his seat on the Cincinnati city council after being caught patronizing a massage parlour, he recovered to become the city's mayor and narrowly failed in a bid to become the Democratic governor of Ohio in 1982. He insists that his show is not a denial of democratic politics but an extension, a way of pursuing the populist project of giving a voice back to all of those whom established politicians too readily dismiss as 'trash' to be discarded, 'Do you ever call a Congressman trash?' he asks. 'It's a euphemism for trailer park, minorities, space between their teeth. We all know it' (Gamson, 1998: 15). He told an interviewer: 'Even in the midst of the craziness of the show – and that's all it is, crazy – my first passion has always been politics' (Borger, 1999: 1).

Jerry Springer, and a number of other American talk shows, including *Oprah* and *Ricki Lake*, are currently available in Europe (sometimes a considerable time after their original airing in the USA), mostly on cable or satellite systems or commercial terrestrial channels. In the autumn of 1998 for example, viewers of commercial channels in the Netherlands could watch all three programmes, together with domestically produced shows strongly influenced by American models. They included *Catherine* (based on *Oprah*) and launched in 1995, *Heartbreak Hotel*, named after one of Elvis Presley's first hits and specializing in personal problems, and *All You Need is Love*, named after the Beatles' song and devoted to reuniting lovers. In contrast, viewers tuning into the public channel AVRO could watch the more news-oriented show *Karel*.

This pattern suggests that European television, in its publicly funded and hybrid forms, is still strongly influenced by public service ideals. So does this mean that European talk shows are less likely to privilege entertainment over information, emotion over rationality? Jerry Springer thinks they are. As he jokingly told the audience for the pilot show of a planned series of *The Jerry Springer Show in the UK*, 'I read that a 12-year-old girl had a baby and her mother is only 26. In the UK you call it a scandal. Back in the States we call it *The Jerry Springer Show*' (Robins, 1999: 10). To answer the question more systematically, let's begin by looking at some other examples from Britain, the European country with the closest cultural and linguistic ties to the United States.

TRANSATLANTIC CROSSINGS: BETWEEN POPULISM AND PATERNALISM

The first British programme to adapt the model pioneered by the early Oprah Winfrey shows, *Day by Day*, was launched by the country's major public service channel, BBC1, in 1986. Hosted by a former Labour Member of Parliament, Robert Kilroy Silk, and broadcast directly after the breakfast news, it concentrated on topical issues, confronting politicians and experts with the experiences and anxieties of ordinary people. Again, it was underpinned by populist politics. As Kilroy Silk freely admits, the shows 'I like best are where people, real people take on those in authority . . . For instance, the soldier talking about bullying in the army and the General interrupts. And the soldier says "Just a minute, I'm speaking,

We're not in the Army now". It's brillant, I love that' (Francis, 2000: 17). However, when it comes to explaining a problem the voice of experience is often obliged to give way to the pronouncements of an expert. Let's take the edition broadcast on 24 January 1993 analysed by Simon Cross (1999) as an example.

It dealt with the government's controversial policy of closing asylums and releasing mental patients into the community. First-hand testimony from people with schizophrenic relatives and representatives of charities caring for the mentally ill were used to illustrate the failure of current policies and construct a critique that was then put to a member of the governing party. But to *explain* what schizophrenia is, as opposed to what it *felt* like to live with it on a daily basis, the host turned to Dr Tim Crowe, who is captioned on screen as a consultant psychiatrist. His contribution comes directly after a series of accounts from schizophrenics describing their experiences of hearing 'voices'.

> *Kilroy-Silk*: Is that typical of what we've heard schizophrenics go through?
> *Dr Crow*: There are many different features of the disease and I think we've heard some of the spectrum so far . . . There are two big categories: hallucinations–disorders of perception; delusions–disorders of belief . . .

As this abrupt introduction of professional terminology (such as 'hallucinations–disorders') makes clear, the programme is an uneasy combination of two traditions of broadcasting. On the one hand, it follows the populist model in giving extended space to speakers and experiences that are seldom heard elsewhere in the schedules and confronting politicians with the everyday consequences of their decisions. On the other, it reinforces a paternalistic belief in the superiority of expert knowledge and relegates first-hand testimony to the role of raw data offered up for authoritative interpretation and analysis.

Andra Leurdijk found the same asymmetry in her study of Dutch talk shows dealing with issues around racism and multiculturalism. Here again, marginalized voices were given extensive opportunities to speak. The 21 programmes she analysed featured 226 lay people (60 per cent of whom were from ethnic minorities). In contrast, there were just 17 academics or other experts (though only one was from an ethnic minority). However, visibility did not guarantee equality. Unlike most participants, experts generally had 'the opportunity to bring forward their expertise and point of view uninhibited by interventions from the studio audience. Also they get more time than the average lay participant' (Leurdijk, 1997: 157). The resilience of this public service paternalism led Leurdijk to conclude that 'most Dutch talk shows can still be considered to be more serious and journalistically inclined than their American counterparts' (1997: 151).

In Britain, however, there are distinct signs that daytime talk shows are moving away from political issues to focus on private anxieties and miseries. Robert Kilroy Silk's programme has followed the American preference for naming the show after the host. Retitled *Kilroy*, it now regularly concentrates on personal relationships, emphasizing emotional sincerity rather than rational analysis, common sense rather than expert opinion. At the beginning of 1996, the topics were still firmly anchored in issues of public concern such as 'Arming the Police' (9 January) and 'Emergency Bed Shortage' (17 January). Two years later the agenda had been stretched to include individual dilemmas such as 'My Husband Wants to Become a Woman' (31 March). Take for example the edition entitled 'I've Lost Contact with my Family' transmitted on 1 June 1999. The centrepiece was the testimony of a woman whose daughter had broken off all communication. After listening to her story, Kilroy invites her to appeal directly to her daughter who she hopes is watching at home.

Kilroy: What do you want to say to her?
Woman: If she's watching this programme, I shall say to her: 'I love her. I miss her. And I'll always, always, be there for her.'
Kilroy: What's her name?
Woman: Michelle. [*She begins to cry. The camera closes in on her face and shoulders as Kilroy places a comforting arm around her.*]
Kilroy: Michelle? You can see how emotional she is. I'm not dwelling on that. But she means that. She felt it.

Kilroy may feel uneasy 'dwelling' on emotion, but newer arrivals have fewer qualms. *Trisha*, broadcast on Britain's major terrestrial commercial channel, and hosted by a young black woman with some training in counselling, follows *Oprah* closely in format and style. The edition transmitted on the same morning as the programme just discussed, is a good illustration. It too dealt with broken family relationships but unlike *Kilroy* displayed no lingering ties to public service paternalism. From the American style title – 'Mum You're Driving Me Mad' – onwards, its orientation was thoroughly populist. In the first act a young woman whose mother had expelled her from the family home when she was 16 tells her story. The host asks the kind of questions a therapist would put: 'Do you love your mum?'; 'How does she make you feel?'; 'What do you want?'

In the second act, the mother is brought on and the two argue, opening up old wounds. In the final act, the host identifies the problem as a 'communication breakdown' and turning to the studio audience, asks 'How are we going to move forward? Does anyone have any ideas?' A middle-aged man (who has previously recounted his own break and reconciliation with his mother) offers his advice:

Can I just say. Let water flow under the bridge. Let bygones be bygones. Look foward. Tomorrow is another day. Why don't you make friends now and just say, 'We'll try our best'.

This string of homespun clichés is greeted with warm applause from the studio audience and brings the segment to an end.

Although this episode does not sensationalize or escalate confrontation, it does lend support to those critics who accuse contemporary talk shows of trivialization. They argue that the situations discussed are stripped of all social and political context. That no attempt is made to probe beneath the surface or challenge common sense. That social problems are comprehensively personalized and solutions reduced to self-help supported by popular therapies. That social change slides off the agenda for debate and the public sphere as a space for exploring issues of common concern is transformed into a succession of private conversations conducted in public.

The audience-building strategies employed by the new talk shows create their own problems. The demands for novel topics and dramatic presentations are not easily met on a daily basis. 'As the emotional situations portrayed become ever more extreme, it becomes more and more difficult to find the man who has slept with all five of his sisters-in-law, cheated on his honeymoon and discovered he is a transvestite' (Bolton, 1999: 7). One solution is to pay people to play the parts, which is what *Trisha* and the BBC's rival show, *Vanessa*, were found to have done early in 1999. The 'real' guests were fakes. Performance had been professionalized. An embarrassed BBC cancelled *Vanessa* soon afterwards.

Elsewhere in Europe however can we still find talk show cultures that remain committed to fostering popular enlightenment through rational debate? Germany, with its strong public service tradition, is a good place to begin looking.

PUBLIC SERVICE TALK

On the basis of a detailed analysis of talk shows broadcast on network television in Germany and the United States in February 1993, Andrea Krause and Elizabeth Goering (1995) identify a number of major differences between the two systems.

American talk shows are named after the host. Their personality and style of performance gives the programme its particular stamp and marks it off from the competition. Like film stars, they offer stable points of identification amidst the continual flux of issues, plots and characters. In return, viewers are encouraged to behave like fans. *The Jerry Springer Show*, for example, opens with shots of Springer entering the studio to a standing ovation from the audience and ends with members of the audience gathered by the stage door saying how far they have come to see him. In marked contrast, none of the German talk shows analysed were named after the host, although one, *Boulevard Bio*, did contain an embedded reference to the presenter, Alfred Biolek. But that was a joke shared with the audience, not a way of fixing the show's character. While American talk shows 'establish the hosts as cultural icons, the German shows emphasize the iconic function of the setting in which the talk is to take place' (Kraus and Goering, 1995: 192). *Boulevard Bio* opens with shots of the city at night, evoking the discussion and debate in pubs and clubs. Similarly, *Presseclub* hints at arguments in editorial meetings over the major news issues of the day. While the setting remains constant in the German shows the presenters may change or rotate. Again this is in marked contrast to the host-centred format of American shows (see also Wieten, Chapter 10 in this volume).

These differences of focus are further underlined by the studio set. Most American shows work with one of three basic sets. Celebrity chat shows usually opt for the informal décor of an imitation domestic lounge with the host in a comfortable chair and the guests seated on a sofa or other chairs. Political interview and discussion shows tend to prefer a more formal, office-like, arrangement, with the presenter behind a desk or both host and guests seated around a boardroom style table. Participatory talk shows, on the other hand, tend to follow the more theatrical model established by Oprah Winfrey, with the guests sitting on chairs on a raised platform facing the studio audience and the host. Although some of the German shows analysed used a living-room set, others evoked the easy communality of conversation in a night club. *Drei nach Neun*, for example, was set in a piano bar with the host and guests seated at a table in the middle and the audience arranged around them sitting at tables with drinks.

These settings hint at the open-endedness of the conversations and on the public service channels it was not unusual for shows to contain one or even two hours of uninterrupted talk. In contrast, the frequent advertising breaks which punctuate programmes on American commercial television oblige producers to work within the three-act structure described earlier and to finish precisely on time, regardless of the state of the debate. This compressed time scale places a premium on action and drama whereas German talk shows are more likely to sustain interest by following the flow of the argument and the interactions of the participants.

These different requirements are reflected in the choice of participants. In American talk shows the guests are generally either celebrities, ordinary people with difficult, often traumatic, experiences to recount, or experts offering advice and analysis. In contrast, the guests on German talk shows appear primarily as mouthpieces for particular positions. Even the best known ones 'are presented less as "experts" and more as "opinion holders", representatives of yet another point of view' (1995: 194). This, Krause and Goering argue, is because German talk shows still operate as 'a forum for the debate of public and political issues that concern people in their lives as part of a collectivity, not as private individuals' (1995: 203). In other words, they resist the American impetus to 'privatize our social concerns' and reduce public issues to personal stories (Abt and Seesholtz, 1994: 177).

Krause and Goering were analysing shows broadcast at the beginning of 1993, before the rise of the new, youth-oriented, American shows and the recent intensification of commercialization in European television. Our earlier survey of the situation in the Netherlands in 1998 suggested that as these movements have gathered momentum so European talk show culture has become more Americanized. Looking at Germany we see the same basic process at work, though it is far from complete, with American-style shows named after the host running alongside older-style public service formats. Take for example the programmes available to viewers in Leipzig on the afternoon of 27 June 1999.

On the main commercial channel, RTL, Bärbel Schäfer, a glamorous blonde of a certain age, was presiding over a heated and sometimes abusive debate about German girls who had formed relations with men from the Turkish migrant community. The topic was local but the format borrowed heavily from America with the show named after the hostess and employing the studio design familiar from *Oprah*, where the guests tell their stories sitting on a raised dais facing an audience who are regularly invited to contribute comments and opinions.

The competing programmes shown one after the other on Pro 7, another commercial channel, also borrowed from American models but owed more to *Rikki* than to *Oprah*. Like Bärbel, all three were named after their hosts (Arabella Kiesbauer, Andreas Türk, and Nicole) but were more firmly aimed at a youth audience. *Arabella*, a young black woman, epitomized street style. Dressed casually but fashionably in a T-shirt and slacks she roamed around a studio set where the guests stood behind a bright red counter mounted on steel legs, designed to evoke a fast-food outlet, an impression reinforced by the advertisements for McDonald's during the commercial breaks. The show's orientation to youth was underlined by always including the guests' ages as well as their relations to each other (such as 'mother' or 'best friend') in the captions that appeared on screen while they were speaking. This was talk about relationships that presented itself as contemporary, entertaining and disposable, aimed at young people, and particularly young women, continually on the move.

The only show broadcast that afternoon that fitted Krause and Goering's description of public service talk was *Der grüne Salon* (The Green Room) on N-TV. The green room is traditionally the place where actors relax and socialize before and after public performances. It is a backstage region, a space for spontaneous talk. The show trades on this connotation but mobilizes the format developed by *Drei nach Neun*. The set is designed to evoke the easy flow of well mannered conversation in a club or upmarket piano bar. It presents itself as a discreet venue for talk about money and power, somewhere professionals might go for a drink after work, an association reinforced by the promotions for computers and banking services that scroll across the bottom of the screen. The lighting is subdued. The male host is dressed in a suit and tie in the contemporary managerial style. He and his guests sit with drinks around a circular table lit by a candle. The main guest is the female Minister of Social Affairs for the state of Brandenburg who is quizzed about her policies. The audience also sit at tables with candles and drinks arranged, at a suitable distance, in a circle around the central table. They are invited to overhear a conversation with a prominent politician speaking off duty. They are not encouraged to comment or ask questions.

The fact that this was the only show broadcast that afternoon that featured a political figure lends support to those who argue that as more and more commercial television services are launched we need public service broadcasting more than ever on the grounds that it is the only institution that can offer a universally accessible public sphere and provide the information and sustained debate on issues facing viewers in their role as citizens. On the other hand, sceptics are more likely to see *Der grüne Salon* as further evidence of paternalism's unresponsiveness to grassroots demands for participation. As Krause and Goering point out themselves, most of the guests on the public service shows they analysed were established figures to whom audiences were expected to listen attentively with few opportunities to speak and contribute comments of their own

TALK SHOWS AND DEMOCRACY

Running through this debate is a sharp division of opinion on how television should function as a public sphere. In Jürgen Habermas's influential model, the public sphere is a space where the tensions between sectional interests and the common good can be rationally debated and a provisional settlement reached. However, as critics have pointed out, his main historical example, the coffee houses of the early nineteenth century, were thoroughly bourgeois and masculine. They were designed as places where the rising generation of merchants, traders and political actors could meet and do business. They were not hospitable to either the poor or to women. These excluded groups gravitated to other public spaces, and particularly to the popular theatre, where the dangers and promises of life in the modern city and the emerging polity were played out in full view. Where the coffee house promoted measured debate, popular theatres encouraged 'rambunctious participatory behaviour . . . quick and immediate responses to happenings on stage [which] made the audience part of the show' (Gamson, 1998: 35).

Contemporary television draws on both of these traditions, and many commentators are inclined to agree with John Keane's view that, 'aside from philosophical prejudice', there is no reason why the contemporary counterparts of these earlier forms of popular participation, including 'the similated uproar of *Rikki Lake* . . . should not be understood as legitimate potential media of power conflicts' (Keane, 1998: 185).

In defence of this position supporters of American talk shows and their European imitators argue that they develop three essential conditions for contemporary democracy that public service models have failed to address adequately: diversity, empathy, and popular critique.

Diversity

Talk shows were one response to the mounting demands for greater representation coming from groups such as women, gays and ethnic minorities who felt that television had either ignored or misrepresented them. By incorporating marginalized lives into a programme form with wide popular appeal, talk shows have undoubtedly helped to make mainstream television more diverse and responsive. On the other hand, participants' life situations have been increasingly removed from their social and political contexts and re-presented as personal dilemmas. As a result, problems are addressed as questions of individual choice rather than social action. Oprah Winfrey expresses this philosophy perfectly when she says: 'if I've learned anything in life it's that you really only have control over yourself. Complaining about what the world is doing doesn't change anything. The only change comes with your willingness, your choice, to change yourself' (Jaggi, 1999: 14). This replaces a political concern with the general distribution of life chances with a consumerist emphasis on the choice between competing lifestyles. Questions of social diversity are translated into maps of market niches. Citizenship is subordinated to shopping.

Empathy

Nurturing a sense of shared community while respecting people's right to difference is one of the central problems of complex democracy. The more contemporary societies fragment, the more difficult it is to say why we should care about the fate of strangers. To close this gap we need to see 'others' not as 'them', over there, nothing to do with 'us', but as people like ourselves with the same basic rights and human qualities. Because it celebrates rational deliberation and rules out emotion, public service talk does little to encourage empathy. As the American writer, Helen Hughes, argued in the 1930s defending human interest stories in the tabloid press: 'Moral speculations are not evoked by news of court procedure; they take form on reading of an intimate story that shows what the impact of law and convention means as a private experience' (Hughes, 1937: 81). Eva Illouz has recently returned to this point, arguing that the emotion talk of American style shows, centred around immediate personal dilemmas and problematic relationships, provides a potent way of 'figuring out the best way to "live together" in an age when people have increasingly lost faith in formal institutions' (1999: 119).

In reply, sceptics argue that far from encouraging genuine empathy, the way these shows dramatize emotional conflicts reinforces the separation between 'us' and 'them' by encouraging voyeurism. As one critic puts it, watching the shows' constant parade of 'confusion, hatred and misery' is like 'staring out of the window at a car accident as you drive past' (Barber, 1998: 8). In the process, an informed tolerance of social differences is edged out by an enveloping indifference. Compassion is eclipsed by spectacle. In the end, 'viewing other people's pain for our own enjoyment leaves us, at best, feeling empty; at worst, feeling soiled' (Anderson, 1995: 172).

Critique

Some supporters of American talk shows compare them to the carnivals of early modern Europe, drawing on the Russian writer, Mikhail Bakhtin's argument that 'Carnival celebrated the temporary liberation from the prevailing truth of the established order: it marked the suspension of all hierarchical rank, norms, and prohibitions' (Bakhtin, 1968: 10). They see the qualities that critics deplore in the new-style shows – their bawdiness, disorderly behaviour, disrespect for authority, and celebration of common sense – as reaffirming populism's refusal to settle for the status quo and its willingness to break the chains of propriety. They insist that these alternative discourses 'don't have to conform to civility nor to the dictates of the general interest. They can be expressed for what they are: particular, regional, one sided, and for that reason politically alive' (Carpignano et al., 1990: 52).

There are several problems with this interpretation. Firstly, as Bakhtin points out, carnivals are temporary. They are safety valves, not alternatives. Secondly, inversions of normality work within prevailing mental maps. They simply attach positive signs to qualities usually regarded as negative. A world turned upside down is not a world deconstructed. Thirdly, the US tradition of carnival is more closely identified with the travelling shows that toured the towns of middle America offering freak shows, contests of strength, and snake oil and patent medicines of dubious effectiveness. Alongside the double-bodied girls, frog boys and other 'freaks of nature', sideshow proprietors offered their customers 'the mother who shocked the world, boy changed into girl' and a range of human 'oddities' that find strong echoes in the parade of guests on the new-style American talk shows (Gamson, 1998: 37). They also gave their more intrepid visitors the chance to go three rounds with a wrestler or boxer in booths filled to capacity with an appreciative audience. Again, the strong continuities with the gladiatorial atmosphere of a number of recent shows, particularly *Jerry Springer*, suggests that they owe rather more to America's native showmen and hucksters than they do to Bakhtin's idealized European instances of popular critique and assertion.

Box 11.1

Europe	America
Bourgeois public sphere	Popular showmanship
Public service broadcasting	Commercial television
Viewers as citizens	Viewers as consumers
Public issues	Private lives
Rationality	Emotion
Expertise	Celebrity
Certified knowledge	Lived experience
Political positions	Personal opinions
Discussion/debate	Stories/confessions/promotions
Search for common ground	Dramatization of conflict
Social change/political intervention	Individual choice

TALKING AT CROSS PURPOSES?

If we look across the range of talk shows currently broadcast on European channels, we can identify two master models, one rooted in an idealized model of the public sphere as pursued in the European public service tradition, the other derived from the traditions of popular theatre and showmanship mobilized by American commercial television, with a number of shows somewhere in between, borrowing elements from both. The basic contrasts between them are summarized in Box 11.1.

As we move towards the new television order described in Chapters 2 and 3, we need to ask whether the classical public service model of the talk show can, and should be preserved. Or is contemporary democracy better served by more Americanized formats or by hybrid forms that incorporate elements from both models? These questions can't be answered in the abstract. As a first step, look carefully at what is on offer in your own country.

ACTIVITIES

Taking talk shows apart:

1 *Mapping*: Choose a week. Using one of the major programme guides, list all the talk shows transmitted on terrestrial, cable and satellite channels, then answer the following questions:

- How many of the programmes are
  - (a) political interview/debate shows?
  - (b) celebrity interview shows?
  - (c) audience participation shows?
- How many of them are domestically produced? How many are imported from the United States? How many are imported from elsewhere?
- Which shows are broadcast in daytime slots, prime-time (6 p.m.–11 p.m.) slots, or late night?
- Are there distinct channel profiles? Do American shows appear mainly or only on commercial channels? Are public service channels more likely to carry political interview/debate shows?
- What are the shows called? How many are named after the host (e.g. *Oprah*) the setting (*Boulevard Bio*) or the activity (e.g. *Question Time*)?

2 *Framing*: For this second, more detailed stage of your analysis, concentrate on audience participation talk shows. Take the two highest rating examples on public service channels and the two highest rating shows on commercial channels. Watch them, and if possible record them on videotape for later re-viewing, concentrating on the following aspects:
- How do the shows begin? What do the title sequences and opening shots show? What expectations are built up?
- What is the host's professional background: politics? journalism? show business? television?
- What themes/issues do the shows deal with? How are the topics described at the outset? Are the programmes on public service channels more likely to deal with political and social issues rather than personal experiences or dilemmas?
- What is the studio set like? What does it remind you of – a domestic interior? an office? a theatre? a leisure location like a night club? a town meeting?
- Does the programme borrow devices from other popular television genres?

3 *Performance*:
- Who is invited to appear as a guest or contributor? How many participants are associated with pressure groups, social movements or political parties? How many are show-business celebrities? How many are academics, experts, or members of professions? How many are ordinary people?
- Who is identified by a caption on the screen? How are they described – by title, job, organizational membership, area of knowledge, opinion, or personal experience?

- How are the relations between guests, host and audience organized? Are the guests and the host separated from the audience? Are guests set apart, with the host standing or sitting with the audience? Or do all the participants share the same space?
- How is the show structured? Is it divided into distinct segments marked by changes of topics or guests or is there a continuous flow of talk?
- Using the classification we introduced at the start of this chapter, which kinds of talk are mobilized in the programme? Is one type dominant? Who gets to speak most and for the longest time?
- Is there a clear division between experience and expertise? Do some speakers simply recount what happened to them or state their views while others offer analysis and interpretation?
- Does the show encourage speakers to look for common ground or does it encourage confrontation? Does it propose solutions?

4 *The Bidding Game*:
Your analysis will give you a good idea of how the talk show genre is currently being used. Imagine that the major public service channel in your country has decided to launch a new hour-long talk show in the slot directly after the early evening news. It wants a programme that plays a positive role in informing viewers about important issues of the day and provides a platform for diverse views and experiences but one which also avoids paternalism and attracts good viewing figures, particularly in the 18–35 age group. You are an independent programme producer and have been asked to bid for the contract. Prepare a programme brief outlining and justifying the main features of your new show.

SUGGESTIONS FOR FURTHER READING

Charaudeu, P. and Ghigkiones, R. (1997) *La Parole confisque. Un genre televisuel: le talk show*. Paris: Dunod.

A French analysis of their talk show genre.

Gamson, J. (1998) *Freaks Talk Back: Tabloid Talk Shows and Sexual Nonconformity*. Chicago: University of Chicago Press.

A well researched and wonderfully readable account of the world conjured up by recent American talk shows, concentrating particularly on their responses to the gay community.

Livingstone, S. and Lunt, P. (1994) *Talk on Television: Audience Participation and Public Debate*. London: Routledge.

A carefully researched and argued study of talk shows in Britain in the mid-1990s.

Shattuc, J.M. (1997) *The Talking Cure: TV Talk Shows and Women*. London: Routledge.

A critical analysis of the ways American talk shows have addressed the concerns of women, from *Oprah Winfrey* and the other major programmes launched the 1980s to the new shows developed in the 1990s, typified by *Ricki Lake*.

CHAPTER 12

TELEVISION CURRENT AFFAIRS: THE CASE OF NORTHERN IRELAND

Greg McLaughlin

All the chapters in this book look at broadcasting in Europe in rapidly changing political and economic environments. Questions such as the impact of the free market, of globalism and transnationalism, of the technological revolution that is digital, on the quality and choice of programming that will be available in the new millennium, seem of paramount importance. In short, if we accept the free market hype, we are apparently heading into an era that promises broadcasting heaven on earth – a transnational, transcultural European broadcasting system, perhaps? Yet we would do well to pause and reflect on other equally important questions: questions about public service and public interest. Where do they lie in the promised land?

Vincent Porter (1992) points to the uneasy co-existence in post-industrial societies of two major regulatory paradigms – 'external pluralist' and 'internal pluralist' models. The 'external' model works on the assumption that pluralism and diversity of opinion in broadcasting can only be generated by unregulated competition between broadcasters (and, in the case of the EU, within and across national and regional boundaries). The 'internal' model, on the other hand, assumes that such diversity needs to be regulated by the state and by broadcasting organizations themselves. What has resulted, however – and this is crucial to an understanding of what has happened in the British case over the past 20 years – is a sort of double-bind whereby economic deregulation has progressed unchecked in tandem with increasing political regulation (1992: 52). This trend was quite evident when Porter wrote in 1992 and it has continued unabated. As he warned us even then, 'political regulation limits the editorial independence of broadcasters and economic regulation [or the lack of it?] reduces the money available for particular strands of programming such as investigative journalism' (1992: 53). However, it seems that in Europe in general, similar trends in economic deregulation of broadcasting have not been accompanied by overt political control: with one exception. As I will show in this chapter, we find a salutary lesson in just this process if we look to the experience of current affairs journalism on British public service television, particularly its treatment of the conflict in Northern Ireland since the 1980s.

I will first of all put this into brief historical context, identifying conflicts between the state and broadcasters in general terms and in terms more specific to coverage of what Rex Cathcart (1984) called 'the most contrary region', Northern Ireland. I will compare specific case studies in this conflict: controversial current affairs treatments of the conflict before and after the public emergence of the 'peace process'. Have they been shaped and influenced as much by the effects of economic and political regulation *per se* as by changing public consensus about the Northern Ireland 'problem'?

HISTORICAL CONTEXT

The public service ethos of British broadcasting, its assumption of impartiality and independence, is meant to protect it from political interference and from the commercial power and influence of big business. From its inception in the 1920s, British broadcasting contrasted with the commercial American media system and the overtly state controlled Soviet media. Public service broadcasting, then, was neither sold as a commercial marketing ploy nor imposed as a political diktat; it was conceived almost as a constitutional right. The main political parties could rest assured that the party in government could not commandeer the fledgling 'British Broadcasting Company' (as it was originally known). In a paradoxical way this reassured its competitors in the press since it would not be depriving them of scarce advertising revenue. Public service principles also apply to the commercial Independent Television network, or ITV, set up in the 1950s. The ITV companies derive their funding from advertising but their news and current affairs output is subject to the same rules of impartiality as the BBC (see Curran and Seaton, 1997; McNair, 1999; and Scannell and Cardiff, 1991).

The public service ethos matured in a post-Second World War social democratic consensus that extended to all spheres of life – economic, social and cultural. However, the consensus strained to breaking point in the 1970s, bringing into question the whole notion of public service. The advent of Margaret Thatcher as the new leader of the Conservative Party actually came about as part of a more fundamental shift in political and economic ideology in Britain. The 'New Right' advocated a break from the ideas of the welfare state and public ownership of services and utilities; society could be organized and run more efficiently by market forces rather than government intervention. It also launched a broadside against those sections of the cultural establishment that appeared to resist its policies for radical reform. Along with sections of academia, the Church of England, even the Conservative Party, the broadcasting institutions stood out as the most visible and potent symbols of establishment opposition to 'Thatcherism'.

There has, of course, always been tension between the state and broadcasters since the system was founded. Among the most famous (or notorious) have been tussles over the General Strike in 1926, the Munich crisis in 1938 and the Suez crisis in 1956. In all these cases, compromises were made and broadcasting independence remained intact, but the sustained assault by successive Thatcher governments on the broadcasters in the 1980s was of a different character. It was not just about coverage of controversial subjects like the Falklands War in 1982, the miners' strike in Britain in 1984, the US bombing of Libya in 1986, or Northern Ireland. It was also about how the New Right saw the broadcasting system evolving in Britain into the next century. The government wanted to push through legislation that would transform broadcasting and pave the way for further new developments in digital technology, and open the market up to satellite and cable television. For the BBC, it was a matter of looking at the question of funding and to a day some time in the future when the public would no longer pay the licence fee. It would have to compete in a marketplace with the commercial ITV network, and the international cable and satellite broadcasters. For the ITV companies, it was a matter of second-guessing proposed legislation on the nature and extent of competition and regulation. Their place in the marketplace was no longer guaranteed. Put simply, broadcasting was under pressure to put its house in order and that meant producing competitive and ultimately safe programmes, not programmes about one of the most controversial and sensitive issues of the day: the conflict in Northern Ireland and the 'war on terrorism'.

However, it was not just economic pressure. Britain in the 1980s was becoming more and more a security state. The 'war on terrorism' was being fought on domestic and foreign fronts – Northern Ireland, Libya and the Middle East – and Margaret Thatcher was affronted by the idea that organizations like the IRA could carry out their campaigns with maximum media exposure. Access to the 'oxygen of publicity', as she called it, helped sustain their propaganda efforts. The government's principal response to this affront was to put political pressure on the media, especially public service television stations like the BBC (Miller, 1994).[1]

The authorities came closest to outright, formal censorship of broadcast material in October 1988 when they introduced a ban on the directly expressed views of paramilitary groups and their political supporters. The effect of this was to shift the onus of censorship on to the broadcasters themselves, to make it so troublesome to include such controversial perspectives that they would find it easier to leave them out. But it was not just these views that suffered. Any news item or current affairs programme remotely critical of the government, or sympathetic or lenient with republican views, came under fire (Henderson et al., 1990).

In some respects, the state's illiberal response throws into question Schlesinger et al.'s (1983) optimistic analysis of British television and its potential to offer a range of political perspectives across the whole spectrum of televisual forms and spaces: official, alternative and oppositional. Schlesinger et al.'s demonstration of television's potential to present perspectives that might challenge or subvert the legitimacy of the state has been taken by many media theorists since as a vital corrective to more instrumental formulations, such as that of Herman and Chomsky (1988), which presumes the media have a straightforward propaganda function. Indeed, such potential is often realized but this is surely determined by the degree of liberal consensus in society at any given time. What happens when the liberal state experiences a crisis of legitimation and resorts to more repressive legal, security and military means to maintain order and conformity? Any analysis of public service broadcasting in this context needs to build in some recognition of wider social, political and cultural flux; to concede that the state's tolerance of broadcasting independence is commensurate with its sense of security in the face of internal and external threat. It seems clear that 'Thatcherism' as it operated in successive Conservative governments in the 1980s suffered a chronic crisis of legitimation on political and economic fronts. I would argue that this explains in *some* measure its turbulent and tempestuous relationship with public service television and, in turn, the effect that had on television's potential for openness and diversity in its treatment of difficult and sensitive political problems like the conflict in Northern Ireland.

PUBLIC SERVICE TELEVISION AND THE CONFLICT IN NORTHERN IRELAND

The current conflict which is now moving towards some kind of resolution began in the 1960s with protests for civil rights, mainly among the large nationalist minority (roughly 40 per cent of the population) who aspired to eventual reunification with the rest of Ireland. They saw themselves as dominated and discriminated against by the majority Unionist population who wanted Northern Ireland to remain British. The protests finally erupted in violence in 1968 and led to an increasingly polarized conflict and the emergence of new political parties and paramilitary groups on both sides. It quickly changed from being one over civil rights to being one of political identities and the right to pursue those identities either by politics or by violence. And because the nationalist community was largely Catholic and the Unionist community largely Protestant in make-up, questions of religion also became entangled in the conflict. The British state, always a political guarantor of Unionist hegemony in Northern Ireland, responded by deploying the army against the paramilitaries,[2] imprisoning 'terrorist suspects' without charge or trial in court, and abolishing the Northern Ireland Parliament in favour of direct rule from Westminster. For successive

British governments, the conflict was essentially a 'war against terrorism' and they enacted a range of 'emergency powers' to give them all possible means of winning that war.[3] As the British media were to discover, especially television news and current affairs, but also drama, attempts by third parties to undermine the war effort and question key policies on Northern Ireland, to challenge the official propaganda, were always controversial. Their record of resisting the political backlash, however, has been rather chequered.

For 25 years, journalists reported on Northern Ireland within the 'anti-terrorism' framework. The cause of the conflict was terrorism: namely, and principally through this prism, that of the Irish Republican Army (IRA) which wanted to drive the British out of Northern Ireland and bring about reunification with the rest of Ireland. The only way to bring peace was to defeat the IRA and promote reconciliation of the two 'tribes': Catholic and Protestant (McLaughlin and Miller, 1996). The peace process has seen a change in this official view. Sinn Fein, the political party most directly associated with the IRA, is no longer a pariah. The legitimate electoral mandate it has won over the previous decade is now accepted and recognized, and in 1998 it negotiated and signed the Good Friday Agreement. As McLaughlin and Miller (1996) have shown, the media, and especially the broadcast news media, were slow to notice this paradigm shift.[4] Nonetheless, the peace process has advanced deadline by deadline and British political culture and public opinion on Northern Ireland have continued to change, helped no doubt by the election of a Labour government with a commanding parliamentary majority. There appears to be a new, more permissive atmosphere for current affairs journalism to probe and investigate, to ask the hard questions at the heart of the process. Two good examples of this have been BBC series on republican and loyalist paramilitaries: *Provos* (BBC1, 1997) and *Loyalists* (BBC2, 1999) respectively.

Presented by journalist Peter Taylor, these series were immediately distinguishable by the unprecedented space they offered recently active and committed paramilitaries to talk about their involvement in violence and their motivations for it. Except for a health warning at the beginning of each programme about strong language and scenes of violence, they suffered none of the broadcasting restrictions or public outrage that constrained so much of news and current affairs output on Northern Ireland at the height of the troubles, for example *Real Lives*: 'At the Edge of the Union' (BBC, 1985), *This Week*: 'Death on the Rock' (Thames Television, 1988), and *The Committee* (Channel Four/Box Productions, 1991).[5]

Indeed, Taylor's programmes seemed to mark a new phase in which public service broadcasting could once again contribute positively to public understanding of the Northern Ireland 'problem' at a crucial phase of political development. But it is easy to get caught up in the magic and miss the illusion. I will show that *Provos* and *Loyalists* are no more or no less 'ground breaking' than 'At the Edge of the Union' or 'Death on the Rock'.

FROM *REAL LIVES* TO *PROVOS* AND *LOYALISTS*

In 1985, a journalist from the *Times* asked Margaret Thatcher at a news conference in New York how she would react if the BBC was to broadcast a programme featuring a prominent member of the IRA. Thatcher replied that it would be intolerable for the national broadcaster to feed terrorists the 'oxygen of publicity'. It appeared at first a hypothetical question and it got a hypothetical response but once it became clear that such a programme had actually been produced, and that it was already scheduled for network broadcast with advance promotion in the *Radio Times*, Home Secretary Leon Brittan was instructed to write to the BBC Board of Governers and ask that it not be broadcast. The Board of Governors requested to view it before transmission and made the unprecedented decision to prevent the programme being broadcast. The BBC's Director-General at the time, Alisdair Milne, was on holiday, and thought it highly irregular of the Board to take such action in his absence and at the government's instigation (Milne, 1988). So what was so controversial that could not be edited or amended? Why the concerted move to ban the programme entirely?

The programme, 'At the Edge of the Union', looked at the lives and outlook of two men at the political extremes of the conflict in Northern Ireland. At one extreme stood Martin McGuinness of Sinn Fein, a committed republican who argues for withdrawal of British forces from 'the north' and eventual Irish unification. At the other extreme was Gregory Campbell, a member of the Democratic Unionist Party (DUP) who professes himself a British citizen and an avowed enemy of McGuinness and the republicanism he represents.

The two men were shown living and working in Derry, Northern Ireland's second city.[6] Indeed, remove the political content and the viewer might conclude that they are ordinary men living ordinary lives in any other large town in Britain or Ireland. In many ways, it was this aspect that ignited the controversy around the programme. Gregory Campbell was seen as just a local Loyalist politician. McGuinness, on the other hand, was by no means 'ordinary' as far as the British government was concerned. Its propaganda output consistently identified him as a key figure of command in the IRA and every effort was made to discredit and undermine his every public appearance and utterance. The portrayal in 'At the Edge of the

Union' of Martin McGuinness as a 'normal' family, churchgoing man did not fit into the dominant propaganda picture of the terrorist as a faceless, psychotic killer isolated from normal society. And it did not conform to Margaret Thatcher's desire to deprive terrorism and its political representatives of the 'oxygen of publicity'. In the end, the *Real Lives* programme was broadcast but only after some extraordinary tussles between the Board of Governors and BBC management and some minor edits and inserts, including extra footage of bombing and shooting and information about the extent of death and injury in Northern Ireland as a result of paramilitary violence (Miller, 1994; Milne, 1988).

The most famous and controversial conflict between ITV and the government over Northern Ireland involved Thames Television and its *This Week* programme, 'Death on the Rock', which set out to investigate the circumstances surrounding the shooting by British undercover soldiers of three members of the IRA in Gibraltar in 1988. The producers came under fire from the right-wing press even before their programme was completed and when it was scheduled to go out, the then Home Secretary Douglas Hurd pressurized the Independent Broadcasting Authority to withhold it. The IBA resisted and allowed the programme to be broadcast as scheduled. Even the government-appointed Windlesham and Rampton inquiry cleared the 'Death on the Rock' producers of any professional misconduct in 1989. However, in 1992, under provisions of the 1990 Broadcast Act, Thames lost its licence in the round of ITV franchise bids. The brand of investigative reporting typical of *This Week* was no more.[7]

Given the hostile political reaction to programmes like 'At the Edge of the Union' and 'Death on the Rock', one would expect a wholesale takeover of the BBC in the wake of *Provos* (BBC, 1997) and *Loyalists* (1999) but, of course, they were broadcast in changing political contexts in Britain and in Northern Ireland itself. The new Labour government was playing a sometimes dynamic, sometimes risky, role in 'promoting the peace process'. Public reaction to both series was muted, although some concern was expressed about the BBC's timing of *Provos*, that it might in some way undermine the peace process in a crucial and delicate phase: the beginning of formal multi-party talks on 15 September 1997. However, the executive producer, Steve Hewlett, thought the scheduling of the series was most appropriate at a time when the issues were high on the political agenda (*Daily Telegraph*, 6 August 1997). There were also fears that the producers were giving air-time to active members of the IRA. Hewlett claimed that the producers did not 'seek interviews with people currently active in the IRA but it is not an open organization; people do not wear badges and there is a distinct possibility that some were not telling the truth. But if we knew they were active, we wouldn't use them' (*Times*, 6 August 1997).

PARAMILITARIES

Television series like *Provos* and *Loyalists* boast all that is best in British broadcasting production values. The programmes are made up of interviews mainly with ex-paramilitaries but there are also contributions from their victims and from other politicians and public figures prominent in the 1960s and 1970s when the violence was at its most sustained. These are intercut with a narrative history of political violence punctuated with some remarkable and hitherto unseen archive film footage of key moments in the history of the conflict and, of course, plenty of footage of bombings and shootings, death and injury. However, in other respects both series are ultimately safe and uncontroversial. They merely confirm prejudice and assumptions rather than challenge them. They are case studies in murder, narratives about 'mad IRA bombers' and 'Loyalist lunatics'. Conducted in stark light against a black background, they are at once interrogative and at times voyeuristic.

The series *Loyalists* in particular features some brutally frank, matter-of-fact admissions of murder from ex-paramilitaries. Jim Light, a former paramilitary with the UFF, the Ulster Freedom Fighters, tells how he carried out the murder of a young Catholic man in retaliation for the murder by the IRA of six Protestant pensioners. It must be said here that the rendering of this interview in print loses the impact gained by viewing this doleful, deadbeat exchange between the interviewer, Taylor, and Light:

> *Taylor*: What did you do?
> *Light*: I went out with a group of other volunteers from the UFF and we picked up a Catholic and we took him away and we executed him.
> *Taylor*: Murdered him?
> *Light*: Yeah.
> *Taylor*: Shot him dead?

Light: Yes.
Taylor: A Catholic?
Light: Yes.
Taylor: Any Catholic?
Light: Yes.
Taylor: Why was he selected?
Light: He was selected for no other reason than he was a Catholic.
Taylor: No reason to believe he was involved in the Republican movement?
Light: No.
Taylor: Just an innocent, 17-year-old student?
Light: Yeah.
[*EDIT*]
Taylor: Who pulled the trigger?
Light: I pulled the trigger.
Taylor: You pulled the trigger?
Light: I did, yes.
Taylor: Without any hesitation?
Light: [*Pause*] No, actually, no. I wouldn't say I had any hesitation at that time.

Of course, this style of interview is quite common in television's 'true crime' genre. It may reveal much about the psychological state of the killer but little of the political impulses behind his action. The focus is on 'coming clean': close-ups invite the viewer to judge the demeanour of the interviewee and render a verdict on their honesty and the plausibility of their remorse. Then, as if to prejudice the verdict, each interview closes with a prison photograph and details of conviction and sentence:

Taylor: Jim Light was sentenced to life for murder.

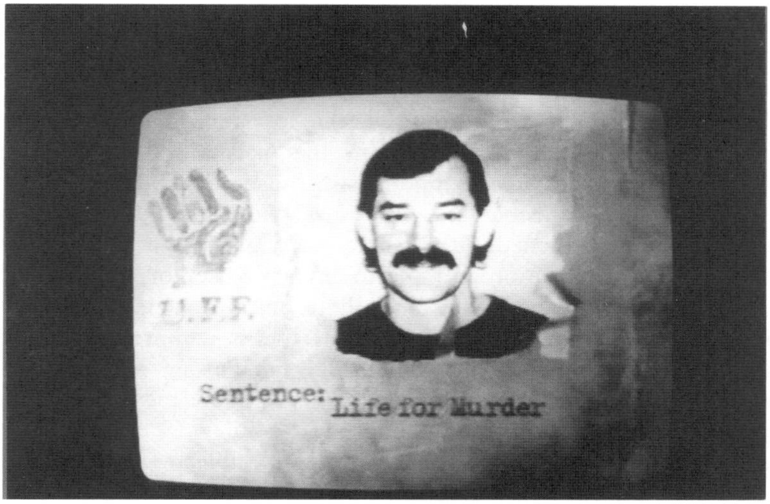

OPPORTUNITIES MISSED

Yet there are entry points for further inquiry that are tantalizingly followed up only for the trail to go cold. Bobby Morton, once a Loyalist paramilitary, tells Taylor that some prominent Unionist politicians of the day had much to answer for in stirring up Loyalist violence:

> *Morton*: They were only too happy to lead us by the nose at one stage – 'Get into them, boys! Protestant Ulster! We will fight and we will die!' Well, *they* never fought and *they* never died. It was left to people like me.

Taylor then takes this point up with the Reverend Ian Paisley of the Democratic Unionist Party, who admits that paramilitaries like Morton were among the ranks of his supporters in those days, but insists that he could not be held responsible for their crimes which, he said, he condemned outright and duly disowned. Other snatches of insight tantalize the viewer with the potential of the programme to embarrass senior members of the Unionist establishment but more crucially to put into some perspective the involvement of Loyalist paramilitaries in the peace process and their implacable opposition today to leaders like Ian Paisley who contest any political settlement in which republicans share some measure of power. However, Taylor consistently works within a framework which interprets Loyalist violence as reactive, in response to republican violence. This is wholly inadequate for explaining paramilitary violence in Northern Ireland over the past 30 years. Loyalist paramilitary violence was rarely reactive or defensive. It was always tactical, always instrumental and it has been used, and may still be used in the future, to sabotage political progress within the framework of the Belfast Agreement of 1998. To see it as merely reactive, or to render it televisually as a matter of individual reckoning and remorse, fails to explain and promote understanding of the politics of paramilitary violence.

DISCUSSION

Both the *Provos* and *Loyalists* series failed to take advantage of the new political dispensation in Northern Ireland, to look at the politics and ideology that motivated and sustained the paramilitaries and see them in some sections as fixed and unbending but in others as fluid and flexible. As I have argued, this has something to do with the changes in patterns of economic regulation in broadcasting over the 1980s and 1990s. For the BBC, it has developed out of the internal reformation of its news and current affairs output: John Birt's 'mission to explain' has shunted broadcast journalism out of political and investigative forms and spaces into something softer, more consumerist in orientation. And this is by no means exceptional. It applies right across the spectrum of news and current affairs output on British television. Both *Provos* and *Loyalists* were screened at irregular, off-peak times in the schedules. The BBC's 'flagship' current affairs programme, *Panorama*, now rests just outside peak time on Monday evenings. Other current affairs series, like BBC2's *Correspondent* and *Storyville*, fit into floating slots on a Saturday evening, subject to other programme priorities like live sporting events. In the years since the 'Death on the Rock' controversy in 1988, a period that has seen two Broadcast Acts in 1990 and 1997, the ITV network has said goodbye to its 'flagship' current affairs programmes, *This Week* and *World in Action*; and it has scrapped its prestige *News at Ten* programme in favour of shorter bulletins at the margins of the evening schedules. The network has launched a new, hour-long, weekly current affairs series, *Tonight*, modelled on the famous American model, *Sixty Minutes* (CBS). It remains to be seen how risky its journalism will be in the long run, but early indications are that it prioritizes human interest and consumer journalism over hard political content. Even Channel Four, always a source of radical alternatives, has shifted its emphasis in this direction, too, although its main news programme, *Channel Four News* (provided by ITN), still remains an example of quality British journalism.

The implications of this for British television news and current affairs are serious enough but they are at their starkest in times of tension between the state and public service broadcasters. The NATO bombing of Serbia is a case in point. Its impact on domestic public opinion in Britain showed again how sensitive government is to the way in which the media report its use of armed force as a means to meet policy objectives and it has highlighted too, how nervous some broadcasters can be in the face of this.[8] None of that, of course, bears any realistic comparison with the battles between the state and broadcasting in the 1980s over presentation and representation of the conflict in Northern Ireland. Is the conflict in Northern Ireland no longer dangerous ground for broadcasting simply because of political progress and paramilitary cease-fires? Or is it just that broadcast journalism in Britain is no longer dangerous?

The 'contrary region' has certainly been a graveyard for public service broadcasting's cherished myths of independent, investigative journalism. The last 20 years of political flak and intimidation and the creeping commercialization of television, in the public service as well as the independent sector, have had the effect of taming political television in general, of encouraging caution rather than risk-taking. Of course, in the case of Northern Ireland, paramilitary cease-fires and progress towards some sort of political settlement have given programme makers much more room to deal with topics that, like 'At the Edge of the Union' and 'Death on the Rock' in the 1980s, would have invited public outrage and a media backlash. Still, the conflict is not over yet. A final permanent settlement in Northern Ireland is even now uncertain and, with some paramilitary groups threatening to go back on the offensive, the peace is an uneasy one. There are also unresolved issues such as decommissioning of weapons and the reform of the police force that threaten to topple the new power-sharing executive. Even leaving Northern Ireland aside, there will be other controversial moments and political crises that will demand and deserve full and serious investigation by news and current affairs journalism. That can only be guaranteed by the survival of public service television in a hostile and ruthlessly competitive broadcasting environment that has little or no room for difficult or controversial political television.

NOTES

1 See Curran and Seaton, 1997; McNair, 1999; and Scannell and Cardiff, 1991.
2 The police force, the Royal Ulster Constabulary (RUC) was also armed and eventually occupied the front line in the conflict, with the army playing a supporting role.
3 This summary sketch is merely designed to show those not familiar with the roots of the Northern Ireland conflict how the British media eventually came to report and explain the conflict within terms broadly defined and shaped by official propaganda.
4 The problem, say McLaughlin and Miller, has been a lack of perspective. Journalists reported the latest briefings with little awareness of their public relations function. They simply reproduced them, verbatim in some cases, as if they were straightforward and unproblematic insights into official government thinking. This was hardly appropriate for journalism steeped in public service values of objectivity and impartiality; see also Butler (1995).
5 The last of these was a controversial programme, broadcast on 2 October 1991, alleging a high-level conspiracy between the Royal Ulster Constabulary (RUC), Protestant business people and Loyalist paramilitaries to murder prominent Irish nationalists and republicans. The filmmakers were forced to hand over sensitive research materials and source information under the provisions of the Official Secrets Act 1989 and the annually renewed Prevention of Terrorism Act (see Miller, 1994: 51–54).
6 Also known by its official British name, Londonderry.
7 However, it should be mentioned that BBC Northern Ireland aired its own investigation into events at Gibraltar as part of its current affairs series, *Spotlight*. It was broadcast around the same period but was much less noticed than 'Death on the Rock' even though it attracted equal condemnation from certain sections of media and pubic opinion in Northern Ireland (*Spotlight*, BBC NI, 1988). For discussions of local broadcast news and current affairs coverage of the conflict see Baker, 1996 and Kyle, 1996.
8 'BBC under pressure over negative reporting', *Guardian*, 30 March 1999.

ACTIVITIES

1(a) Carry out your own study of television current affairs and documentary output according to the following guidelines:

- *Monitor* the schedules of the principal TV network(s) in your country or region over a limited time period, e.g. two weeks or one month. (This is your sample period.)
- *Identify* (and possibly video-record) current affairs programmes (not TV news bulletins). (This is your sample.)
- *Note* the place in the schedules of each programme you identify (peak time or off-peak time?) Note the length of each programme you identify. Note the type of television channel on

which the programme appears (public service or commercial? terrestrial, satellite or cable?) and find out its current weekly viewing figures. Note the day on which each programme is broadcast (weekday, Monday–Friday? or weekend, Saturday and Sunday?). Note the subject of each programme according to categories such as politics, economics, international relations, consumer affairs, and human interest.

(b) Now answer the following questions:

- What is the total share of programming time given over to current affairs output in your sample period?
- What relationship, if any, is there between total programming share and type of broadcaster?
- What is the dominant category of current affairs and documentary output in your sample overall? How does that break down according to (1) channel and (2) place and time in the schedules?

2 With reference to the results of your study, above, and to the available literature, discuss the nature and extent of current affairs television in your country/region; assess whether its quantity and quality will be affected by rapid developments in broadcasting both within the European Union and worldwide.

SUGGESTIONS FOR FURTHER READING

Drummond, P., Paterson, R. and Willis, J. (eds) (1992) *National Identity and Europe: The Television Revolution*. London: BFI.

For a better grasp on the subject of economic deregulation of broadcasting and political control of the broadcasting environment.

Miller, D. (1994) *Don't Mention the War: Northern Ireland, Propaganda and the Media*. London: Pluto Press.

A detailed examination of the British propaganda machine.

Whyte, J. (1990) *Interpreting Northern Ireland*. Oxford: Clarendon.

A good book for those who are interested in a fuller background and explanation of the conflict between Northern Ireland and the UK.

CHAPTER **13**

TELEVISION NEWS: THE CASE OF THE FRENCH ROAD BLOCKADES

Sari Näsi

French lorry drivers were on strike for a period of twelve days in November 1996. According to estimates some 50,000 drivers and their vehicles were involved in forming road blockades on the most important highways and roads of France. The lorry drivers initiated the actions in order to put pressure on negotiations between their unions and their employers. The drivers were dissatisfied with their salary, retirement age and long working hours. The dispute was picked up by international media, because many non-French drivers got stuck in a blockade in France and could not deliver their cargo to its destination. On the 26th of November, the ninth day of the strike, the news broadcasts predicted that the dispute could last for several more weeks if a satisfactory solution was not reached soon. The strike was expected to spread to other sectors and to paralyse the whole transportation sector in France. The right-wing government of Alain Juppé wished to avoid the spreading of the labour unrest. The government was at the same time trying to decide on important cuts in the national budget, and a possible wave of wage increases was less than welcome at that point. Towards the end of the strike the French authorities met with hardened criticism from neighbouring countries who argued that the French government did less than it could to end the strike. The French franc was losing ground as the strike continued. When an agreement was finally reached, most of the demands were met: lorry drivers with 25 years of work could retire at the age of 55, drivers would get a double end of year bonus and compensation for sick days. Also, foreign lorries would not be allowed to pass through France on Sundays.

The French road blockades of November 1996 provide an interesting opportunity to analyse television news reporting from (at least) two different theoretical perspectives. In the first place this is a labour conflict. Media reporting of (British) labour disputes is an area in which the Glasgow University Media Group has done research since the mid-1970s. One of the conclusions of their research is that media tend to report such conflicts from the perspective of management. Secondly, we have a labour dispute here with effects across the French borders. It was covered in neighbouring and more distant European countries. This offers a chance to find out if out if the theory of globalization and increasing uniformity of news would apply here. That theory has been criticized and amended by Gurevitch et al. (1991), and other authors. Put (a little too) simply, we expect to learn something from this comparative research, and the confrontation of these theoretical perspectives, about biases in news reporting and their origins.

The Glasgow University Media Group has studied the interaction that takes place between media organizations and society. In works such as *More Bad News* (1980) their focus was on the reporting of industrial conflict (around the so-called 'Social Contract' in 1975). The institutional forms of journalism are an important factor in creating what is called 'common sense' and also contribute to the reinforcement of the preferred social order. News vocabulary reflects a collective value system and choices that are made, but news producers' intentions do not necessarily play a role. The focus in the Glasgow University Media Group's research was on those conventions which, whether articulated or not, define and delineate the vocabulary. Their most widely discussed conclusion was that the vocabulary in use amounts to a 'preferred' view of industrial disputes which corresponds with a particular version of a *managerial ideology*. The disputes are reported from the perspective of the management, who serve as the order-maintaining force in society, the workers being the ones who cause disruption. The Glasgow University Media Group concludes that the omission of detailed descriptions of the claims of the workers and summary references to their proposals lead to an image of an action without cause – an explanatory vacuum which is then filled by the inferential frameworks of the broadcasters which match with popular misconceptions and stereotypes of industrial action. In other words, the managerial ideology presented in television news could just as well be called the 'unreasonable worker' ideology (Glasgow University Media Group, 1980: 155–160). Why should a strike, for example, not be reported as 'a consequence of bad management' instead of the usual 'workers demanding more cash'? In terms of this managerial ideology, the 'unreasonable demands' of workers have become common sense and an institutionalized form of reporting industrial conflicts (cf. McLaughlin, Chapter 12 in this volume).

One of the consequences of a highly developed news exchange system is that news organizations around the world have access to the same material. A relatively small group of news personnel function as 'gate-keepers', sorting out the information flow from all over the world. In a picture-driven medium, the available dramatic footage competes with, and often supersedes, other news considerations. Television news services distribute the same images of news events of potentially global interest to customers around the world. Gurevitch et al. (1991) have analysed this 'global newsroom'. Their analysis is firmly located in the perspective of news as storytelling. This approach borrows its concepts and strategies from literary criticism, and proposes that specific news stories should be examined as related to myths or a superstory or cultural theme, as these appear in different cultures, much in the same way as documented historical facts and incidents. They argue that for an event to be judged newsworthy it must be anchored in narrative frameworks that are already familiar to journalists as well as to audiences situated in particular cultures. Gurevitch et al. (1991) offer this as an 'antidote' to a rather naive notion of universalism – that events reported carry their own meanings, and that meanings embedded in news stories produced in one country can therefore be generalized to news stories told in other societies (cf. Roe and De Meyer, Chapter 8 in this volume). Despite the similarities in form of news programmes all over the world, a uniquely national character is still present in every news programme and organization (Heinderyckx, 1993). This can be achieved, for instance, by casting faraway events in frameworks that render these events comprehensible, appealing and 'relevant' to domestic audiences. Or the meanings of these events are constructed in ways that are compatible with the culture and the 'dominant ideology' of the societies they serve. It has been argued that television maintains both global and culturally specific orientations (Gurevitch et al., 1991). In the case of the French road blockades it is interesting to study whether there are differences in the manner of presenting this industrial dispute in different countries. How would it be 'domesticated', in terms of the notion in Gurevitch et al. (1991), and what differences are there in presentation and ideological content? We expect this case study to be instructive on how to detect these aspects in news broadcasts.

A study of news is a study of 'news discourse'. Our way of viewing the world, the values and morals which are considered to be important in the culture where the news is produced, determine to a large extent what the evening news is to consist of. This 'news discourse' is typical of the society in which it is situated. It is also influenced by the institutional forms of the medium in question, e.g. resources, journalistic practices, ideological sympathies or orientations and traditions in making the news. Television, and television news in particular, now draw public attention to and shape the understanding of the political situations it chooses to cover. A specific mode of narration, style and content of the news was first developed in print media. The subjective origin of the news 'story' was suppressed and this practice gradually developed a mode of address, resembling 'discourse' (Morse, 1986: 86).

Certainly in industrialized societies discourse is not only a product of culture, but even more a product of that society and its power structure. A discourse will always have a socially and politically identifiable origin and it will serve the interests of the groups around that point of origin by making their sense of the real appear as common sense. Therefore, according to Fiske (1987), it is never enough to study a sign and the view of the world that it represents; one must recognize that someone's view of the world is implicitly or explicitly, obviously or subtly, inscribed in it. Revealing the 'who' within the 'what' is possibly the most important task of this kind of criticism (Fiske, 1987: 42).

ANALYSING THE CASE: THE FRENCH ROAD BLOCKADES

As noted, for instance in Wallis and Baran (1990), there have been few international comparative studies of television and radio news output. All kinds of practical reasons make this sort of research difficult. There are important national and systemic differences in the storage of material, not to mention the logistical problems in acquiring tapes and transcripts from different countries. Nevertheless, for this particular study a limited amount of international material has been available in the form of videotaped television news bulletins of the same day (26 November 1996) from several European countries (Table 13.1). These countries and programmes are: France (Antenne 2, *Le Journal*, public), Belgium/Flanders (BRTN, *Journaal en sport*, public), Netherlands (RTL4 *Nieuws*, commercial; NOS, *Journaal*, public), UK (BBC, *Breakfast News*, public), Germany (ZDF, *Heute*, public; ARD, *Tagesschau*, public) and Finland (YLE1, *Uutiset ja sää*, public; MTV3, *Kymmenen uutiset*, commercial). The CNN *World News* item of the subject was also taped.[1]

When defining the perspective from which a news item about a labour conflict has been made, the definition of the *who* is crucially important. Whether the voice and the face appearing on the screen belong to a representative of the management or of the union makes a difference to the way in which the audience will interpret it. A spoken word broadcast unedited, just as the person said it, is considered to be more reliable and important than a quotation expressed by the reporter. This is why politicians attempt to include 'sound-bites' in their speeches, which can be easily edited into the news as a few seconds' illustration to a story. Journalists and news personnel are willing to insert these unedited pieces into news broadcasts, because they add to the authenticity of the programme.

In the case of the French road blockades we can observe the same news item from several national perspectives. The *who* (actor in the news story) within the *what* (news story) could be defined differently in different countries. The angle of the news report may vary a lot from focusing on the motives of the French drivers for the strike to what it meant to the British drivers, for instance, who were kept from doing their work, although they had nothing to do with it in a direct sense.

One way of revealing the who within the what is to analyse which of the actors are considered to be 'us' and which are 'them'. 'Us' are the actors in the news with whom the viewers are able, or expected, to identify: the 'good guys'. 'Them' are the actors in the story who threaten the status quo in some way, for instance by supporting and expressing opposite ideas, values or policies, and taking some form of action in order to achieve their goals. This division can take an explicit or an implicit form.

In Todorov's view (1977) the basic narrative structure consists of a state of equilibrium which is later disrupted, usually by some 'bad guy'. The forces of disruption are worked through until a resolution and a new state of equilibrium are reached. This new equilibrium can be identical to or

TABLE 13.1 An overview of the material

Country/broadcaster	Time/duration	Rank order of the item	Length of the item (min.)
France Antenne 2 *Le Journal* public	22.00 30 min.	1/13	10.32
Belgium/Flanders BRTN *Journaal en sport* public	19.30 30 min.	2/14	4.00
Netherlands RTL4 *Nieuws* commercial	19.30 30 min.	2/10	4.32
Netherlands NOS/NL1 *Journaal* public	20.00 20 min.	1/10	6.52
UK BBC *Breakfast News*[2] public	different format	different format	3.51
Germany ZDF *Heute* public	19.00 25 min.	9/15	0.25
Germany ARD *Tagesschau* public	20.00 15 min.	6/14	2.18
Finland[3] YLE1 *Uutiset ja sää* public	20.30 25 min.	6/14	0.31
Finland MTV3 *Kymmenen uutiset* commercial	22.00 20 min.	7/15	0.21
International CNN[4] *World News* commercial	20.30 30 min.	4/7	0.33

closely resemble the first one. According to Fiske (1987: 139), Todorov's model is particularly useful for its ability to explain news stories and to model news as the social narrative of a conflict between the social order and disruptive forces. Todorov specifies two kinds of elements in a narrative: a state (of equilibrium or disequilibrium) and a passage from one state to another, usually through an event or a chain of events. Newsworthy events are those which disrupt or restore equilibrium. The state of equilibrium is not in itself newsworthy and is never described, except implicitly in its opposition to the state of disequilibrium which, typically, is described in detail. Here, the ideological work is at its clearest in the selection of which events are considered to disrupt or restore which equilibrium and in the description of what constitutes disequilibrium. Thus the event conventionally selected as a cause of an industrial dispute is an action of a worker or a union, whereas the event selected to restore order is equally conventionally an act of management or a government agency. In the narrative structure of news about industrial disputes unions are given the roles of villains and management those of heroes. Similarly, the description of the disequilibrium will usually be in terms of the dispute's effect upon consumers, and rarely in terms of the hardships undergone by the striking union-members. This again serves to position the reader with the good guys (i.e. management and consumers) and in hostility to the union, the bad guys (Fiske, 1987: 139). Fiske's interpretation closely resembles the 'managerial ideology' described by the Glasgow University Media Group.

THE FRENCH ROAD BLOCKADES AS DOMESTIC NEWS ITEM

In the material five different perspectives on the labour conflict were clearly identified. The news item in the French *Le Journal* will give us an opportunity to study whether the managerial ideology is present in a television news item as the Glasgow University Media Group concluded. For the French the issue is clearly a domestic one and therefore more comparable to Glasgow University Media Group's findings than the other items in the material. The perspective found in the French news broadcast may serve as an example of an implicit way of naming the heroes/victims and the villains in this news item.

Lorry drivers (French) are interviewed on several occasions in this ten-minute-long report and their demands and motives for the strike are widely reported. The journalists seem to show sympathy for the situation of the poorly paid, overtime-working drivers. The material is carefully chosen and altogether ten reporters have been working on the item providing five different 'on-location' reports. The drivers themselves and their unions are given voice on seven different occasions. The government or local administrators state their opinion on three occasions, including the unedited speech of Minister of Transport, Pons. This is the final part of the report and it is not commented upon at all by any of the journalists. Representatives of the employers are missing completely, which suggests that the drivers' motivations for the strike are seen as reasonable and acceptable by the media. *Le Journal* for instance shows a short interview with a child who had just brought some food that his mother had prepared for the drivers who had put up a blockade outside their village. The purpose of the interview is obviously to win the sympathy of the audience. Despite the rationing of fuel, undelivered goods and higher prices for some commodities, everybody is shown to support the strike.

The perspective of exnomination and nomination as ideological practices, reflected visually and aurally in the news, is helpful in this case (cf. Fiske, 1987). The union members and workers are nominated, as they have a voice and a face in the broadcast. The management is exnominated: the journalist explains the management's point of view but the representatives of management are not actually seen in person. In the French news broadcast, not a single management representative was mentioned by name, whereas the drivers and union members were mentioned several times in the text and their names and functions were shown on the screen. Fiske (1987) argues that the nomination/exnomination division is a tactic of a hierarchy of discourses. Nominating discourses places them low in the hierarchy and thus licenses them to speak oppositionally or radically. The exnominated discourse, however, speaks the final 'truth', against which the partiality of the subordinated discourses can be assessed. Nominating disruptive discourses and exnominating that of social control is a common tactic of semiotic and ideological containment (Fiske, 1987: 290). If the French news broadcast is analysed beyond the seemingly balanced layer in terms of Fiske's tactics of hierarchy it would be possible to argue that the management was after all exnominated and was given a dominant position. But when you take into account the imagery and the vocabulary used to tell this story, with sympathy for the workers' side, it is not so clear that management is the dominant actor.

Because this strike is a domestic issue for the French news broadcaster, the international implications are briefly mentioned, but in the form of neutral comments on the counter-blockade the Spanish drivers had initiated in Spain close to the French border. This strike was not meant to support the demands of the French drivers, but to show that the Spanish drivers were not at all happy with the effects of the French action on their business. In the following extract from *Le Journal* the news anchor explains the situation at the French/Spanish border and also reminds us that the French citizens themselves are still supporting the strikers.

News anchor in studio: Les entreprises de transport routier européennes anglaises, espagnoles, portugaises, allemandes réclament à leurs gouvernements de demander des indemnités à la France pour cette grêve. Et à la frontière franco-espagnole, côté Espagne, et bien des cammioneurs espagnols protestent contre le blocage des routes en France qui les empêchent d'exporter plusieurs centaines de milliers de tonnes d'agrumes vers les différents marchés européens. Dans certaines régions de France où les grévistes sont présents sur la route depuis plus d'une semaine maintenant, neuf jours plus exactement, des communes vivent à l'heure des routiers et de leurs revendications. C'est le cas à St André sur Ornes près de Caen en Normandie, une commune de 1500 habitants, dont la principale artère est bloquée par une quarantaine de poids lourds . . .

European haulage companies in England, Spain, Portugal, Germany ask their governments to demand compensation from France for this strike. And at the French–Spanish border, Spanish side, quite a few Spanish truck drivers protest against the blockade of the roads in France which prevents them from exporting several hundreds of thousands of tons of citrus fruit to the different European markets. In certain French regions where the strikers have been present on the road for more than a week now, nine days to be precise, communities live at the schedule of the truckers and their demands. That is the case in St André sur Ornes near Caen in Normandy, a municipality with 1500 inhabitants, whose main artery is blocked by about 40 trucks . . .

THE FRENCH ROAD BLOCKADES AS A FOREIGN NEWS ITEM

BBC *Breakfast News*, 26 November, 1996

News anchor in studio: France can face a general strike tomorrow. After talks aimed at ending the lorry drivers' dispute failed to settle matters, tens of thousands of vehicles are now involved in almost 200 blockades of major routes across France. Here the . . . transport associations warned that small businesses face a catastrophe because of the action.

[*Voice-over film of English truckers*] *Jeremy Cooke*: Another night of misery and frustration. For hundreds of British lorry drivers the road home remains blocked. There was hope that talks between French truckers and the Paris authorities could bring an end to the blockade, but overnight negotiations have broken down, and now the French union is calling for a nation-wide general strike. [*Film: at night, a group of people outdoors talking to each other, a fire, a man in uniform in front of a truck, text on the screen: No way home.*] In haulage companies across the UK, that is not what they want to hear. Lorries stuck in France mean losses that could be measured in the millions before it is all over. In Aberdeen this haulage firm is trying to pop routes around the blockades. The priority is to avoid confrontation. [*Film: the office of haulage company, people on the phones, a chart in the background wall showing which of the company's trucks are stuck where.*]

Jim Wilson, Dee Glen Haulage [*in picture*]: There's been quite a lot of violence in France in the last week. Trucks having their tyres slashed, and things have been put on the roads. That if the trucks drive across them, they bust all their tyres. There's been three . . . trucks, has kept them aside last week, it's quite serious.

[*Voice-over*] *Jeremy Cooke*: A handful of trucks has made it through the blockade. This Derby firm was delighted when one of its trucks pulled into the yard, even though it was six days late. For everyone in the business it is a difficult time, but here thoughts are for the self-employed drivers, who own their own lorries. [*Film: a truck arriving at its destination, the parking lot of the haulage company, the driver carrying out his arrival routines in the cabin of his vehicle.*]

John Cooper, Stone & Ogan [*in picture*]: All the drivers must be thinking about going bankrupt, because they just can't afford it. It's a cash flow, if you ever think about it, there is not sufficient profit in transport to stand a truce like this for eight days and what looks being even longer. [*Film:*

Cooper standing in front of a truck which has Stone & Ogan logos on the sides.]

[*Voice-over*] *Cooper*: Back at the port, British drivers hope that the French authorities will pay them compensation. Some of them warn they will go out of business, unless there's a settlement soon. Jeremy Cook, BBC News. [*Film: people gathered around a fire, night.*]

News anchor in studio: British lorry drivers stranded at Calais have been threatening to block tourist routes into the port as they did yesterday. They have become increasingly frustrated with the time it is taking to solve this dispute. More talks to try to find a solution are due to resume in Paris this afternoon after being adjourned in the early hours. Our correspondent Chris West is in Calais. Chris, good morning to you.

[*Duo-picture. News anchor in studio/Chris West in Calais.*]

News anchor in studio: Absolutely no progress at all in those talks, it seems?

Chris West [*in Calais*]: Nothing at all and no likelihood of any progress, it seems at all. The drivers here are very frustrated, they spent another very bitterly cold night, stuck in the cabs of their lorries, they are not going anywhere. All around me hundreds of lorries, just like a huge car park. They can't get up to the Netherlands, they can't go to Belgium, they're just stuck and it seems like it's going on for days.

News anchor in studio [*duo-picture*]: Understandably, Chris, they are frustrated and angry, but frankly, it seems, from the way we're looking at it here, and I would have thought where you're looking at it there, there is very, very little they can do about it.

West [*in Calais*]: Very little they can do at all, you know they are in the hands of the French government and the hands of the employers and the unions. Of course the British can't really see the point, a lot of the people here are self-employed truckers, they are losing their livelihoods, they're seeing money going down the drain for every hour they sit here. They are saying 'Why can't the French government do anything about it?' It is really a huge political game, which the men stuck here just don't understand.

News anchor in studio [*duo-picture*]: And briefly Chris, what are the thoughts there on the question of compensation? Understandably lots of the people involved will want to be compensated. What are the French unions saying about that, and any word of the French?

West [*in Calais*]: That's a long way in the future. At the moment they're trying to get the dispute solved. The question of compensation will come later and if the previous workings of the French courts are anything to go by, that could take a very long time indeed.

News anchor in studio: Chris West in Calais, thank you very much indeed.

In this extract from the BBC *Breakfast News*, there are many details that appeal to the viewers so that they can relate to the situation of the British truckers. The news anchor presents the story from the perspective of the British lorry drivers. The use of the words 'night', 'misery', 'frustration', 'road home' tells a story of British lorry drivers, who are dramatically caught in this uncomfortable situation away from home. The footage supports this story with the theme: 'fellow countrymen in need far away from home'. The fire around which people are gathered and a man in uniform add to the drama of being caught in the French road blockades.

The talks between the unions and the French government have failed and this causes more discomfort for the British drivers. What the French drivers' demands are and why they are so persistent in continuing the strike does not come up in this extract of BBC news at all. Reference to the violent acts that have occurred during the past days emphasizes the 'us' and 'them' division in this item. The British lorry drivers, despite the fact that the strikers are their colleagues, are an opposing group to the French drivers and show no sympathy at all for their motives. The BBC news does not give voice to any French actor: the drivers, union representatives, employees and the government are all put into one group, called 'the French/them', whose actions lead to discomfort and financial losses for 'the British/us'. This is made very explicit in this report. The division is supported by footage which clearly illustrates how the strike afflicts the British drivers (*dark, cold nights*), and it is also supported by the choice of words when talking about 'them', the French.

> [*Chris West reporting from location in Calais*]: . . . They [the British drivers] are saying: 'Why can't the French government do anything about it?' It is really a huge political game, which the men stuck here just don't understand.

The hero/victim and villain division takes on a national, almost patriotic shape, where all the British are in the role of the heroes/victims of the dispute and all the French are presented as the villains who are unable or unwilling to solve their problem.

Like the BBC, the German *Tagesschau* begins its report with the consequences of the blockade to Germany itself. A German driver who is stuck in the blockades somewhere in France states that from his point of view it resembles a 'hostage situation'. A French colleague argues in another segment that the French truckers are determined to 'continue the strike until a positive solution is found'.

German lorry driver [*commenting on the situation to the reporter*]: Was hier passiert das ist ja also direkt Geiselnahme.
[What happens here is nothing other than being held hostage.]

French lorry driver [*commenting on the situation to the reporter, dubbed in German*]: Wir sind . . . entschlossen, haben nichts mehr zu verlieren, bleiben bis zu einen positiven Antwort.
[We are determined, we have nothing to lose and we will stay till we get a positive answer.]

A journalist also quotes a statement of the French drivers in which they call for solidarity from their foreign colleagues: 'We are all Europeans and strict about not letting foreign drivers break the front.'

Voice-over [*footage of German drivers*]: Die streikenden Franzosen sagen 'Wir sind alle Europäer und achten strikt darauf das kein Ausländer die Streikfront durchbricht'.
[The striking French say 'We are all Europeans and we will see to it that not a single foreigner breaks the front.']

A third kind of perspective is found in the Dutch RTL4 news, which introduces the item from the French government's point of view. The news anchor explains the pressure the government now faces because of the failed negotiations: the strike is about to expand to other sectors and there is a fuel shortage in many places in France. The government is trying to find a solution that would satisfy both sides in the dispute: the employers and the workers. This point of view seems to put the French government in a central role in this conflict. It is given the role of an impartial party that is working to mediate a solution that will satisfy everybody. The government's role as a mediator does not come up in any other items in the material. In the other news broadcasts the government is more or less seen as one of the parties that are preventing a positive result in the negotiations. The RTL4 *Nieuws* was the only case in the material, where the typology of the managerial ideology was visible. The disrupting force are the workers with their 'unreasonable demands', whereas the government seems to be the order-maintaining force.

> *Voice-over*: De staking brengt de Franse regering in een moeilijk parket. Zouden de chauffeurs hun zin krijgen, dan schept dat verwachtingen bij andere werknemers. De stakers willen meer loon, kortere werktijden en pensioen vanaf hun 55ste. Dat terwijl de Franse regering wil bezuinigen.
> [The strike brings the French government to a difficult situation. If the drivers have their way, then other employees will expect something too. The strikers want higher wages, shorter working days and retirement at the age of 55. This at a time when the French government wishes to cut its budget.]

The management and employers were exnominated. The issue was domesticated in the same way as it was in the British news: that is, the Dutch drivers had no sympathy for their French colleagues at all. Nevertheless, the criticism was directed towards Dutch authorities and to the French truck drivers as well. This criticism was also used as a means of domestication as it was partly directed against an organization in the home country. In this case, the division between heroes/victims and villains does not follow national borders as it does in other items in the research material. The villains are both the French drivers and the Dutch help organizations, and the heroes/victims are the Dutch drivers and a French government that is doing its best to find a solution.

A fourth perspective was detected in the Dutch NOS *Journaal* and Belgian BRTN *Journaal en sport* broadcasts. The implications for the lorry drivers of each country are the most important and most strongly emphasized theme. A large part of the coverage is dedicated to the French drivers and their motives are presented clearly. Sympathy for the Dutch drivers is achieved by showing a truck loaded with young chickens that are now facing premature extermination since the lorry cannot reach its destination in France. The Dutch/Belgian drivers are also interviewed on several occasions. The broadcasters had sent reporters and a camera crew to the location. The dispute has also affected the Belgians in a more direct way, because French people are crossing the border into Belgium to buy petrol for their cars. The Belgian harbours are overflowing with lorries that are crossing the Channel to the UK. Interestingly, the Dutch NOS *Journaal* quotes a manager of a transport company, who sympathizes with the claims of the French drivers but expresses cautious criticism of the harsh measures against foreign drivers in France. This situation is curious: the Dutch manager expresses some sympathy with French lorry drivers instead of with his own colleagues, the French employers.

[*Voice-over*] *Grijpma* [*reporter*]: De firma Hendrix heeft van haar kant wel begrip voor de eisen van de Franse chauffeurs, maar vindt het middel van de blokkades te zwaar. Teveel mensen tegelijk de dupe. [*Film: a lorry departing from company's parking lot.*]

[On the other hand the Hendrix transport company has some sympathy for the demands of the French drivers, but finds the method of blockading too strong. Too many people at once become victims.]

The fifth perspective is present in the two Finnish news broadcasts and the CNN item, which are all considerably shorter and more superficial than the other samples in the material. This can be explained by the geographical and economical 'distance' from the dispute. For Finnish society national interest was not involved. The dispute is worth mentioning but not important enough for coverage of its backgrounds or for more than 10 seconds of valuable news time to be dedicated to it. Both Finnish news broadcasts used almost identical footage, which was neutral in a sense that no people were visible, only long lines of lorries standing on the road in an unidentified location. The short news story in all three broadcasts was clearly based on material received from the same source.

CNN

News anchor in studio: Transportation problems in France are about to get worse. The country's airline pilots' union has called a two days' strike for Wednesday and Thursday. It is expected to sharply cut French flights. French officials are already working on a nine-day truckers' strike. Truckers have set up nearly 200 barricades, creating traffic chaos and angry neighboring countries. Britain has warned the French that they face compensation claims for goods spoiled or not delivered because of the strike. Truckers are demanding better pay and the chance to retire early.

DISCUSSION

The managerial ideology, of the Glasgow Media Group's *More Bad News* (1980), is not evident in most of the news coverage in different European countries of the French road blockades of 1996. In the material that we analysed we found two layers of actors: the workers and their unions, employers and the government are represented both nationally, e.g. Dutch or Belgian, and internationally, in this case their French counterparts. The national perspective did not set the two conventionally opposing sides against each other. Instead a division was made between 'the French' and the others. The dominant theme in the non-French news broadcasts was the national interest. The BBC report was explicitly biased in favour of the British drivers and criticism was directed towards every party in France with no distinction made between the workers, employers and the French government. The French news covered the demands of the drivers and the consequences of the strike widely, but the overall conclusion was that the claims made by the drivers were justified and reasonable. Cultural and historical differences between the two countries might help explain these two very different approaches to the same issue. But we should be aware, of course, of the limitations of our material, which is too thin for any general conclusions. Despite all this, the French news broadcast was more balanced in presenting different viewpoints than the British news. Yet there is room to argue that the managerial perspective was somewhat neglected in the French coverage. The issue of the foreign drivers, who got stuck in France and were forced to go along with the strike, is completely absent. Correspondingly, the BBC broadcast totally ignored the French points of view throughout its report. The German broadcast did present viewpoints of French drivers, but selectively: only expressions of their determination to go on as long as was necessary and their demand for understanding and solidarity from their foreign colleagues. The main concern of the *Tagesschau* was the damage caused by the blockades to the German economy. The French, Belgian, Dutch and German broadcasts had as a shared element in their broadcast the everyday difficulties inflicted on ordinary French citizens, in the form of fuel rationing and increased prices, whereas the BBC news coverage of the topic did not touch on consequences of the dispute to French society at all, but concentrated only on how the strike affected the British transportation sector and the British lorry drivers personally.

Although much of the visual material, used in many of the broadcasts, was of a similar kind (and some was identical),[5] it was possible to distinguish five different approaches in the news bulletins. This supports the suggestion made by Gurevitch et al. (1991) that global events are shaped and reshaped by television news reporters and producers in ways that make them comprehensible and palatable to domestic audiences. Although images may have global currency, the meanings given to them may not necessarily be shared globally. Even in European countries that are culturally relatively close to each other, the perspectives which are presented in the news are not necessarily the same, even when dealing with the same kinds of implications of the same event. The 'story' of the French lorry drivers' strike was domesticated with the relevance of the actions to individuals and to the whole of society in each country as a starting point.

Television news coverage of labour conflicts in different countries seems to follow a similar type of format and contain similar kinds of codes. In our material the news was constructed to a considerable extent according to the same formats that have been presented by the Glasgow Media Group (1980). Signs of a managerial ideology are visible, but these ingredients do not add up, at least in these newscasts, to the kind of ideological structure, the managerial ideology, of *More Bad News*. Striking workers are nominated, as Fiske (1987) suggested, and managers and employers are exnominated, but when labour conflicts are reported in an international context, this duality may receive different interpretations than have been found in news reports of labour conflicts in a domestic context. What is exnominated is not necessarily higher in the hierarchy of discourses than what is nominated. Or, as we saw in this material, what is exnominated is not always presented as the natural 'truth'. It may be treated more respectfully because of a higher social status, but it can still be criticized. Indeed it has been challenged, by French lorry drivers one day in November 1996 on television across Europe.

NOTES

1 The news bulletins were videotaped at the Department of Communication, Universiteit van Amsterdam. Ms Liisa Riekki kindly videotaped the two Finnish

newscasts. The material was gathered originally for a comparative study of one day of European TV news. We are, of course, aware of the limitations of an analysis based on news reporting of a single day in a long-lasting dispute.

2 We have used the BBC *Breakfast News* because the French road blockades were not in the evening news. On that day, the government faced a catastrophe, when details of the budget were leaked to the media. The issue of the leakage and the budget itself completely dominated the evening news.

3 In both Finnish news broadcasts foreign items were presented at the beginning of the broadcast. Domestic items followed. The French road blockade was the last of the foreign news items (6th) in YLE's broadcast but came before any domestic issue. In MTV3 the road blockades were placed after four foreign items and two domestic items. This is an example of different news cultures; in all the other material domestic issues were presented first, followed by foreign issues approximately halfway through the broadcast, then moving back to minor domestic issues.

4 CNN news channel differs in format from the other channels. Most of the programme consists of constant news broadcasts linked with previews and commercials. Although their news broadcast lasts 30 minutes, it is interrupted by commercial breaks, so the actual time dedicated to news is not 30 minutes, but 12 minutes.

5 A curious example of how the same footage can serve different ends is provided by camera shots of a crowd of truckers being addressed by a strike leader. It was used by Dutch commercial broadcaster RTL4 in its item about the French road blockades, but by German public broadcaster ZDF to illustrate similar actions by Danish lorry drivers on the Danish–German border.

ACTIVITIES

1 Go through the transcript of the BBC *Breakfast News*.

- Analyse, what kinds of view are represented as 'common sense'.
- What is considered to be the 'truth' by the news writers?

2 Study the extract from RTL4 *Nieuws* and try to find signs of a 'managerial ideology'.

3 This particular case raises other questions that are not discussed in this chapter, such as: why was this news item selected at all (or not, as in the case of the BBC evening newscasts); what explains the differences in the amount of time taken to discuss the event, or its rank order in the news bulletins? Studies of international news have come up with theories about the differential selection and treatment of international events.

- Try to find answers that would apply in this case.
- Find out if they apply in other recent cases of international reporting as well.

SUGGESTIONS FOR FURTHER READING

Fiske, J. (1987). *Television Culture*. London: Methuen (later, Routledge).

Still one of the most readable books about television, its narrative forms and its role in constructing genres such as the news.

Glasgow University Media Group (1980) *More Bad News*. London: Routledge and Kegan Paul.

This diagnosis of media reporting of the economic crisis and the unrest surrounding the Social Contract in Britain is one of the most interesting critical studies of this productive research team.

Gurevitch, M., Levy, M.R. and Roeh, J. (1991) 'The global newsroom: convergencies and diversities in the globalization of television news', in P. Dahlgren and C. Sparks (eds), *Communication and Citizenship. Journalism and the Public Sphere in the New Media Age*, pp. 195–216. London: Routledge.

One of the most interesting conclusions of this international comparative research is that television news maintains both global and culturally specific orientations by placing distant events in domestically relevant frameworks and by constructing meanings that are compatible with the culture and ideology of the societies they serve.

REFERENCES

1 THE STATUS OF TV BROADCASTING IN EUROPE

Achille, Y. and Miège, B. (1994) 'The limits to the adaptation strategies of European public service television', *Media, Culture and Society*, 16: 31–46.

Biltereyst, D. (1995) *Hollywood in het avondland: over de afhankelijkheid en de impact van Amerikaanse televisie in Europa* (Dependence and impact of American TV in Europe). Brussels: VUB-Press.

Blumler, J.G. and Gurevitch, M. (1995) *The Crisis of Public Communication*. London: Routledge.

Brants, K. (1998) 'Who's afraid of infotainment?', *European Journal of Communication* 13 (3): 315–337.

British Annan Committee (1997) Cmnd 6753 Report of the Committee on the Future of Broadcasting. London: HMSO.

Corcoran, F. (1996) 'Arts Council of the air: switching attention from the service to the programme', *Javnost/The Public*, 3 (2): 9–23.

Council of Europe (1994) *The Media in a Democratic Society*. Draft Resolutions and Draft Political Declaration, 4th European Ministerial Conference on Mass Media Policy, Prague, 7–8 December. Strasbourg: Council of Europe, MCM–CDMM 3 prov 1.

De Bens, E. de (1998) 'Television programming: more diversity, more convergence?', in K. Brants, J. Hermes and L. van Zoonen (eds), *The Media in Question*. London: Sage, pp. 27–38.

D'Haenens, L. and Saeys, F. (eds) (1998) *Media Dynamics and Regulatory Concerns in the Digital Age*. Berlin: Quintessenz Verlag.

Euromedia Research Group (ed. Bernt Stubbe Østergaard) (1997) *The Media in Western Europe: The Euromedia Handbook*, 2nd edition, London: Sage.

European Audiovisual Observatory (1999) *Statistical Yearbook '99. Film, Television, Video and the New Media in Europe*. Strasbourg: Council of Europe.

Golding, P. (1994) 'Telling stories: sociology, journalism and the informed citizen', *European Journal of Communication*, 9 (4): 461–484.

Herman, E.S. and McChesney, R.W. (1997) *The Global Media: The New Missionaries of Corporate Capitalism*. London: Cassell.

Jankowsky, J. and Fuchs, D.(1995) *Television Today and Tomorrow*. New York: Oxford University Press.

Kelly, M. (1983) 'Influences on broadcasting policies for election coverage', in J.G. Blumler (ed.), *Communicating to Voters: Television in the First European Parliamentary Elections*. London: Sage, pp. 65–82.

Krüger, U. (1998) 'Programm-Analyse: Tendenzen in den Programmen der grossen Fernsehen 1985–1995' (Trends in TV programming), *Media Perspektiven*, 98: 417–440.

McQuail, D. (1992) *Media Performance. Mass Communication and the Public Interest*. London: Sage.

McQuail, D. (1998) 'Commercialization and beyond', in D. McQuail and K. Siune (eds), *Media Policy, Convergence, Concentration and Commerce*. London: Sage, pp. 107–128.

Mitchell, J. and Blumler, J.G. (eds) (1994) *Television and the Viewer Interest*. (European Institute for the Media.) London: John Libbey.

Peacock, A. (1986) *Report of the Committee on Financing the BBC*. Cmnd 9824. London: HMSO.

Robillard, S. (1995) *Television in Europe: Regulatory Bodies. Status, Function and Powers in 35 European Countries*. European Institute for the Media. London: John Libbey.

Ros, G. (1998) 'Broadcasting in the Federal Republic of Germany', in D'Haenens and Saeys (eds), pp. 215–237.

Siune, K. and Hultén, O. (1998) 'Does public broadcasting have a future?', in D. McQuail and K. Siune (eds), *Media Policy*. London: Sage, pp. 22–38.

Tunstall, J. (1997) 'The United Kingdom', in Euromedia Research Group, *The Media in Western Europe*, pp. 244–260.

2 KEY TRENDS IN EUROPEAN TELEVISION

Graham, A. and Davies, G. (1997) *Broadcasting, Society and Policy in the Multimedia Age*. Luton, UK: John Libby.

Hultén, O. (1996) 'Public service och den mediepolitiska utvecklingen i Norden', in O. Hultén et al. (eds), *Nordisk forskning om public service*. Göteborg: Nordicom.

Hultén, O. and Siune, K. (1998) 'Does public broadcasting have a futrure?', in D. McQuail and K. Siune (eds), *Media Policy*. London: Sage.

Hultén, O. and Brants, K. (1992) 'Public service broadcasting: reactions to competition', in K. Siune and W. Treutzschler (eds), *Dynamics of Media Politics*. London: Sage.

Humphreys, P.J. (1996) *Mass Media and Media Policy in Western Europe*. Manchester: Manchester University Press.

Ishikawa, S. (ed.) (1996) *Quality Assessment of Television*. Luton: John Libby Media.

McQuail, D. (1998) 'Commercialisation and beyond', in D. McQuail and K. Siune (eds), *Media Policy*. London: Sage.

Murdock, G. (1990) 'Television and citizenship: in defence of public broadcasting', in A. Tomlinson (ed.), *Consumption, Identity and Style*. London: Routledge.

Raboy, M. (ed.) (1996) *Public Broadcasting for the 21st Century*. Luton, UK: John Libby.

Sveriges Television (1999) *Public-service-uppföljning och årsredovisning*. Stockholm: Swedish Television.
Tracey, M. (1998) *The Decline and Fall of Public Service Broadcasting*. Oxford: Oxford University Press.

3 DIGITAL FUTURES: EUROPEAN TELEVISION IN THE AGE OF CONVERGENCE

Allen, R. (1998) 'This is not television . . .', in J. Steemers (ed.), *Changing Channels: The Prospects for Television in a Digital World*. Luton: University of Luton Press, pp. 59–71.
Anders, J. (1999) 'Crossed wires', *Cable and Satellite Europe*, July: 50–52.
Beavis, S. (1998) 'Slow start for digital television in view', *Guardian*, 25 March: 21.
Birt, Sir J. (1999) *The Price and the Prize: The Social, Political and Cultural Consequences of the Digital Age*. London: BBC. The New Statesman Media Lecture.
Chalaby, J.K and Segell, G. (1999) 'The broadcasting media in the age of risk: the advent of digital television', *New Media and Society*, 3: 351–368.
Chaudhary, V. (1999) 'Now armchair fans get to control what they watch', *Guardian*, 13 August: 3.
Clegg, J. and Kamall, S. (1998) 'The internationalisation of telecommunications services in the European Union', *Transnational Corporations*, 7 (2), August: 39–96.
Clemens, J. (1996) 'Database marketing and the future of public service', *Intermedia*, 24 (2), April/May: 6–9.
Economist (1999) 'European media: flirtation and frustration', *Economist*, 11 December: 99–102.
Economist (2000a) 'How Wired is Britain?', *Economist*, 19 February: 38–40.
Economist (2000b) 'Le cyber challenge', *Economist*, 11 March: 53.
European Commission (1997a) *Green Paper on the Regulatory Implications of the Convergence of the Telecommunications, Audiovisual and Information Technology Sectors: Towards a Common Approach to Information Society Services*. Brussels: European Commission, 29 September.
European Commission (1997b) *Green Paper on the Convergence of the Telecommunications, Media and Information Technology Sectors, and the Implications for Regulation: Towards an Information Society Approach*. Brussels: European Commission. COM(97)623.
Feldman, T. (1997) *Introduction to Digital Media*. London: Routledge.
Gibbons, T. (1998) 'De/re-regulating the system: the British experience', in J. Steemers (ed.), *Changing Channels: The Prospects for Television in a Digital World*. Luton: University of Luton Press, pp. 73–96.
Golding, P. and Murdock, G. (2000) 'Culture, communications, and political economy', in J. Curran and M. Gurevitch (eds), *Mass Media and Society*. London: Arnold.
Harding, J. (2000) 'Murdoch offers stake to Gates', *Financial Times*, 29 February: 19.

Harding, J. and Larsen, P.T. (2000) 'BSkyB unveils internet strategy', *Financial Times*, 2 February: 23.
House of Commons (1998) *Select Committee on Culture, Media and Sport: Fourth Report: The Multi-Media Revolution*. London. House of Commons Select Committee on Culture, Media and Sport.
Hutton, W. (2000) 'The buck stops with big corporations', *Financial Times*, 28 February: 23.
Kilgarriff, R. (2000) 'It's a teen thing. Oldies not wanted', *Independent Tuesday Review*, 8 February: 8.
Kleinsteuber, H.J. (1997) 'Crippled digitalization? Superhighways or one-way streets? The case of German digital television', in H. Kubicek, W.H. Dutton and R. Williams (eds), *The Social Shaping of Information Superhighways: European and American Roads to the Information Superhighway*. Frankfurt: Campus Verlag, pp. 79–96.
Middleton, C. (2000) 'Beyond 2000', in *Coming to a Town Near You*. London: BBC.
Murdock, G. (1999) 'Rights and representations: public discourse and cultural citizenship', in J. Gripsrud (ed.), *Television and Common Knowledge*. London: Routledge, pp. 7–17.
Murdock, G. and Golding, P. (1999) 'Common markets: corporate ambitions and communication trends in the UK and Europe', *Journal of Media Economics*, 12 (2): 117–132.
Negroponte, N. (1995) *Being Digital*. London: Hodder and Stoughton.
Norris, P. (2000) 'The Internet in Europe: A New North-South Divide?', *Press/Politics*, 5 (1): 1–12.
Papathanassopoulos, S. (1998) 'The development of digital television in Europe', *Media International Australia*, 86 (February): 77–86.
Pons, J.F. (1998) 'The application of competition and anti-trust policy in media and telecommunications in the European Union', speech to the International Bar Association, Vancouver, British Columbia, 14 September.
Reith, J.C.W. (1924) *Broadcast Over Britain*. London: Hodder and Stoughton.
Rose, F. (2000) 'TV or not TV', *Wired*, March: 246–251.
Sutherland, F. (1999) 'Finding your niche', *Cable and Satellite Europe*, May: 52–54.
Walmsley, N. (1999) 'Enhancing the value of branded content in the digital age', *Cable and Satellite Europe*, June: 29.
Wired (2000) 'Rupert discovers the Internet', *Wired*, March: 252–253.

4 PROGRAMMING AND CHANNEL COMPETITION IN EUROPEAN TELEVISION

Achille, Y. and Miège, B. (1994) 'The limits of adaptation strategies of European public service television', *Media, Culture & Society*, 16 (1).
Andersen, R. (1995) *Consumer Culture & TV Programming*. Boulder, CO: Westview Press.
Ang, I. (1985) 'The battle between television and its audiences', in P. Drummond and R. Patterson (eds), *Television in Transition*. London: BFI.
Ang, I. (1991) *Desperately Seeking the Audience*. London: Routledge.

Bono, F. and Bondebjerg, Ib. (eds) (1994) 'Nordic television: history, politics and aesthetics', *Sekvens*, Special Edition, Department of Film & Media Studies, University of Copenhagen (together with Festival Nordico, Prix Italia, RAI).

Caldwell, J.T. (1995) *Televisuality: Style, Crisis and Authority in American Television*. New Brunswick, NJ: Rutgers University Press.

Carlsson, U. (ed.) (1997) *Radio Research in Denmark, Finland, Norway and Sweden*. Gothenburg: Nordicom.

Carroll, R.L. and Davis, D.M. (1993) *Electronic Media Programming, Strategies and Decision Making*. New York: McGraw-Hill.

Corner, J. (1999) *Critical Ideas in Television Studies*. Oxford: Clarendon Press.

De Bens, E., Kelly, M. and Bakke, M. (1992) 'Television content: Dallasification of culture?', in K. Siune and W. Treutzschler (eds), *Dynamics of Media Politics, Broadcast and Electronic Media in Western Europe*. London: Sage.

Eastman, S.T. (1993) *Broadcasting/Cable Programming Strategies and Practices*. Belmont, CA: Belmont.

Ellis, J. (1992) *Visible Fictions*. London: Routledge (revised edition).

Feuer, J. (1995) *Seeing Through the Eighties, Television and Reaganism*. Durham: Duke University Press.

Gitlin, T. (1994) *Inside Prime Time*. London: Routledge (revised edition).

Hellman, H. (1999) 'From companions to competitors: the changing broadcasting markets and television programming in Finland', *Acta Universitatis Tamperensis* 652, University of Tampere.

Hellman, H. and Sauri, T. (1997) 'Hybridikanavien nousukausi: Kilpailu ja television ohjelmarakenteen muutos Pohjoismaissa 1988–1995' [The boom of hybrid channels: competition and change of TV programme structure in the Nordic countries 1988–1995], *Tiedotustutkimus*, 2 (1997), pp. 20–39 (in Finnish).

Hultén, O. and Brants, K. (1995) 'Public service broadcasting: reactions to competition', in K. Siune and W. Treutzschler (eds), *Dynamics of Media Politics: Broadcast and Electronic Media in Western Europe*. London: Sage, pp. 116–128.

Jensen, K.B. (1994) 'Reception as flow: the "new television viewer" revisited', *Cultural Studies*, 8 (2): 293–305.

Lähteenmäki, M. (1999) *Kruununjalokivi, merkkipaalu ja veturi. Uutiset ja kaaviovetoinen ohjelmointi kanavilla TV1, TV2, MTV3 ja Nelonen 1978–1998* [Crown jewel, milestone and locomotive. News and schedule driven programming on channels TV1, TV2, MTV3 and Channel 4 in 1978–1988]. MA thesis, Department of Journalism and Mass Communication, University of Tampere.

Moran, A. (1998) *Copycat TV: Globalisation, Program Formats and Cultural Identity*. Luton: University of Luton Press.

Nordenstreng, K. (1972) 'Policy for news transmission', in D. Mcquail (ed.), *Sociology of Mass Communications*. Harmondsworth: Penguin Books, pp. 386–405.

Nordic Baltic Media Statistics 1998 (1999). Gothenburg: Nordicom.

Pringle, P.K., Starr, M.F. and McCavitt, W.E. (1995) *Electronic Media Management* (3rd edn). Boston: Focal Press.

Ridell, S. (1996) 'Resistance through routines: flow theory and the power of metaphors', *European Journal of Communication*, 11 (4): 557–582.

Solla, K. (1999) *Saippuadokumenttisarjat – television faktan ja fiktion uudenlainen sekoitus* [Docusoaps – a new mixture of fact and fiction on TV]. MA thesis, Department of Journalism and Mass Communication, University of Tampere.

Søndergaard, H. (1994) *DR i tv-konkurrencens tidsalder* (DR in the era of TV competition]. Frederiksberg: Samfundslitteratur.

Syvertsen, T. (1996) *Den store TV-krigen, Norsk allmennfjernsyn 1988–96* [The

big TV war, Norwegian public service television in 1988–96]. Bergen-Sandviken: Fagboklaget (in Norwegian).
Vane, E.T. and Gross, L.S. (1994) *Programming for TV, Radio, and Cable*. Boston: Focal Press.
Williams, R. (1974) *Television: Technology and Cultural Form*. London: Fontana/Collins.
Ytreberg, E. (1999) *Allmenkringkastingens autoritet, Endringer i NRK Fjernsynets tekstproduksjon 1987–1994* [The authority of public service broadcasting, changes in the text production of NRK's television in 1987–1994]. Oslo: Mediestudier, Skriftserie fra Institutt for medier og kommunikasjon, Universitetet i Oslo.

5 POPULAR DRAMA: TRAVELLING TEMPLATES AND NATIONAL FICTIONS

Ang, I. (1991) *Desperately Seeking the Audience*. London: Routledge.
Beck, C. (1984) *On Air: 25 Years of TV in Queensland*. Brisbane: One Tree Hill Publishing.
Hofmann, M. (1988) 'The Federal Republic of Germany', in A. Silj (ed.), *East of Dallas: The European Challenge to American Television*. London: British Film Institute, pp. 141–164.
Hofmann, M. (1992) 'Germany', in A. Silj (ed.), *The New Television in Europe*. London: John Libbey, pp. 525–596.
Kingsley, H. (1989) *Soap Box: The Australian Guide to Television Soap Opera*. Melbourne: Sun Books.
Kreutzner, G. and Seiter, E. (1995) 'Not all "soaps" are created equal: towards a cross-cultural criticism of television series', in R. Allen (ed.), *To be Continued . . . Soap Opera Around the World*. London: Routledge, pp. 234–255.
Madsen, O. (1994) 'On the quality of soap', in T. Elsaesser, J. Simons and L. Bronk (eds), *Writing for the Medium: Television in Transition*. Amsterdam: Amsterdam University Press, pp. 49–53.
Moran, A. (1985) *Image and Industry: Australian Television Drama Production*. Sydney: Currency Press.
Moran, A. (1993) *Moran's Guide to Australian TV Series*. Sydney: Australian Film, Television and Radio School.
Oxley, H. (1979) 'Okerism: the Cultural Habit', in P. Spearitt and D. Walker (eds), *Australian Popular Culture*. Sydney: George Allen and Unwin, pp. 105–1390.
Windshuttle, K. (1979) *Unemployement: A Social and Economic Analysis of the Economic Crisis in Australia*. Ringwood, Victoria: Penguin Books.

6 PROGRAMME MAKING ACROSS BORDERS: THE *EUROSUD* NEWS MAGAZINE

Bilbao-Fullaondo, J. (1993) *Television transfronteriza: Imagenes reciprocas en los medios de comunicacion social*. Universidad del Pais Basco, servicio editorial.

Ladmiral, J.R. and Lipiansky, E.M. (1989) *Communication interculturelle* (Intercultural communication). Paris: Armand Colin.

Marchetti, P. (1997) *La Production d'œuvres audiovisuelles dans l'Union européenne*. Paris: Economica.

Schlesinger, P. (1997) 'L'Identité culturelle européenne: au-delà du slogan' (European cultural identity: beyond the slogan), in Marchetti (1997).

Winkin, Y. (1996) *Anthropologie de la communication. De la théorie au terrain* (Anthropology of communication. From theory to practice). Paris and Brussels: Deboeck University.

Wolton, D. (1990) *Eloge du grand public. Une théorie critique de la télévision*. Paris: Flammarion.

7 TELEVISION AUDIENCES

Ang, I. (1991) *Desperately Seeking the Audience*. London: Routledge.

ARF/ESOMAR (1992) *Worldwide Broadcast Audience Research Symposium, Toronto (Canada) 1st–3rd June 1992*. Amsterdam: ESOMAR Central Secretariat.

Barwise, P. and Ehrenberg, A. (1988) *Television and its Audience*. London: Sage.

Bechtel, R.B., Achelpohl, C. and Akers, R. (1972) 'Correlates between observed behavior and questionnaire responses on television viewing', in E.A. Rubinstein, G.A. Comstock and J.P. Murray (eds), *Television and Social Behavior. Reports and Papers, Volume IV; Television in Day-to-day Life: Patterns of Use*. A technical report to the Surgeon General's Scientific Advisory Committee on Television and Social Behavior, pp. 274–344. Rockville, MA: National Institute of Mental Health.

Becker, L.B. and Schoenbach, K. (eds) (1989) *Audience Responses to Media Diversification. Coping with Plenty*. Hillsdale, NJ: Lawrence Erlbaum.

Beville, H.M. Jr. (1988) *Audience Ratings: Radio, Television, and Cable*, revised student edition. Hillsdale, NJ: Lawrence Erlbaum.

Blumer, H. (1939) 'Collective behavior', in A. McClung Lee (ed.), *New Outline of the Principles of Sociology*. New York: Barnes and Noble, pp. 167–224.

Blumler, J.G. (ed.) (1992) *Television and the Public Interest. Vulnerable Values in West European Broadcasting*. London: Sage.

Collett, P. (1987) 'The viewers viewed', *Et cetera*, 44 (3): 245–251.

Cooper, R. (1996) 'The status and future of audience duplication research: an assessment of ratings-based theories of audience behavior', *Journal of Broadcasting and Electronic Media*, 40: 96–111.

Dahlgren, P. (1998) 'Critique: elusive audiences', in R. Dickinson, R. Harindranath and O. Linné (eds), *Approaches to Audiences. A Reader*. London: Arnold, pp. 298–310.

EBU (1997) *Guidelines for the Setting Up and Operating of TV Audience Measurement Peoplemeter Systems*. Geneva: European Broadcasting Union.

Ettema, J.S. and Whitney, D.C. (eds) (1994) *Audiencemaking: How the Media Create the Audience*. Thousand Oaks, CA: Sage.

Ferguson, D.A. and Perse, E.M. (1993) 'Media and audience influences on channel repertoire', *Journal of Broadcasting and Electronic Media*, 37: 31–47.

Festinger, L. (1957) *A Theory of Cognitive Dissonance*. Stanford, CA: Stanford University Press.

Gunter, B. and Svennevig, M. (1987) *Behind and in Front of the Screen. Television's Involvement with Family Life*. London: John Libbey.

Gunter, B. and Wober, M. (1992) *The Reactive Viewer. A Review of Research on Audience Reaction Measurement*. London: John Libbey.

Höijer, B. (1998) 'Social psychological perspectives in reception analysis', in R. Dickinson, R. Harindranath and O. Linné (eds), *Approaches to Audiences. A Reader*. London: Arnold, pp. 166–183.

Jensen, K.B. and Jankowski, N.W. (eds) (1991) *A Handbook of Qualitative Methodologies for Mass Communication Research*. London: Routledge.

Jensen, K.B. and Rosengren, K.E. (1990) 'Five traditions in search of the audience', *European Journal of Communication*, 5: 207–238.

Katz, E., Blumler, J.G. and Gurevitch, M. (1974) 'Utilization of mass communication by the individual', in J.G. Blumler and E. Katz (eds), *The Uses of Mass Communications: Current Perspectives on Gratifications Research*. Beverly Hills, CA: Sage, pp. 19–32.

Lazarsfeld, P.F., Berelson, B. and Gaudet, H. (1944) *The People's Choice. How the Voter Makes Up His Mind in a Presidential Campaign*. New York: Duell, Sloan & Pearce.

Lemish, D. (1982) 'The rules of viewing television in public places', *Journal of Broadcasting*, 26: 757–781.

Liebes, T. and Katz, E. (1986) 'Patterns of involvement in television fiction: a comparative analysis', *European Journal of Communication*, 1: 151–171.

Lindlof, T.A. (ed.) (1987) *Natural Audiences: Qualitative Research of Media Uses and Effects*. Norwood, NJ: Ablex.

Lindlof, T.A. (1988) 'Media audiences as interpretive communities', in J.A. Anderson (ed.), *Communication Yearbook*, 11: 81–107.

Lindlof, T.A. (1991) 'The qualitative study of media audiences', *Journal of Broadcasting and Electronic Media*, 35: 23–42.

Livingstone, S.M. (1992) 'The resourceful reader: interpreting television characters and narratives', in S.A. Deetz (ed.), *Communication Yearbook*, 15: 58–90.

Lull, J. (1990) *Inside Family Viewing. Ethnographic Research on Television's Audiences*. London: Routledge.

Lunt, P. and Livingstone, S. (1996) 'Rethinking the focus group in media and communications research', *Journal of Communication*, 46 (2): 79–98.

McQuail, D. (1994) *Mass Communication Theory. An Introduction*, 3rd edn. London: Sage.

McQuail, D. (1997) *Audience Analysis*. Thousand Oaks, CA: Sage.

Merton, R.K. (1987) 'The focused interview and focus groups. Continuities and discontinuities', *Public Opinion Quarterly*, 51: 550–566.

Mitchell, J. and Blumler, J.G. (eds) (1994) *Television and the Viewer Interest. Explorations in the Responsiveness of European Broadcasters*. London: John Libbey.

Morley, D. (1988) 'Domestic relations: the framework of family viewing in Great Britain', in J. Lull (ed.), *World Families Watch Television*. Newbury Park, CA: Sage, pp. 22–48.

Morley, D. (1992) *Television, Audiences and Cultural Studies*. London: Routledge.

Morrison, D.E. (1998) *The Search for a Method: Focus Groups and the Development of Mass Communication Research*. Luton: University of Luton Press.

Neuman, W.R. (1992) *The Future of the Mass Audience.* Cambridge: Cambridge University Press.
Press, A. (1989) 'Class and gender in the hegemonic process: class differences in women's perception of television realism and identification with television characters', *Media, Culture and Society*, 11: 229–251.
Schulz, W. (2000) 'Changes of mass media and the public sphere', in S. Splichal (ed.), *Public Opinion and Democracy.* Hampton Press (forthcoming).
Television 98. European Key Facts, 5th edn, August 1998. Kronberg: IP Group.
Webster, J.G. and Lichty, L.W. (1991) *Ratings Analysis. Theory and Practice.* Hillsdale, NJ: Lawrence Erlbaum.
Webster, J.G. and Phalen, P.F. (1997) *The Mass Audience. Rediscovering the Dominant Model.* Mahwah, NJ: Lawrence Erlbaum.
Webster, J.G. and Wagschlag, J.J. (1985) 'A theory of television program choice', *Communication Research*, 10: 430–446.
Wolf, M.A. (1987) 'How children negotiate television', in T.A. Lindlof (ed.), *Natural Audiences: Qualitative Research of Media Uses and Effects.* Norwood, NJ: Ablex, pp. 58–94.
Zillmann, D. and Bryant, J. (eds) (1985) *Selective Exposure to Communication.* Hillsdale, NJ: Lawrence Erlbaum.

8 MUSIC TELEVISION: MTV-EUROPE

Aufderheide, P. (1986) 'Music videos: the look of the sound', *Journal of Communication*, 36 (1): 57–78.
Banks, J. (1996) *Monopoly Television: MTV's Quest to Control the Music.* Boulder, CO: Westview Press.
Baxter, R.L., De Reimer, C., Landini, A., Leslie, L. and Singletary, M.W. (1985) 'A content analysis of music videos', *Journal of Broadcasting and Electronic Media*, 29 (3): 333–340.
Bekaert, M. (1998a) *Hoe Europees is MTV-Europe?* Leuven: Departement Communicatiewetenschap.
Bekaert, M. (1998b) 'De Regionalisering van muziekzenders in Europa', *Mediagids*, 2: 43–51.
Broadcasting and Cable (1990) *MTV: Moving with the Music*, 2 July: 39–40.
Brown, J.D. and Campbell, K. (1986) 'Race and gender in music videos: the same beat but a different drummer', *Journal of Communication*, 36 (1): 94–106.
Brown, J.D and Schulze, L. (1990) 'The effects of race, gender, and fandom on audience interpretations of Madonna's music videos', *Journal of Communication*, 40 (2): 88–102.
Brown, J.D., Campbell, K. and Fischer, L. (1986) 'American adolescents and music videos: why do they watch?', *Gazette*, 37: 19–32.
Burnett, R. (1990) 'From a whisper to a scream: music video and cultural form', in K. Roe and U. Carlsson (eds), *Popular Music Research.* Göteborg: NORDICOM.
Burnett, R. (1996) *The Global Jukebox.* London: Routledge.
Caplan, R.E. (1985) 'Violent program content in music video', *Journalism Quarterly*, 62 (2): 144–147.

Denisoff, S.R. (1988) *Inside MTV*. New Brunswick, NJ: Transaction Books.

Elg, P-E. and Roe, K. (1986) 'The music of the spheres: satellites and music video content', *The NORDICOM Review of Nordic Mass Communication Research*, 2: 15–19.

Hansen, C.H. and Hansen, R.D. (1990) 'The influence of sex and violence on the appeal of rock music videos', *Communication Research*, 17 (2): 212–234.

Hansen, C.H. and Krygowski, W. (1994) 'Arousal-augmentation priming effects: rock music videos and sex object schemas', *Communication Research*, 21 (1): 24–47.

Hartman, J.K. (1987) 'I want my ad-TV', *Popular Music and Society*, 11 (2): 17–24.

Kaplan, E.A. (1987) *Rocking Around the Clock: Music Television, Postmodernism, & Consumer Culture*. New York: Methuen.

McKee, K.B. and Pardun, C.J. (1999) 'Reading the video: a qualitative study of religious images in music videos', *Journal of Broadcasting and Electronic Media*, 43 (1): 110–122.

Montavelli, J. (1986) 'MTV sees low cost programming ingenuity as key to sustaining high profitability', *Cable Vision*, 15 September: 26–28.

Pittman, R.W. (1990) 'The television generation speaks a different tongue', *New York Herald Tribune*, 25 January: 5.

Riley, P. and Monge, P.R. (1998) 'Communication in the global community', *Communication Research*, 25 (4): 355–358.

Roe, K. (1985) 'The school and music in adolescent socialization', in J. Lull (ed.), *Popular Music and Communication*. Newbury Park, CA: Sage.

Roe, K. (1992) 'Different destinies – different melodies: school achievement, anticipated status and adolescents' tastes in music', *European Journal of Communication*, 7 (3): 335–357.

Roe, K. (1993) 'Academic capital and music tastes among Swedish adolescents: an empirical test of Bourdieu's model of cultural reproduction', *Young: The Nordic Journal of Youth Research*, 1 (3): 40–55.

Roe, K. (1994) 'Music use and social mobility', in K.E. Rosengren (ed.), *Media Effects and Beyond*. London: Routledge.

Roe, K. and Cammaer, G. (1993) 'Delivering the young audience to advertisers', *Communications: The European Journal of Communication*, 18 (2): 169–177.

Roe, K. and Lövgren, M. (1988) 'Music video and educational achievement', *Popular Music*, 7 (3): 303–313.

Roe, K. and Wallis, R. (1989) '"One planet one music": the development of music television in Western Europe', *The NORDICOM Review of Nordic Mass Communication Research*, 1: 34–39.

Savage, J. (1987) 'Latched onto the loop', *The Observer*, 16 August.

Seidman, S. (1992) 'An investigation of sex-role stereotyping in music videos', *Journal of Broadcasting and Electronic Media*, 36 (2): 209–216.

Sherman, B.L. and Dominick, J.R. (1986) 'Violence and sex in music videos', *Journal of Communication*, 36 (1): 79–93.

Straw, W. (1988) 'Music video in its contexts: popular music and post-modernism in the 1980s', *Popular Music*, 7 (3): 247–266.

Sun, S-W. and Lull, J. (1986) 'The adolescent audience for music videos and why they watch', *Journal of Communication*, 36 (1): 115–125.

Tapper, J., Thorson, E. and Black, D. (1994) 'Variations in music videos as a function of their musical genre', *Journal of Broadcasting and Electronic Media*, 38 (1): 103–113.

Tomlinson, J. (1999) *Globalization and Culture*. Cambridge: Polity Press.
Waisbord, S. (1998) 'When the cart of media is put before the horse of identity', *Communication Research*, 25 (4): 377–398.
Wheeler, D.K. (1998) 'Global culture or global clash', *Communication Research*, 25 (4): 359–376.

9 ARTS TELEVISION: QUESTIONS OF CULTURE

Bakke, M. (1986) 'Culture at stake', in D. McQuail and K. Siune (eds), *New Media Politics. Comparative Perspectives in Western Europe*, London and Beverly Hills: Sage, pp. 130–151.
Blumler, J.G. (1992) 'Vulnerable values at stake', in J.G. Blumler (ed.), *Television and the Public Interest. Vulnerable Values in West European Broadcasting*. London: Sage, pp. 22–42.
Carlsson, U. and Harrie, E. (eds) (1997) *Media Trends 1997 in Denmark, Finland, Iceland, Norway and Sweden*. Göteborg: NORDICOM, Göteborg University.
De Bens E. et al. (1992) 'Television content: Dallasification of culture?', in K. Siune and W. Treutzchler (eds), *Dynamics of Media Politics. Broadcast and Electronic Media in Western Europe*. London: Sage, pp. 75–100.
European Broadcasting Union Statistics Group (reference year 1998) *Questionnaire for TV-programmes' Output and Origin*.
Heilbrun, J. and Gray, C.M. (1993) *The Economics of Art and Culture. An American Perspective*. New York: Cambridge University Press.
Hermans, H. (1988) 'The arts on television', *EBU Review*, 39 (6), November: 42–45.
Hoffmann-Riem, W. (1992) 'Defending vulnerable values: regulatory measures and enforcement dilemmas', in J.G. Blumler (ed.), *Television and the Public Interest. Vulnerable Values in West European Broadcasting*. London: Sage, pp. 173–201.
Kroeber, A.L. and Kluckhohn, C. (1963) *Culture. A Critical Review of Concepts and Definitions*. New York: Vintage Books.
McQuail, D. and van Cuilenburg, J.J. (1983) 'Diversity as media policy goal: a strategy for evaluative research and a Netherlands case study', *Gazette*, 31: 145–162.
Murdock, G. (1992) 'Citizens, consumers, and public culture', in M. Skovmand and K. Schröder (eds), *Media Cultures*. London and New York: Routledge, pp. 17–41.
NRK (1987) *NRK – framtid, oppgave, tiltak. Om kringkastingens stilling og utvikling*. Brev til Kultur- og vitenskapsdepartementet, 19 June. Oslo.
NRK (1994) *NRKs virksomhet i 1993*. Oslo.
Syvertsen, T. (1991) '"Culture" vs. "business": structural changes in Norwegian broadcasting', in H. Rønning and K. Lundby (eds), *Media and Communication. Readings in Methodology, History and Culture*. Oslo: Norwegian University Press, pp. 331–344.
Tuchman, G. (1983) 'Consciousness industries and the production of culture', *Journal of Communication*, Summer: 330–341.
UNESCO (1998) *Background Document* for Intergovernmental Conference on Cultural Policies for Development, Stockholm, 30 March–2 April.

Vercruysse, J. (1992) 'Vercruysse statement about Documenta 9', *Art Monthly*, September: 14.
Walker, J.A. (1994) *Art in the Age of Mass Media*. London: Pluto Press.
Williams, R. (1967) 'Culture and civilization', in *The Encyclopedia of Philosophy*, Vol. 2, pp. 273–276. New York and London: Macmillan & The Free Press.
Yinger, J.M. (1960) 'Contraculture and subculture', *American Sociological Review*, 25 (5): 625–635.

10 BREAKFAST TELEVISION: INFOTAINERS AT DAYBREAK

Alasuutari, P. (1997) 'Why does the radio go unnoticed?', in U. Carlsson (ed.), *Radio Research in Denmark, Finland, Norway and Sweden*. Special issue *Nordicom Review* 1/1997: 161–171.
Allan, S. (1998) 'News from NowHere: televisual news discourse and the construction of hegemony', in A. Bell and P. Garrett (eds), *Approaches to Media Discourse*. Oxford: Blackwell, pp. 105–141.
Altman, R. (1986) 'Television/sound', in T. Modleski (ed.), *Studies in Entertainment. Critical Approaches to Mass Culture*. Bloomington: Indiana University Press, pp. 39–53.
Bardoel, J. (1998) 'The dead pope "live". Television news, technology and journalism in the Netherlands, 1956–1996', paper presented at the IAMCR conference, Glasgow, 26–30 July.
Barwise, P. and Ehrenberg, A. (1988) *Television and its Audience*. London: Sage.
BBC News (1998) *BBC News: The Future. Public Service News in the Digital Age*. London: BBC.
Boyd, A. (1998) *Broadcast Journalism. Techniques of Radio and TV News*, 4th edn. Oxford: Focal Press.
Corner, J. (1995) *Television Form and Public Address*. London: Edward Arnold.
Cottle, S. (1993) 'Mediating the environment: modalities of TV news', in A. Hansen (ed.), *The Mass Media and Environmental Issues*. Leicester: Leicester University Press, pp. 107–133.
Cottle, S. (1995) 'The production of news formats: determinants of mediated public contestation', *Media, Culture & Society*, 17: 275–291.
Dahlgren, P. (1995) *Television and the Public Sphere. Citizenship, Democracy and the Media*. London: Sage.
Day-Lewis, S. (ed.) (1989) *One Day in the Life of Television*. London: Grafton Books.
Ellis, J. (1982) *Visible Fictions. Cinema, Television, Video*. London: Routledge & Kegan Paul.
Fairclough, N. (1995) *Media Discourse*. London: Edward Arnold.
Feuer, J. (1983) 'The concept of live television: ontology as ideology', in E.A. Kaplan (ed.), *Regarding Television: Critical Approaches – an Anthology*. Los Angeles: University Publications of America, pp. 12–22.
Fiske, J. (1987) *Television Culture*. London: Methuen.
Franklin, B. (1997) *Newszak and News Media*. London: Arnold.
Fry, T. (1983) 'The latest technology for the latest news. A BBC-designed electronic newsroom for *Breakfast Time*', in *EBU Review*, 34 (4), July: 13–16.

Hallin, D. (1994) *We Keep America on Top of the World. Television Journalism and the Public Sphere*. London: Routledge.
Hamm, I. (1990) 'Das Fernsehen als Informationsquelle. Zum Verhältnis von Gestaltung und Rezeptionserfolg', *Rundfunk und Fernsehen*, 38 (2): 201–221.
Hartley, J. (1982) *Understanding News*. London: Methuen.
Heinderyckx, F. (1993) 'Television news programmes in Western Europe: a comparative study', *European Journal of Communication*, 8: 425–450.
Kepplinger, H.M. (1991) 'The impact of presentation techniques: theoretical aspects and empirical findings', in F. Biocca (ed.), *Television and Political Advertising*, Vol. 1: *Psychological Processes*. Hillsdale NJ: Lawrence Erlbaum, pp. 173–194.
Levo-Henriksson, R. (1994) *Eyes upon Wings. Culture in Finnish and US Television News*. Helsinki: Finnish Broadcasting Company.
Madge, T. (1989) *Beyond the BBC. Broadcasters and the Public in the 1980s*. Houndmills: Macmillan.
Morley, D. (1980) *The 'Nationwide' Audience*. London: British Film Institute.
Morse, M. (1986) 'The television news, personality and credibility. Reflections on the news in transition', in T. Modleski (ed.), *Studies in Entertainment. Critical Approaches to Mass Culture*. Bloomington: Indiana University Press, pp. 55–79.
Munson, W. (1993) *All Talk. The Talkshow in Media Culture*. Philadelphia: Temple University Press.
Pedersen, V. (1999) 'Invasion of the body-stockings. The threat of femininity in the old public service television', *Nordicom Review*, 20 (2): 93–100.
Perse, E.M. (1998) 'Implications of cognitive and affective involvement for channel changing', *Journal of Communication*, 48 (3): 49–68.
Phelan, J.M. (1991) 'Selling consent: the public sphere as a televisual market-place', in P. Dahlgren and C. Sparks (eds), *Communication and Citizenship. Journalism and the Public Sphere*. London: Routledge, pp. 75–93.
Scannell, P. (1996) *Radio, Television and Modern Life. A Phenomenological Approach*. Oxford: Blackwell.
Van Zoonen, L. (1991) 'A tyranny of intimacy? Women, femininity and television news', in P. Dahlgren and C. Sparks (eds), *Communication and Citizenship. Journalism and the Public Sphere*. London: Routledge, pp. 217–235.
Williams, R. (1974) *Television. Technology and Cultural Form*. London: Fontana.
Wilson, E. (1984) 'All in the family: Russel Grant on *Breakfast Television*', in L. Masterman (ed.), *Television Mythologies: Stars, Shows and Signs*. London: Comedia, pp. 7–9.

11 TALK SHOWS: DEMOCRATIC DEBATES AND TABLOID TALES

Abt, V. and Seesholtz, M. (1994) 'The shameless world of Phil, Sally and Oprah: television talk shows and the deconstruction of society', *Journal of Popular Culture*, 28 (1): 171–191.
Anderson, R. (1995) *Consumer Culture and TV Programming*. Oxford: Westview Press.
Bakhtin, M. (1968) *Rabelais and his World*. Cambridge: MIT Press.
Barber, N. (1998) 'It's a piece of faith-cake', *Independent on Sunday: Culture*, 11 October: 8.

Barthes, R. (1973) *Mythologies*. London: Paladin.
Bauman, Z. (1999) 'Let the good times roll', *Guardian Saturday Review*, 19 June: 8.
Bolton, R. (1999) 'And what television needs to do about it', *Guardian*, 15 February: 6–7.
Borger, J. (1999) 'Springer for Senate shock', *Guardian*, 5 August: 1.
Brecht, B. (1979–80) 'Radio as a means of communication: a talk on the function of radio', *Screen*, 20 (3/4): 24–28.
Carpignano, P. et al. (1990) 'Chatter in the age of electronic reproduction: talk show television and the "public mind"', *Social Text*, 25–26: 33–55.
Corner, J. (1999) *Critical Ideas in Television Studies*. Oxford: Clarendon Press.
Cross, S. (1999) 'Mediating madness: mental illness and public discourse in current affairs television', University of Loughborough Department of Social Sciences, doctoral thesis.
Duncan, A. (1999) 'Interview with Oprah Winfrey', *Radio Times*, 27 February–5 March: 1619.
Fairclough, N. (1995) *Media Discourse*. London: Edward Arnold.
Francis, P. (2000) 'Kilroy: "I wanted to be PM"', *TV Times* (London), 12–18 February: 15–17.
Gamson, J. (1998) *Freaks Talk Back: Tabloid Talk Shows and Sexual Nonconformity*. Chicago: University of Chicago Press.
Greenberg, B.S. et al. (1997) 'Daytime television talk shows: guests, content and interactions', *Journal of Broadcasting and Electronic Media*, 41 (3): 412–426.
Guardian Saturday Review (1999) 'Can we trust anything we see on television?', 20 February: 2.
Hughes, H.M. (1937) 'Human interest stories and democracy', *Public Opinion Quarterly*, April: 73–83.
Illouz, E. (1999) '"That shadowy realm of the interior": Oprah Winfrey and Hamlet's glass', *International Journal of Cultural Studies*, 2 (1): 109–131.
Jaggi, M. (1999) 'The power of one', *Guardian*, 13 February: 10–16.
Joyner Priest, P. (1995) *Public Intimacies: Talk Show Participants and Tell-All TV*. Cresskill, NJ: Hampton Press.
Keane, J. (1998) *Civil Society: Old Images, New Visions*. Cambridge: Polity Press.
Krause, A.J. and Goering, E.M. (1995) 'Local talk in the global village: an intercultural comparison of American and German talk shows', *Journal of Popular Culture*, 29 (2): 189–207.
Landman, J. (1996) 'Identity on trial: narration, gossip, and confession on the day-time chat show', *Australian Journal of Communication*, 23 (1): 1–14.
Leurdijk, A. (1997) 'Common sense versus political discourse: debating racism and multicultural society in Dutch talk shows', *European Journal of Communication*, 12 (2): 147–168.
Livingstone, S. and Lunt, P. (1994a) *Talk on Television: Audience Participation and Public Debate*. London: Routledge.
Livingstone, S. and Lunt, P. (1994b) 'Psychologists on Television', *The Psychologist*, May: 207–211.
Marshall, A. (1999) 'C'mon Jerry, are you just faking it?', *Independent on Sunday*, 6 June: 24.
Meyrowitz, J. (1994) 'The life and death of media friends: new genres of intimacy and mourning', in S.J. Drucker and R.S. Cathcart (eds), *American Heroes, in a Media Age*. Cresskill, NJ: Hampton Press, pp. 62–81.
Richardson, K. and Meinhof, U.H. (1999) *Worlds in Common? Television Discourse in Changing Europe*. London: Routledge.

Robins, J. (1999) 'Toilet talk from Jerry Springer', *Independent on Sunday*, 12 September: 10.
Shattuc, J.M. (1998) '"Go Riki": politics, perversion and pleasure in the 1990s', in C. Geraghty and D. Lusted (eds), *The Television Studies Book*. London: Arnold, pp. 212–225.
Squire, C. (1997) 'Empowering women? *The Oprah Winfrey Show*', in C. Brunsdon, J. D'Acci and L. Spigel (eds), *Feminist Television Criticism: A Reader*. Oxford: Clarendon Press, pp. 98–113.
Tavener, J. (2000) 'Media, morality and madness: the case against sleaze TV', *Critical Studies in Media Communication*, 17 (1), March: 63–85.
Tran, M. (1999) 'Oprah sets up women's channel', *Guardian Europe*, 25 November: 6.

12 TELEVISION CURRENT AFFAIRS: THE CASE OF NORTHERN IRELAND

Baker, K. (1996) 'Reporting the conflict', in M. McLoone (ed.), *Broadcasting in a Divided Community: Seventy Years of the BBC in Northern Ireland*. Belfast: Institute of Irish Studies, pp. 118–126.
Butler, D. (1995) *The Trouble with Reporting Northern Ireland*. Aldershot: Avebury.
Cathcart, R. (1984) *The Most Contrary Region: The BBC in Northern Ireland 1924–1984*. Belfast: Blackstaff Press.
Curran, J. and Seaton, J. (1997) *Power without Responsibility*, 5th edn. London: Routledge.
Curtis, L. (1984) *Ireland: The Propaganda War*. London: Pluto.
Henderson, L., Miller D. and Reilly, J. (1990) *Speak No Evil: The British Broadcasting Ban, the Media and the Conflict in Ireland*. Glasgow: Glasgow University Media Group.
Herman, E.S. and Chomsky, N. (1988) *Manufacturing Consent*. New York: Pantheon.
Kyle, K. (1996) 'The media and Northern Ireland: some personal reflections', in M. McLoone (ed.), *Broadcasting in a Divided Community: Seventy Years of the BBC in Northern Ireland*. Belfast: Institute of Irish Studies, pp. 105–117.
McLaughlin, G. and Miller, D. (1996) 'The media politics of the Irish peace process', *International Journal of Press/Politics*, 1 (4), Cambridge, MA: MIT Press.
McNair, B. (1999) *News and Journalism in the UK*, 3rd edn. London: Routledge.
Miller, D. (1994) *Don't Mention the War: Northern Ireland, Propaganda and the Media*. London: Pluto Press.
Milne, A. (1988) *DG: The Memoirs of a British Broadcaster*. London: Coronet.
Porter, V. (1992) 'Broadcasting pluralism and the freedom of expression in France, Germany and Ireland', in P. Drummond, R. Paterson and J. Willis (eds), *National Identity and Europe: The Television Revolution*. London: BFI.
Scannell, P. and Cardiff, D. (1991) *A Social History of British Broadcasting: Vol. 1 1922–1939*. Oxford: Blackwell.
Schlesinger, P., Murdock, G. and Elliot, P. (1983) *Televising 'Terrorism': Political Violence in Popular Culture*. London: Comedia.
Whyte, J. (1990) *Interpreting Northern Ireland*. Oxford: Clarendon.

Fiske, J. (1987) *Television Culture*. London: Routledge.
Glasgow University Media Group (1980) *More Bad News*. London: Routledge and Kegan Paul.
Gurevitch, M., Levy, M.R. and Roeh, J. (1991) 'The global newsroom: convergencies and diversities in the globalization of television news', in P. Dahlgren and C. Sparks (eds), *Communication and Citizenship. Journalism and the Public Sphere in the New Media Age*. London: Routledge, pp. 195–216.
Heinderyckx, F. (1993) 'Television news programmes in Western Europe: a comparative study', *European Journal of Communication*, 8: 225–250.
Morse, M. (1986) 'The television news, personality and credibility. Reflections on the news in transition', in T. Modleski (ed.), *Studies in Entertainment. Critical Approaches to Mass Culture*. Bloomington: Indiana University Press, pp. 55–79.
Todorov, T. (1977) *The Poetics of Prose*. Oxford: Blackwell.
Wallis, R. and Baran, S. (1990) *The Known World of Broadcast News*. London: Routledge.

INDEX

Aamu-TV 183
access 5, 32, 52–4, 162
accountability 14–15
actors 239, 249
advertising 13–14, 52, 115, 153
AGB 117
Aijälä, Tauno 176
Americanization 19, 21, 61, 77–80, 147, 164
analogue broadcasting 35, 43–4
Anglo-American music 147
Arabella 213
ARD (Germany) 13
ARTE 173
arts 138, 159, 162
audience
  analysis 115–23
  arts 162
  availability 128
  behaviour 123–30
  breakfast television 176
  as commodity 132
  control 73–4
  as customers 41
  fragmentation 13, 31, 46, 64, 132
  markets 132
  MTV 145–7
  orientation 76
  polarization 133
  qualitative research 120–3
  reach 75–6
  research 130–3
  talk shows 203, 204
  targetting 191
Australia 62, 84–6

Bakhtin, Mikhail 216
Barr, Roseanne 206, 207
Barthes, Roland 207
BBC (UK) 19, 37, 42, 182, 226–7, 243–5
  digital channels 54–5
BBC Worldwide 42
block programming 73
Boulevard Bio 211–12
The Brains Trust 202
breakfast magazines 177–9
Breakfast News 175, 184–5, 190, 194
breakfast television 138–9, 175–97
Breakfast Time 182, 187
bridging 73
Britain 208, 209–10, 222–4
broadcasting 7–22, 70
  analogue 35, 43–4
  culture 164–5
  trends 60
  see also commercial broadcasting; digital television; public service broadcasting
BSkyB 19, 37, 46, 48

cable networks 4, 10–11, 29
CADs *see* conditional access systems
Campbell, Gregory 227
Canal Plus 14
censorship 223
Channel 4 (UK) 21, 183
channels
  abundance 46
  competition 70, 75
  repertoire 128
chat shows 203
CIRCOM 97
citizen mode 172
CNN 248
collaboration 63, 94

commercial broadcasting 4, 10, 27
  accountability 14–15
  advertising 13
  digital 47–8
  programmes 17–19
commercialization 24, 26, 28, 213
commissions 80
commodification 42–3
commodity model of audience 132
communication systems 37–8
compatability 72, 176
competition 64, 137
compression 45–7
computers 53
conditional access systems (CADs) 48
confession 199–200
consolidation 47–50
consumer mode 172
consumerism 27–8
control 162–3
  see also regulation
convergence 5, 36–9, 44, 78
conversation 199
corporate ownership 38–9, 47–8, 49, 50
corporatization 42
Council of Europe 9
counterprogramming 73
critique 216–17
cross border collaboration 63
crossed looks 63, 96, 101
cultural content 166–73
cultural diversity 4, 27–8, 151, 162
cultural forms 36–7
cultural goods 161
cultural identity 162, 165
cultural imperialism 62, 84, 164
cultural policy 138, 158, 160–3
  PSB 158, 165–6
cultural references 85–6
cultural studies 121
cultural-pedagogic logic 16, 27
culture 163–4
current affairs programmes 232–3

DAVID 95
debate 202
democracy 31–2, 214–16
demographics 127
Denmark 82
deregulation 4, 23–7, 139, 221
diaries 119
digital television 4–5, 11, 35–57
direct-to-home (DTH) 29
distribution 37–8
diversity 26, 166, 215
documentaries 173
docusoaps 62, 79–80
domestic news 241–3
Donahue 204, 206
Drei nach Neun 212
DTH *see* direct-to-home
dual broadcasting systems xi, 21

early morning television *see* breakfast television
Eastman, Susan Tyler 71
eavesdropping research 128
EBU *see* European Broadcasting Union
editorial independence 9
EEC television 110
effects research 123
electronic commerce 5, 51
electronic programme guides (EPGs) 48
empathy 215–16
English 53–4, 138, 147
enhancement 45
entertainment programmes 18, 21
EPGs *see* electronic programme guides
equilibrium 240–1
ESCORT classification system 171–2
Euro Media Research Group x
Euro puddings 94, 106
European Broadcasting Union (EBU) 14, 160, 167, 179
Eurosport 14
Eurosud 63, 64, 94–112

feminist research 121
fiction 169
finance 12–14, 31
Finland 65–8, 74, 76, 80, 82, 183
five minute rule 147
flow 70, 73, 189, 190–1
fly-on-the wall documentaries 62
focus group 122
foreign investment 29
foreign news 243–8
format development 74
France 12, 15, 100, 236–52
France 3 (France) 95
frequency 117
frequency allocation 8

Germany 13, 15, 18, 26, 89–92, 211–12, 245–6
Glasgow University Media Group 237
globalization 28, 138, 140, 237
  MTV 150–1, 154, 155
  see also transnationalization
GMTV 183, 192
Goede Tijden, Slechte Tijden 87–9
Good Friday Agreement 225

Good Morning America 182
Greece 15
gross rating points (GRP) 117
Der grüne Salon 213
guests 203
Gute Zeiten, Schlechte Zeiten 89–92

habit formation 72
hammocking 73
Heller, Caroline xi
Hjarvard, Stig 24
household meter 119
human interest programmes 169
Huomenta Suomi 183
hybrid channels 78–9
hybrid programmes 62, 137, 179

Illouz, Eva 215
imported fiction 19, 21
information programmes 18, 18–19, 169
infotainment 137, 138, 169, 179, 191, 193–4
interactivity 51–2
intercultural communication 97
international news 140
Internet 36, 38, 44, 48, 53, 64
interpretive community 121, 132
interviews 120, 201
investigative journalism 233
Italy 25, 54
ITV (UK) 12, 13, 21, 228

Jerry Springer Show 207–8, 211
journalism 233

Kilroy Silk, Robert 208–9, 210
KRO (The Netherlands) 183

labour disputes 236–52
Lake, Ricki 206
language 53–4, 90, 144
  MTV 147–50, 152
  translation 105
  see also English
Laybourne, Geraldine 205
lead-in 73
lead-off 73
least objectionable programming (LOP) 76
leisure 27–8
Lescue, Pierre 41
liberalization 40
licence fees 12–13, 14
light entertainment 169
live transmissions 173
LOP *see* least objectionable programming

Loyalists 229–32
Luxembourg 15, 21

McGuinness, Martin 227
managerial ideology 237, 249
marginalization 30, 46
market forces 4, 26, 32
market model of audience 132
marketing 88, 132
marketization 39–43
Me TV 46
media, role of 16–17, 224
media environment 127–8
Media-programme 20
Microsoft 49
mission 16–17, 27, 32
mix 68
mobile telephones 37
monopolies xi, 24
movie channels 14
MTV (Finland) 12, 21, 65, 69, 183, 186, 192
MTV (Music Television) 137–8, 141–57
multiculturalism 162
Murdoch, Rupert 38
music 147, 161–2, 169
music videos 144, 145

narrative structure 239
national identity 166
nationalization 85
Netherlands 12, 87–9, 183, 208, 209, 246–8
New Right 222
news 72, 138, 139–40, 177
  collaboration 95
  domestic 241–3
  foreign 243–8
  international 140
  labour disputes 237, 239–41
  perspective 241–8, 249–50
news discourse 238
newsdesk 185
niche channels 173
Nielsen 117
Northern Ireland 139, 221–35
Norway 66, 82, 165–6
Norwegian Broadcasting Corporation 165–6
NRK (Norway) 66, 165–6
Nyhetsmorgon 183

The Oprah Winfrey Show 205–6
Ontbijt TV 183
Oxygen 205

Paglia, Camille 207
panel 116

participatory talk shows 203–4, 205
paternalism 16, 76, 209
pay TV 11, 14, 24
pay-per-view channels 11
peace process 225
peoplemeter 116–18
persistence threshold 116
personalized viewing regimes 46
perspective, news 241–8, 249–50
Pittman, Robert W. 144
pluralism 76, 166
political accountability 15
politics 9, 16, 25, 139, 221
Portugal 15, 100
presenters 187–90, 203
Presseclub 212
prime time 18, 72, 73
privatization 40, 55
producer choice 80
programmes 17–19
  appreciation 119
  choice 126–8
  conservation 74–5
programming 52, 54, 65–83, 144, 165
  cultural content 166–73
propaganda 224
proportion 68
Provos 232
PSB *see* public service broadcasting
public culture 32
public service broadcasting (PSB) xi, 3, 8, 61–2
  accountability 15
  breakfast television 178
  Britain 222–4
  cultural policy 165–6, 172–3
  culture 158, 160
  finance 12–13
  goals 9
  hybrid programmes 137
  mission 16–17, 27, 32
  Northern Ireland 224–6
  programmes 17–19
  regulation 24
  trends 29–31, 54–6
public service talk 213

qualitative audience research 120–3
qualitative ratings 119
quality 26, 61, 165
Question Time 203

RAI (Italy) 54
Rapport Morgon 183
ratings 64, 113–23
reach 117
reality television 75, 77
reception analysis 121
regionalization 155
regulation x-xi, 31, 40–2
  see also deregulation
Reith, John 42
religious programming 66–8, 72, 169
repetition 62, 74
reruns *see* repetition
The Restless Years 62, 84–6
Ricki Lake Show 206
road blockades 236–52
RTE (Spain) 13
RTL (The Netherlands) 12, 246–8
RTP (Portugal) 95, 99–100

sales pitches 201–2
sampling error 116
satellite television 4, 10, 29
satellite-cable system relay 29
segmentation 190–1
selective exposure 126
self-censorship 63
self-help 205
Serbia 233
serialization 62, 72
set, breakfast television 185–7
set-top boxes 48
sets 212
share 117
soap operas 85–92
social changes 27–8
social cohesion 17
social responsibility 16, 25
social themes 86
sofa 185
Spain 12, 13, 100
spin-offs 62
sponsoring 13
sports programmes 14, 66–8, 167, 169
Springer, Jerry 207–8, 211
state intervention 9
storytelling 201, 237
stripping 62, 72, 73
stunting 73
SVT (Sweden) 183
subscription channels 11
surveys 120
Sweden 82, 183
symbols 184–5

tabloidization 193, 200
talk shows 139, 172, 198–220
talking heads 198
Taylor, Peter 226
technology 29, 31, 35–7, 45, 132

telecommunications 40, 49–50
telephone systems 37
television
  EEC 110
  social uses of 130
television journalism 179
Television Without Frontiers 9, 19
templates 84
tent-poling 73
terrorism 225
Thatcherism 222–3
thematic channels 14
therapy 200–1
time 175
time-budgeting 72
TMF (The Music Factory) 149
Today 181–2
translation 105
transnational news magazines 96
transnationalization 4, 24, 28, 31
trends
  broadcasting 60
  digital television 43–5
  PSB 29–31, 54–6
Trisha 210
Truth or Consequences 200
TV3 25
TV4 (Sweden) 21, 183
TV-am (UK) 182
TV babies 144
TVE (Spain) 95, 99–100

United Kingdom 12, 13, 15, 50, 182–3
United States 8, 19, 71–5, 145, 211–14
universalism 32, 42
uses-and-gratification 127

Vanessa 211
viewing behaviour 124, 128–9
viewing patterns 123–6
VIVA (Germany) 148–9

Wheel of Fortune 7
Williams, Raymond 68
Winfrey, Oprah 200, 202, 205–6
world wide web 38

YLE (Finland) 65–8, 74, 76, 80, 183
youth culture 88
youth market 144, 206

ZDF (Germany) 13